आ नो भद्राः क्रतवो यन्तु विश्वतः ।

ā no bhadrāḥ kratavo yantu viśvataḥ

Let noble thoughts come to us from every side

- Ṛg Veda I - 89-i

BHAVAN'S BOOK UNIVERSITY

LIVING BIOGRAPHIES OF

GREAT PHILOSOPHERS

by

HENRY THOMAS and DANA LEE THOMAS

BHAVAN'S BOOK UNIVERSITY

LIVING BIOGRAPHIES OF
GREAT PHILOSOPHERS

HENRY THOMAS

and

DANA LEE THOMAS

2010

BHARATIYA VIDYA BHAVAN

Kulapati Munshi Marg

Mumbai - 400 007

First Edition: 1956
Second Edition: 1960
Third Edition: 1965
Fourth Edition: 1970
Fifth Edition: 1988
Sixth Edition: 1993
Seventh Edition: 2010

Price : Rs. 200/-

Typesetting by Samir Parekh,
at Creative Page Setters,
Fort, Mumbai-1 T.2282 5784

PRINTED IN INDIA by Nilesh Parekh, at Paras Prints,
34, Cowasji Patel Street, 17, Lakhani Terrace, Fort, Mumbai - 400001
and Published by P. V. Sankarankutty, Deputy Registrar (Publications),
Bharatiya Vidya Bhavan, K.M. Munshi Marg, Mumbai - 400007.
E-mail : brbhavan@bom7.vsnl.net.in
Web-site : http://www.bhavans.info

KULAPATI'S PREFACE

The Bharatiya Vidya Bhavan – that Institute of Indian Culture in Bombay – needed a Book University, a series of books which, if read, would serve the purpose of providing higher education. Particular emphasis, however, was to be put on such literature as revealed the deeper impulsions of India. As a first step, it was decided to bring out in English 100 books, 50 of which were to be taken in hand, almost at once. Each book was to contain from 200 to 250 pages and was to be priced at Rs. 2.50.

It is our intention to publish the books we select, not only in English but also in the following Indian languages: Hindi, Bengali, Gujarati, Marathi, Tamil, Telugu, Kannada and Malayalam.

This scheme, involving the publication of 900 volumes, requires ample funds and an all-India organisation. The Bhavan is exerting its utmost to supply them.

The objectives for which the Bhavan stands are the reintegration of the Indian culture in the light of modern knowledge and to suit our present-day needs and the resuscitation of its fundamental values in their pristine vigour.

Let me make our goal more explicit:

We seek the dignity of man, which necessarily implies the creation of social conditions which would allow him freedom to evolve along the lines of his own temperament and capacities; we seek the harmony of individual efforts and social relations, not in any makeshift way, but within the framework of the Moral Order; we seek the creative art of life, by the alchemy of which human limitations are progressively transmuted, so that man may become the instrument of God and is able to see Him in all and all in Him.

The world, we feel, is too much with us. Nothing would uplift or inspire us so much as the beauty and aspiration which such books can teach.

In this series, therefore, the literature of India, ancient and modern, will be published in a form easily accessible to all. Books in other literatures of the world, if they illustrate the principles we stand for, will also be included.

This common pool of literature, it is hoped, will enable the reader, eastern or western, to understand and appreciate currents of world thought, as also the movements of the mind in India, which though they flow through different linguistic channels, have a common urge and aspiration.

Fittingly, the Book University's first venture is the *Mahabharata*, summarised by one of the greatest living Indians, C. Rajagopalachari; the second work is on a section of it, the Gita by H.V. Divatia, an eminent jurist and student of philosophy. Centuries ago, it was proclaimed of the *Mahabharata*: "What is not in it, is nowhere." After twenty-five centuries, we can use the same words about it. He who knows it not, knows not the heights and depths of the soul; he misses the trials and tragedy and the beauty and grandeur of life.

The *Mahabharata* is not a mere epic: it is a romance, telling the tale of heroic men and women and of some who were divine; it is a whole literature in itself, containing a code of life, a philosophy of social and ethical relations and speculative thought on human problems that is hard to rival; but above all, it has for its core the *Gita* which is, as the world is beginning to find out, the noblest of scriptures and the grandest of sagas in which the climax is reached in the wondrous Apocalypse in the Eleventh Canto.

Through such books alone the harmonies underlying true culture, I am convinced, will one day reconcile the disorders of modern life.

I thank all those who have helped to make this new branch of the Bhavan's activity successful.

K. M. Munshi

INTRODUCTION

Every biography is a story of adventure. The energetic personalities of the world represent an adventure in living. The philosophical personalities, on the other hand, represent an adventure in thinking. And when we examine the lives of the philosophers we find that the procession of a man's thoughts can be as exciting a spectacle as the pageantry of a man's deeds. It is just as enchanting to plunge into new ideas as it is to penetrate into new lands. Our world becomes wider, our imagination richer and our life more coloured and more zestful as the result of our companionship with the travellers of the spirit and the pioneers of thought.

In conformity with our general purpose in the writing of the present biographical series, we have tried to place the accent upon the thinkers rather than upon their thoughts. We have endeavoured to avoid technical expositions, critical analyses or metaphysical excursions into any of the philosophical systems. But on the other hand we have attempted to introduce the reader not only into the homes of philosophers but into their minds as well. For in order to understand the dreamers of the absolute we must allow them to invite us into the garden of their dreams. It is possible, we believe, to get a revealing picture of the beauty of a garden and to enjoy a healthy whiff of its fragrance without a technical study of the botanical structure of the flowers or an expert knowledge of their scientific names. We have therefore tried in such of these biographies to reproduce the gist of the philosopher's thought simply, informally and — we hope — vividly.

And as we gain an insight into the minds of the various philosophers we make an interesting and important discovery. All these philosophers, in spite of their extrinsic quarrels, exhibit an intrinsic unanimity of thought. This is especially true in the field of ethics. Here we find the different schools of philosophy in practical agreement with the different systems of religion. The philosophers and the prophets alike are united in their belief as to the fundamental purpose of life. And this purpose is — to insure the happiness of man through the co-operation of mankind.

H. T.

D. L. T.

CONTENTS

1

PLATO

427 B.C. – 347 B.C.

THERE was a banquet at the house of the Athenian poet Agathon. This man had won the first prize for his drama at the Greek Theatre, and he had invited his best friends to join him in the celebration of his victory. The guests were discussing one of their favourite subjects – love. Each one, in turn, was trying to explain his own idea as to the meaning of this all-absorbing topic.

"Love," said Phaedrus, "is the oldest of the gods, and one of the most powerful. It is that principle which turns ordinary young people into heroes. For the lover is ashamed to act the coward in the presence of his beloved. Give me an army made of lovers, and I can conquer the world."

"Yes," agrees the next speaker, Pausanias, "but you must distinguish between earthly love and heavenly love – the attraction between two bodies on the one hand and the affinity between two souls on the other. The vulgar love of the body takes wings and flies away when the bloom of youth is over. But the noble love of the soul is perpetual."

And then comes the comic poet Aristophanes with a brand — new theory about love. "In the olden days," he tells us, "the two sexes were united into one body. This body was round like a ball, with four hands, four feet and two faces. It moved about with amazing rapidity, using its eight limbs like the spokes of a wheel in a continual series of somersaults. Terrible was the strength of this race of men-women and boundless was their ambition. They were planning to scale the heavens and to attack the gods when Zeus hit upon a happy plan. 'Let us cut them in two,' he said, 'and then they will have only half their strength and we shall have twice as many sacrifices.'

"And so he split them apart into male and female and from that day onwards the two halves of the once-united body have been consumed with a longing to be reunited into one. And this longing for the reunion of the sexes is what we call *love.*"

This humorous interpretation of love is followed by several other interesting definitions until finally the guest of honour, Socrates, is requested to make a few remarks on the subject.

"After all this eloquence," begins Socrates, "I am turned into a stone and struck dumb. For how can my foolishness compete with such wisdom?"

And having unburdened himself on this Socratic preface of ironic modesty, he proceeds to confute all their "wisdom" with his "foolishness." He tears down their arguments with a series of unanswerable questions-Socrates was the founder of the *quiz* method in education — and then he follows this destructive process with a constructive theory of his own. "Love," he observes, "is the hunger of the human soul for divine beauty. The lover is eager not only to *find beauty* but to *create* it, to *perpetuate* it, to plant the seed of immortality in the mortal body. This is why the sexes love each other – to reproduce themselves and thus prolong time into eternity. And this is why parents love their children. For the soul of the loving parent creates not merely children but seekers and partners and co-workers and successors in the eternal quest for beauty."

And what is this beauty that we are all seeking to perpetuate through love? It is wisdom and virtue and honour and courage and justice and faith. In a word, *beauty* is *truth.* "And truth is the way that leads directly to God.

The guests applaud the speech of the barefoot philosopher and then they proceed to the more prosaic business of the evening. They enter into a drinking contest which lasts all through the night. One by one the revellers drop out of the contest until at cock-crow there are only three left – Aristophanes, Agathon and Socrates. They are drinking out of a large goblet which they pass around, and Socrates is explaining to the two poets, who are half asleep, that the great writer of comedy should also be a great writer of tragedy. And first Aristophanes falls asleep; and then, as the day is dawning, Agathon. Socrates lays them gently to rest, takes a final drink in honour of the wine god, Dionysus, and goes off to his daily business of spreading wisdom among the citizens of Athens.

One of the guests at this famous banquet was a disciple of Socrates, a young man who was later to immortalize the mental prowess and the physical endurance of his master. The name of this young man was Plato.

II

PLATO was one of the favourite children of heaven. Like Goethe, he was endowed with every gift that the gods could bestow upon a mortal – noble ancestry, wealthy parents, good looks, a sound mind in an athletic body (he was nicknamed *Plato,* it was said, because of his broad shoulders) and a passionate love for wisdom. In his quest for wisdom he came, at the age of twenty, under the influence of Socrates, who was sixty-two years old at the time (407 B.C.).

Plato worshipped Socrates from the very first. He joined the group of brilliant young intellectuals who followed the "gadfly" through the streets of the city and listened with amazement and delight as he "stung" the wisest men of Athens into an admission of their ignorance. Socrates was ugly as a satyr and gentle as a saint. One of his ablest students, Alcibiades, compared him to those trick statues that were sold in the market place of Athens. "They have the exterior of a Silenus (a mythological clown), but open them up and you find inside of them the image of god."

Yet it was no godly heights of superhuman wisdom that Socrates was trying to attain. Instead he modestly devoted himself, as he remarked, to the very human task of asking questions. "There is only one thing I know," he said, "and that is, that I know nothing." And then he sat out to prove to all and sundry that they too, like himself knew nothing. It was his business to learn and to enable others to learn. "My mother," he said, "was a midwife, and I am trying to follow in her footsteps. I am a mental obstetrician, helping others to give birth to their own ideas."

And so he went about the streets of Athens, this philsopher with the homely phrases and the homely features, Saint Socrates with the flattened nose, the thick lips, the projecting eyes, the uncouth body and the divine thoughts. And everywhere he asked his elementary question, *to ti,* what is the meaning of this? What is piety? What is democracy? What is virtue? What is courage? What is honesty? What is justice? What is truth ? And — what is your business and what knowledge and skill have you brought to it? Are you a statesman? If so, what have you learned about government? Are you a lawyer ? What study have you made of human motives for human actions? Are you a teacher? What steps have you taken to conquer your own ignorance before you can presume to attack the ignorance of others? *To ti,* information, please?

With such questions as these he cross-examined the pundits and exposed their ignorance. But he did this in no vicious mood. He was just as eager to expose his own ignorance. His one object was to acquire truth through the elimination of error, "I pursue the trail of truth like a bloodhound." In the pursuit of truth he neglected his interests, neglected his business — he was a sculptor by trade — neglected his family. And his shrewish wife Xanthippe never lost an opportunity to remind him of this neglect. Socrates was a martyr to philosophy. And what, he asked, is philosophy? That process of thought which enables us to become acquainted with our own personality, *Gnothi seauton,* know thyself.

But most people, when they become acquainted with themselves, are rather disappointed with their new acquaintances. When Socrates removed the mirror of self-flattery from the eyes of the Athenians and held up before them the glass of truth, they were shocked at the result. For they saw in this glass not the reflection of men but the image of beasts. And like beasts they began to prosecute Socrates. For a number of years they were content to let him off with ridicule, invective and occasional blows. But then there came a conflagration in the moral atmosphere of Athens and many of the finer feelings of the citizens were turned into ashes. The Athenians had been defeated in the Peloponnesian War (404 B.C.) – a war that had been fought between the dictatorship of Sparta and the democracy of Athens. Human decency, the dignity of life and the sense of individual liberty had received a mortal blow. The tyrant Critias (the leader of the Fifth Columnists in Athens) had overthrown the free government. And when Critias was overthrown in his turn the state was plunged into a revolution in which the basest passions of humanity had been let loose. Athens was no safe place for a philosopher to live in – especially for a philosopher who still dared to insist upon the free expression of his thought. One morning, as Socrates came into the market place, he found the following indictment posted up against him:

Socrates is guilty of crime: first for not worshipping the gods whom the city worships, but introducing new divinities of his own; next, for corrupting the youth. The penalty due is – death.

The chief instigator of this accusation was a leather merchant by the name of Anytus. This man had a personal grudge against Socrates. For Socrates had advised the son of Anytus to give up the tannery business of his father and to devote himself to the study of philosophy. This criminal corruption of youth, insisted Anytus, deserved nothing less than the death penalty.

It was a case of leather against learning. And leather won. Socrates was arrested and placed on trial for his life.

Socrates had it within his own power to escape the death penalty. For, in accordance with Athenian law, a man condemned to death was permitted to choose exile as an alternative. Furthermore, a number of his wealthy friends, including Plato, has succeeded in bribing the jailer. Socrates could escape if he wished. But he did not wish to escape. His time had come and he was prepared to go. Throughout his life he had been ready to face danger and, if necessary, death. As a young man he had won the prize for bravery in battle. In his middle age he had dared, as a senator, to defy the entire populace who were clamouring for the death of an admiral accused of cowardice. Several years later he was equally courageous in defying the tyrant Critias. This tyrant had commanded him to bring back to Athens a "democratic rebel" by the name of Leon who had escaped to Salamis. But Socrates refused to carry out the tyrant's command. "Perhaps I should have suffered death on account of this," Socrates tells us, "if the government of Critias had not soon been broken up."

And now that he was actually condemned to death he did not flinch. Better to die now, while his strength was still intact, than to live on into the helpless decrepitude of excessive old age. Always proud of his physical endurance – he alone in Athens had been able to walk barefoot over the ice in the dead winter – he couldn't bear the thought of life without activity. "Let us face death, as we have faced life, courageously......The difficulty, O my judges, is not to escape from death, but from guilt. For guilt is swifter that death, and catches up with us much more rapidly..... I have been overtaken by death; but my accusers, by wickedness....... I submit to my punishment and they to theirs."

On the last day of his life a number of his disciples visited him in the prison. Plato describes the scene in his *Phaedo,* a work which ranks with the great epics of the world. The disciples are clustering about their beloved master. Socrates calls one of them to his side and strokes his hair as he explains his ideas about life and death and the immortality of the soul. Death is either an eternal sleep – a sweet immortal forgetfulness in which there is no persecution, no justice, no disappointment, no suffering, no grief – or else it is a gateway through which we pass from earth to heaven, a vestibule which leads into the palace of God. "And there, my friends, no one is ever put to death for his opinions.... So be of good cheer, and do not lament my passing...... When you lay me down in my grave, say that you are burying my body only, and not my soul."

And now the hour of sunset is near. The jailer enters with the hemlock. "Pray do not be angry with me, O Socrates; for others, as you are aware, are the guilty cause of your death, and not I."

So saying, the jailer holds out the cup to Socrates and bursts into tears as he turns away.

"And the rest of us, too could no longer forbear, and in spite of ourselves our tears were flowing fast..... Socrates alone retained his calmness." "What is all this nonsense!" he said. "I have sent away the women mainly in order to avoid such a scene as this..... Be quiet, then, and let me die in peace."

"When we heard this we blushed and restrained our tears..... And Socrates, having drunk the hemlock, had laid himself down upon the cot. For the jailer had told him to do so." Little by little the poison reached up from his feet towards his heart. "And then there was a convulsive movement, and Socrates fixed his eyes.... This was the end of our master, whom I may truly call the wisest and the best of all the men whom I have ever known."

III

WHEN Socrates died (398 B.C.) Plato found it expedient to leave Athens. For his efforts to save Socrates had made him a marked man. He started on a journey "around the world"— that is, the world known at that period. Just what countries he visited we cannot say. It is quite probable, however, that he went to Italy, where he became acquainted with the mystical philosophy of Pythagoras, "the founder of mathematics and the father of music." From there he is said to have travelled to Sicily, to Cyrene, to Egypt, to Judea and even to the banks of the Ganges. If he didn't visit all these countries in person, he certainly visited them in his thoughts. For when he returned to Athens, after a pilgrimage of twelve years, his mind had become a treasure-house of all the accumulated wisdom of the world.

But Socrates was still his supreme master. His life henceforth was to be dedicated to the teaching of the Socratic truths. For this purpose he opened up a school of philosophy in the public garden of Athens known as the Academia, an enchanting spot planted with trees and adorned with temples and statues. Here, on the bank of a river, with

A sound of a hidden brook
In the leafy month of June,
Which to the sleeping woods all night
Singeth a quiet tune,

he established his academy and proceeded to expound the Socratic doctrine. Or, as we call it today, the *Platonic* doctrine. For Plato presented all his idea in dialogue form through the mouth of Socrates, so that to this day we do not know just where the thought of Socrates leaves off and the thought of Plato begins. But this we do know--- that to Plato, as well as to Socrates, the meaning and the mission of all philosophy is the establishment of justice among men. "Justice," said Socrates, "is the only real happiness. The unjust alone are unhappy." And, adds Plato, speaking as usual through the mouth of Socrates, "No one has ever yet condemned injustice or praised justice (apparently he is unaware of the teachings of the Hebrew prophets).... No one has ever yet investigated.... how it happens that injustice is the greatest of all evil that the soul has within it, and justice the greatest good."

And it is in order to ascertain the nature of justice that Plato composed his immortal *Dialogues.* Referring to these *Dialogues*, Emerson repeats the words of Omar about the *Koran:* "Burn the libraries; for their value is in this book." Plato was perhaps the most comprehensive of the world's great thinkers. "Out of Plato---" we are again quoting Emerson— "come all things that are still written and debated among men of thought." Indeed, there is hardly a subject of human interest that Plato did not touch upon in his lifelong quest for the principles of justice. The universal brotherhood of man, eugenics, socialism, communism, feminism, birth control, free love, free speech, the double and the single standards of morality, the public ownership of wealth, of women, of children -- these are only a few of the problems that he discusses in his *Dialogues,* But underlying all these discussions there is a single purpose, his steadfast desire to see *rightness* – or, as we term it today, *righteousness* – established upon the earth. Rightness in the individual and righteousness in the state. He wants to see a state in which Socrates would not be murdered but instead would be elected king.

He pictures this imaginary land of the heart's desire in his *Republic,* the first Utopia in history.

IV

IN order that we may get an adequate idea of Plato's *Republic,* let us examine the life of its citizens, from their birth onward.

The children born in the Republic are to be the result of communal mating. The best men are to be mated with the best woman for the sole purpose of producing superior offspring. The men are to possess these women in common; there must be no individual marriages and no private families. As soon as the children are born they are to be taken away from the parents and placed in a state nursery. "It is essential that the parents should not know their own children, or the children their parents. In this way only can universal brotherhood ever become a fact instead of a theory. For everybody in this communal state may truly be regarded as everybody else's brother."

As for the parents, they need not confine their sexual experiences to their allotted mates. If, after they have given children to the state, they wish to "range at will," they may do so — provided "they try their utmost to abort any embryo which may thus come into being." The matter of free love is thus left to the discretion of the individual, and this applies to women as well as to men. The private life of the citizens is none of the state's business. All that the state requires is that the citizens should not injure one another in the pursuit of their individual happiness.

But let us return to the children.

From their very birth, as we have seen, they are delivered into the keeping of the state. Up to the age of twenty they all receive the same education. This preliminary education consists largely of gymnastics and music— gymnastics to develop the symmetry of the body, and music to develop, the harmony of the soul. "The man that hath no music in his soul is not to be trusted." For his mind is crippled, his passions are unbalanced and his sense of right and wrong is forever distorted. Music-and to Plato music meant all harmony, whether audible or not— is the underlying principle which keeps the world from falling into disjointed chaos. It is the soul of the universe, just as the planets and the stars are its body. Without it the earth would be a burnt-out cinder and the heavens a handful of dead ashes.

Music, therefore, is an essential part of everybody's education. Before they reach the age of twenty all boys and girl are to be thoroughly grounded in music---and in gymnastics. The schools in which they study these subjects are to be co-educational. Boys and girls must work and play together. The girls, as well as the boys, must strip when they take their exercises; for, as Plato puts it, the citizens of his ideal state are "sufficiently clad in the garment of virtue." There must be no foolish sense of shame or clownish jeering at the sight of the human body.

Furthermore, the education of the children must not only be free from prudery but it must also be divorced from drudgery. Learning is to be made a pleasure rather than a torture. Under the right kind of teachers a normal child will enjoy the gymnastics of his mind fully as much as the exercises of his body. A school, therefore, should be a mental gymnasium, an intellectual playground where the children try to excel one another in the fascinating sport of exchanging ideas.

This, then, is to be the education in the Republic up to the age of twenty. After that there comes a great weeding out. Those who are incapable of further education are relegated into the lowest class – that is, the farmers, the labourers and the businessmen. These constitute the "baser metal" of the state.

Those who are left after the elimination of the baser metal are to continue with their training. For the next ten years – that is, from the age of twenty to the age of thirty – they are to take up the study of the sciences: arithmetic, geometry and astronomy. These subjects, however, are to be mastered mainly for aesthetic rather than for practical purposes. Plato thought it beneath the dignity of the better citizens of his Republic to use arithmetic for barter or for the building of bridges or the making of machines. In this respect he was no different from the other Greeks of his day. The Greeks were not interested in mechanical inventions or in material progress. They preferred abstract speculation to concrete knowledge. The study of numbers, according to Plato, was good for only two things – to enable the philosopher to envision the actual unity through the apparent diversity of things and to enable the military commander to array his soldiers into squads, platoons, companies and regiments. Philosophers and soldiers, therefore, are the only ones who need to make any extensive study of mathematics.

When the study of the sciences is completed at thirty there is to be another weeding out. Those who fail to pass the test for still higher training are to be mustered into the middle class–the soldiers. They are to be the guardians of the state. The soldiers play a very important role in Plato's Republic. They are to form not a force of aggression but a power for defence. Plato hated war, but he realized that the best way to discourage a threatening invader is to wield before his eyes the counter-threat of an invincible sword.

We have then, in his Republic, a middle class of soldiers – or, as Plato calls them, guardians – in addition to the lowest class – of farmers, labourers and buinessmen, the lowest class, we remenber, consists of those who at the age of twenty have been found to possess inferior minds. The middle class contains all those who at thirty have demonstrated that they are incapable of further mental development. Those of superior mentality who are left after the two eliminations are now ready to take up the study of Philosophy. They are thirty years old. These are the men and the women who will be trained to become the rulers of the state. In Plato's Republic, as we have seen there is complete equality between the sexes. They get the same training, and they are allowed to enter the same positions when they are ready to take up the serious business of life. After a five years' course of philosophy these picked men and women are thorough with their theoretical training. But not with their practical educaion. They must now go through a post – graduate course in good government. They must come down from the heights of their contemplation into the rough-and-tumble world of everyday life. They must get the "feel" of life before they are allowed to take a hand in directing it. For fifteen years they must engage in practical affairs until, at fifty, they are at last ready to assume the role of philosopher— kings. For, in the ideal Republic, the philosopher alone is worthy of being the ruler. "Unless philosophers become rulers, or rulers study philosophy, there will be no end to the troubles of men."

And how is the philosopher differentiated from his fellow men? In his ability to understand God's perfect Idea of which the material world is but an imperfect copy. The Idea of God, the Divine Secret of life, is like a shining light in heaven. But our ordinary minds here below are distorted bits of mirrors in which the Idea becomes broken up into blurred and grotesque and unrecognizable reflections. It is the business of the Philosopher so to shape and to polish the mirror of his mind as to get a clear image of the Idea of God, the Divine Secret, the Light of Reason that guides the stars in the heavens and the affairs of men. And having received this clear indication of God's purpose, it is the further business of the philosopher to incorporate it into the best possible government for his ideal state.

For the ideal state must always be governed by the best. And in Plato's Republic the philosophers are, both by training and by natural ability, the "choicest of the best" men and women that the state has been able to produce. These philosopher-rulers from the highest class, and the other two classes must obey them at all times. In order to insure the honesty of these public officials there must be no private property among them. They are to own everything in common. They will take their meals in public dining rooms and sleep together in barracks. Having no personal interests, these rulers will be above bribery and they will have but a single ambition – to establish and to perpetuate justice among men.

V

WE now have the complete structure of our ideal state. Let us inscribe upon its gates, "This is the City of Justice," and let us enter it in order that we may examine a few of its more interesting features. First of all we find that the philosopher-rulers have driven out of this city their epic poet, Homer, together with his pagan system of polytheism. It insults their intelligence to believe in the childish tales about the Olympian gods who strut about with their silly human weaknesses throughout the pages of the *Iliad.* Religion must be purified of all its savage myths and superstitious miracles. We must have only the religion which is compatible with human reason.

So much for the treatment of the gods in Plato's Republic. How about the dealings between man and man? These dealings are all based upon a strict observance of fair play. Business is looked upon as degrading, because maintains Plato – it is impossible for a businessman to be both successful and honest at the same time. Criminals in Plato's Repubic are regarded as an object of pity. They are restrained, not punished. For viciousness is the result of ignorance. If a man commits a crime, it is because he has not been properly educated. He is a pitiable creature who understands neither his own interests nor the interests of his fellows. You cannot make a violent horse docile by whipping it, and you cannot make an antisocial man gentle by treating him as an outcast. If a criminal is mad, you must cure him of his madness. If he is illinformed, you must teach him. Stamp out the crime with the medicine of wisdom, but do not scourge the criminal with the whiplash of revenge.

Physical sickness, like moral sickness, is due to ignorance. Proper education will eliminate disease to a large extent. Those, however, who are incurably sick must be mercifully allowed to die. For a speedy death is better than a lingering disease.

Lawyers in Plato's Republic are an unnecessary evil. Where there is knowledge there is no need for litigation. The laws that govern the people are few now in number and easy to interpret. For the rulers of the state know that every new law is likely to breed a new class of lawbreakers. These rulers teach their citizens to govern themselves, so that the necessity of policing them is reduced to a minimum.

The main business of the government in the Republic is to insure the happiness of the governed, to give them health and contentment and leisure. "Give me health and a day," writes the Platonist, Emerson, "and I will make the pomp of emperors ridiculous." Health, contentment and a day — a lifelong blue–and–golden day of beauty — this, to Plato, is the sum of human happiness. A life of *beauty*, a life of *justice*, a life of *love*. The three words, beauty, justice, love, are almost synonymous in the philosophy of Plato. The good man, the happy man — for to be good is to be happy — is the just man, the harmonious man, the man whose perfectly attuned character always plays the right note in the symphony of social cooperation. This ideal man of Plato's ideal Republic is consecrated to the creation of beauty, either in living offspring or in works of art or in noble deeds. For beauty is the password to immortality. By creating a thing of beauty we conquer death.

VI

SUCH was the philosophic dream of Plato, the high priest in the religion of Beauty. He built a city of supermen, dedicated it to his godfather Apollo, the Lord of Light, and placed it among the stars that the architects of the future might look to it as a model for their own attempts to bring the earth nearer to heaven.

Plato was not satisfied, however, with the mere creation of a dream. Like that Chinese philosopher Confucius, he attempted to put his philosophical theories into practice. At the invitation of Dionysius he went to Syracuse and tried to show this monarch how to rule like a wise man. Dionysius, however, was merely a king and no philosopher. He took fright at some of Plato's radical ideas and threatened to put him to death. At the intercession of some of Plato's friends, however, he spared his life but sold him into bondage. And thus, instead of transforming Dionysius into a philosopher-king, Plato was himself transformed into a philosopher-slave.

Fortunately for Plato, the man who had bought him for the education of his children was not only a lover of wisdom but a lover of justice. He released Plato and allowed him to go back to Athens.

On his return to his native city Plato received an apologetic letter from Dionysius. The whole episode, explained the tyrant, had been a ghastly mistake, and he therefore hoped that Plato would forgive him and think well of him. To which letter Plato contemptuously replied, "I am too busy with my philosophy to waste my time thinking about Dionysius."

For a long time he continued his quiet philosophical conversations in the garden of his Academy— conversations that were like heavenly discourse. Indeed, "had Jove descended to the earth, he would have spoken in the style of Plato."

But Plato was a *mortal* Jove. One day, in his eighty first year, he was present at the wedding feast of a young friend. The noise of the revellers fatigued him. He asked to be excused and went into another room 'to take a little nap,' as he said. The merry-making became more and more boisterous. The wedding guests forgot about the tired old philosopher who was trying to rest through all this hubbub.

At last the bridegroom tiptoed into the next room to have a look at his master. Plato was sound asleep. The meaningless noises of the world no longer disturbed him. The philosopher-king, the king of philosophers, had been summoned at last to enter into the peaceful Republic of Death.

***

IMPORTANT WORKS BY PLATO

Republic.
Symposium
Phaedrus
Phaedo
Apology of Socrates
Crito
Timaeus
Critias
Philebus
Theaetetus
Lysis
Laches
Charmides
Gorgias.
Parmcnides
Euthydemus
Sophist
Protagoras
Cratylus
Ion
Meno
Euthyphro
Laws ·

2

ARISTOTLE

384 B.C. – 322 B.C.

ON a midsummer day in the year 366 a young man applied for matriculation at Plato's Academy. He had come from the Macedonian city of Stagira, the "Wild West" of the Athenian world. Yet there was nothing of the cowboy about this elegant youngster. He was the very picture of refinement, for he had been brought up in a cultured atmosphere. His father, who was now dead, had been court physician to Amyntas, king of Macedonia and grandfather of Alexander. From early childhood young Aristotle had been trained to a life of mental discipline and physical comfort.

His arrival at the Academy created a stir among the other students. For here was an aristocrat of the aristocrats—suave, dapper, graceful, soft-spoken, gentle, polite, the very model of sartorial and ethical propriety. Indeed, he was somewhat of a fop. He spoke with an affected lisp, and he paid more attention to his clothes-as Plato complained – than was becoming for a sincere lover of wisdom.

But he displayed an intellect of incredible versatility.

It seemed almost impossible for one mind to be open to so many facets of knowledge. Politics, drama, poetry, physics, medicine, psychology, history, logic, astronomy, ethics, natural history, mathematics, rhetoric, biology– these were but a few dishes in the diversified banquet with which the young student tried to feed his voracious appetite for learning. Plato once humorously remarked that his Academy consisted of two parts – the body of his students, and the brain of Aristotle.

As was to be expected, the greatest master and the most brilliant student of Athens couldn't get along together. When Greek meets Greek, especially on a level of mental quality, there is bound to be a clash. The old and the young philosoher constantly quarrelled and always adored each other.

When Plato died (347 B.C.) Aristotle was thirty-seven years old. He had rightfully expected to be chosen as Plato's successor to the presidency of the Academy. But in this expectation he was disappointed. The trustees of the Academy passed over him as a "foreigner" and elected a native Athenian instead. Angry over his failure, Aristotle looked for an opportunity to leave Athens. And the opportunity came by way of invitation from one of his former classmates, Hermeias. This philosopher-politician had acquired the lordship of a large territory in Asia Minor. Like Dionysius, the king of Syracuse, he was eager to try an experiment in wise government, provided the wisdom wouldn't interfere with his wealth. And so he invited Aristotle to teach him how to reconcile abstract Justice with concrete plunder.

But Aristotle was interested only in justice. He therefore failed in his mission to divert his friend from the pursuit of riches to the quest for righteousness. He succeeded, however, in marrying Pythias, the niece and adopted daughter of Hermeias. Though he loved the lady for herself, he offered no objection to the handsome dowry which she brought along with her. Aristotle, as we shall see, was not averse to "a fair measure" of prosperity. Indeed, he regarded it as one of the essentials of a happy life.

He married Pythias, invested his money and spent his honeymoon collecting sea shells for his scientific studies.

After the honeymoon he returned to the court of Hermeias. But his stay at that court was brief. The intrigues of Hermeias had aroused the anger of the Persian king. The Persians invaded his country, took Hermeias prisoner and crucified him.

Once more Aristotle found himself without a country and without a job. But once more a royal friend came to the rescue. This time it was King Philip of Macedonia, the son of Amyntas and the father of Alexander. He invited Aristotle to his palace as the tutor of Alexander.

When Aristotle returned to the court in which his father had served as the royal physician he felt "like a fish out of the water." The Macedonian atmosphere at that moment was no fit place for philosophical meditation. It was an atmosphere of inordinate ambition, barbaric splendour and barbaric vulgarity. King Philip was a man of superior intelligence but inferior education. His language bristled with grammatical errors. "I ain't no barbarian," he insisted, and he didn't want his son, either, to be, "no barbarian." Indeed, he wanted Alexander to grow up as a refined philosopher. As well try to transform a seething maelstrom into a placid lake. Alexander was the untamed cub of a ferocious lion. In fact, the entire court was like a jungle of snarling beasts. Quarrels, duels, debaucheries, assassinations--- these were the order of the day. Olympias, the wife of King Philip, bordered on the verge of insanity, and Philip and Alexander were not far removed from that irrational borderland. At one of the royal banquets Philip tried to stab Alexander because the boy had insulted him. And Alexander, not to be outdone, made a murderous assault upon his father. Fortunately for the two, but unfortunately for the world, the attendants succeeded in tearing them apart.

Such was the turbulent household which Aristotle had been commissioned to soothe with the "sweetness of wisdom." But to no avail. Philip had long entertained a dream of world wide conquests. He was now engaged in carrying out the first part of this imperialistic dream— the subjugation of the Greek states. One by one he held out to them a policy of 'appeasement,' and when the Greek states (like the European states in 1938-40) were lulled into a false sense of security by his insincere promises, he gobbled them up one by one. And then, in the midst of this triumph he was assassinated; and Alexander, the pupil of Aristotle, abandoned the theoretical philosophy of his teacher for the practical dreams of his father. He completed Philip's interrupted campaign against the Greeks and then he set out to conquer the rest of the world. As a spur against his own impetuosity he took along with him the philosopher Callisthenes, who was the pupil and nephew of Aristotle. But Callisthenes didn't put an end to

Alexander's impetuosity. On the contrary, Alexander put an end to Callisthenes' life. Infuriated at the young man's refusal to regard him as a god, he ordered Callisthenes to be hanged.

Again Aristotle was left to his own resources. He had come to Macedonia in quest of political glory. He now returned to Athens a sadder politician and a wiser philosopher. Enough of practical life. From now on he would devote himsef to his studies.

Fortunately he was able to plunge into his studies on a tremendous scale. Aside from his own funds, which were by no means negligible, he had received from King Philip a sum of eight hundred talents- equal in modern purchasing power to about $4,000, 000-for his scientific investigations. Hiring nearly thousand assistants, he sent them off into every part of the world to collect material and specimens for a comprehensive encyclopedia of philosophy and science.

But Aristotle was more than a research scholar. He was primarily a teacher. Still smarting under his defeat as a candidate for the presidency of the Academy, he opened a rival school, the Lyceum (so - called because it was situated in the grove dedicated to Apollo Lyceus, the defender of the flock against the wolves). Here he gathered his flock of students and prepared them to fight against the wolves of ignorance. In the morning he offered technical courses to his advanced students and in the afternoon he delivered popular lectures to the general public.

His contemporaries have handed down to us a vivid picture of Aristotle as a lecturer. Bald and somewhat pot-bellied (for he was now turning fifty), carefully and even ostentatiously dressed, thin of leg but keen-eyed and sharp-tongued, he still talked with that boyhood lisp of his as he guided and cajoled and satirized his audiences into the paths of wisdom. Restless by nature, he was unable to sit still as he lectured to his students, especially in the morning when his classes were small. He paced up and down among the colonnades with his pupils, expounding his views and answering their questions, and thus gained for his Lyceum the nickname of the *Peripatetic* school— the school of *strolling Philosophers.* To this day the Aristotelian philosophy is known as the *Peripatetic* system.

Let us attend a few of the sessions at this school in order that we may get a glimpse into the Aristotelian system of philosophy. We shall not go into his voluminous scientific observations, fascinating as they are, since these observations form a catalogue of unorganized facts rather than a synthesis of organic thought. Let us, however, explain in passing that the inadequacy of Aristotle's scientific knowledge was due not to the imperfection of his mind but to the absence of the necessary scientific instruments. Without a telescope on the one hand or a microscope on the other, he could get no idea either of the vastness of the universe or of the minuteness of its parts. Due to this handicap the science of Aristotle is of historical interest but of no practical value today.

When we come to his speculative philosophy, however, we find ourselves on more universal ground. For he discusses three topics that concern our present generation as vitally as they concerned the generation of Aristotle. These three topics are *God*, the *State* and *Man*. What is the nature of God? What is the best sort of government for the State? And what is the most desirable conduct for man? Aristotle considers the nature of God in his *Metaphysics,* the government of the State in his *Politics* and the morals of Man in his *Ethics.*

II

In the philosophical system of Aristotle, God is not the Creator of the universe but the Cause of its motion. For a creator is a dreamer, and a dreamer is a dissatisfied personality, a soul that yearns for something that is not, an unhappy being who seeks for happiness-in short, an imperfect creature who aims at perfection. But God is perfect, and since he is perfect he cannot be dissatisfied or unhappy. He is therefore not the Maker but the Mover of the universe.

But what sort of Mover? To this question Aristotle replies that God is the *Unmoved Mover* of the universe. Every other source of motion in the world, whether it be a person or a thing or a thought, is: (according to Aristotle) *a moved mover.* Thus the plough moves the earth, the hand moves the plough, the brain moves the hand, the desire for food moves the brain, the instinct for life moves the desire for food and so on. In other words, the cause of every motion is the result of some other motion. The master of every slave is the slave of some other master. Even the tyrant is the slave of his ambition. But God can be the result of no action. He can be the slave of no master. He is the source of all action, the master of all masters, the instigator of all thought, the Unmoved Mover of the world.

Furthermore, God is not interested in the world, though the world is interested in God. For to be interested in the world means to be subject to emotion, to be swayed by prayers or imprecations, to be capable of changing one's mind as a result of somebody else's actions or desires or thoughts–in short, to be imperfect. But God is passionless, changeless, perfect. He moves the world as a beloved object moves the lover. A beautiful woman is walking down the street. She is completely absorbed in her own thoughts. Her gaze is fixed upon the ground. She doesn't look at anybody. But everybody is looking at her. The presence of her beauty has turned all eyes, has stirred all hearts into action, all minds into thought. Such is the nature of the beauty of God. Without being moved itself, it "produces motion within all of us by being loved."

This Aristotelian God, who is loved by all men but who is indifferent to their fate, is a cold, impersonal and, from our modern religious standpoint, "perfectly" unsatisfactory type of Supreme Being. He resembles the Primal Energy of the scientists rather than the Heavenly Father of the poets. The human minds, divorced of all emotion, may be able to conceive of such a disinterested ruler of the universe. But the human heart, with its burden of sorrow and its gift for compassion, insists upon a God who is a Loving Friend in heaven rather than a loveless abstraction in the metaphysical speculations of a Greek philosopher. And perhaps the heart is nearer than the mind to the ultimate mystery of the world.

As for the scientific validity of the Aristotelian speculation about the Unmoved Mover, or the Uncreated Cause of all motion, the weakness of Aristotle's position is well summarised in the words of the little girl who asked "But, Mother, who made God?"

III

WHEN Aristotle moved down from heaven to earth his thought becomes more logical, more understandable, more concrete. One by one he takes up the various forms of government that have been tried out in the world– dictatorship, monarchy, oligarchy (the rule of the few) and democracy. He analyses each of them in turn, admits their strong features and points out their weaknesses. Of all the forms of government, dictatorship is the worst. For it subordinates the interests of all to the ambition of one. The most desirable form of government, on the other hand, is that which "enables every man, whoever he is, to exercise his best abilities and to live his days most pleasantly." Such a government, whatever its name, will always be a *constitutional* government. Any government without a constitution is a tyranny, whether it is the government of one man, a few men or many men. The unrestrained will of a handful of plutocrats or of a horde of proletarians is just a tyranny as the unrestrained will of one man. The dictatorship of a class is no better than the dictatorship of an individual.

From this point Aristotle goes on to describe what he considers as the perfect type of undictatorial government:

In the first place the government should not be– like Plato's Republic– communistic. The common ownership of property, and especially of women and of children, would result in continual misunderstandings, quarrels and crimes. Communism would destroy personal responsibility. "What everybody owns, nobody cares for." Common liability means individual negligence. "Everybody is inclined to evade a duty which he expects another to fulfil." You can no more hope to communise human goods than you can hope to communise human character. Aristotle advocates the private development of each man's character and the private ownership of each man's property.

But just as each man's private character must be directed to the public welfare, so too must each man's private property be employed for the public use. "And the special business of the legislator is to create in all men this co-operative disposition." It is the legislator's *entire* business to provide for the *public* interest through the unselfish interplay of the *private* interests of the citizens. To this end there should be no hard-and-fast distinction between classes, particularly between the classes of the rulers and the class of the ruled. Indeed, all the citizens alike should take their turn of governing and being governed, with the general proviso that "the old are more fitted to rule, the young to obey."

The ruling must be vitally concerned with the education of the young. And this education must be both practical and ideal. It must not only provide the adolescent citizens with the means for making a living but it must also teach them how to live within their means. In this way the state will be assured of an enlightened, prosperous, co-operative and contented citizenry.

Above all, the rulers must aim at the contentment of the ruled. Contentment through justice. For only in this way can they avoid revolutions. "No sensible man, if he can escape from it or overthrow it, will endure an unjust government." Such a government is like a fire that heats the pent-up resentment of the people to the bursting point. It is bound, sooner or later, to result in a violent explosion. Judged from the standpoint of fairness toward its citizens, "democracy appears to be safer and less liable to revolution than any other form of government." The countries that are most likely to explode into early rebellion are those that are governed by dictators. 'Dictatorship" observes Aristotle, "are the most fragile of governments."

IV

THE aim of government, writes Aristotle, is to insure the welfare of the governed. And thus politics is translated into ethics. The state exists for man and not man for the state. Man is born for only one purpose-to be happy.

But what is happiness? It is that pleasant state of mind which is brought about by the habitual doing of good deeds. But to be happy it is not sufficient merely to be *good.* It is necessary also to be blessed with a sufficiency of goods — that is, good birth, good looks, good fortune and good friends. Above all, a long and healthy life is necessary for the attainment of happiness. "One swallow does not make a summer, nor does one day." To make a perfect summer of our life we need many days, a sufficiency of sunlight and a full measure of song.

Yet even in a short life, and in the midst of misfortune it is possible for the noble man to be happy. For the noble soul can cultivate an insensibility to pain, and this in itself is a blessing. In other words, we may sometimes *attain* happiness by *renouncing* it. Furthermore, no man can be called unhappy if he acts in accordance with virtue. For such a man "will never do anything harmful or mean." And happiness, as we have already observed, consists in the doing of good deeds. But the only *completely* happy man is he "who is active in accordance with complete virtue and is sufficiently equipped with wealth and health and friendship, not for some chance period but throughout a complete life."

But if happiness is the result of virtue, what then is virtue? To the ancients this word did not mean, as it does to us, *moral* excellence alone. It meant any kind of excellence. Thus a Greek Casanova might have been called a virtuous lover because he was an *efficient* lover. A ruthless but competent general would in Athens have been regarded as a virtuous soldier. Indeed, the Greek word for virtue *arete*, was derived from Ares, the god of war. We get our own term, *virtue*, from the Latin translation for *arete-virtus*, which means *the quality of manliness*. A virtuous person, in Aristotle's philosophy was a person who possessed physical prowess, technical competence and mental virtuosity. To these three qualities Aristotle now added a fourth requisite for happiness — moral nobility. This all-round excellencc, therefore, was needed for Aristotle's "happy warrior" in the battlefield of life.

Aristotle summarised this manifold excellence in his famous doctrine of the "golden mean." The happy man, the virtuous man, is he who preserves the golden mean between the two extremes of ignoble conduct. He is the man who steers the middle course between the shoals that threaten on either side to wreck his happiness. In every act, in every thought, in every emotion, a man may be overdoing his duty or underdoing it or doing it just right. Thus, in sharing his goods with other people, a man may be *extravagant,* which is overdoing it, or *stingy,* which is underdoing it, or liberal, which is doing it just right. In the matter of facing the dangers of life a man may be *foolhardy* or *cowardly* or *brave.* In the handling of his appetites he may be *gluttonous* or *abstemious* or *moderate.* In every case the rational way of life is to do nothing too much or too little but to adopt the middle course. The virtuous man will be neither supernormal nor subnormal but justly and wisely normal. He will act "at the right times, with reference to the right objects, towards the right people, with the right motive and in the right way." In short, he will at all times and under all conditions observe the golden mean. For the golden mean is the royal road to happiness.

And now, having paved the road to happiness, Aristotle describes the ideal man who is most worthy of being happy. This ideal man, the Aristotelian gentleman, "does not expose himself needlessly to danger but is willing in great crises to give his life if necessary. He takes joy in doing favours to other men, but he feels shame in having favours done to him by other men. For it is a mark of superiority to confer a kindness, but inferiority to receive it." His unselfishness, however, is but a higher form of selfishness, of *enlightened* selfishness. The doing of a kind deed is not an act of self-sacrifice but of self-preservation. For a man in not *individual* self but a *social* self. Moreover, every good deed is a profitable investment. It is bound, sooner or later, to be returned with interest. "The ideal man, therefore, is altruistic because he is wise... He does not speak evil of others, even of his enemies, unless it be to themselves... He never feels malice and away forgets injuries... In short, he is a good friend to others because he is his own best friend."

V

THIS picture of the Athenian gentleman is in reality the self- portrait of Aristotle. Gentle, unperturbed and wise, he continued to point out to his fellow men the middle course of safety that lay between the rashness of conquest on the one hand and the cowardice of submission on the other. But the times were out of joint. The Athenians were in no mood to listen to wisdom. They accused Aristotle of being a pro-Macedonian spy. They couldn't forget the fact that he had been the teacher of Alexander. As for Alexander himself, he too had grown hostile towards Aristotle. Wisdom and war were two irreconcilable enemies. Moderation, calmness, the golden mean — this was too dangerous a doctrine to be heard amidst the clash of conquering arms. Alexander had already killed Callisthenes, the nephew of Aristotle. It would be safer for Alexander if Aristotle, too, could be put out of the way.

And so the gentle philosopher was beset by dangers on either side. One of these dangers was eleminated when Alexander died as a result of a drunken debauch. But the other danger, stemming from the suspicion of the Athenians, kept constantly growing until finally Aristotle was threatened with arrest.

Mindful of the fate of Socrates, Aristotle left the city before it was too late. He wouldn't give the Athenians "a second chance of sinning against philosophy," he said.

Aristotle had escaped from the judges, but he couldn't escape from death. It lay in wait for him in his exile. He died only a year after his departure from Athens.

Just before his death he wrote the greatest of his works–a brief but epoch-making will in which he provided for the deliverance of his slaves. It was the first emancipation proclamation in history.

****

Important Works By Aristotle

158 Constitutions (including The Constitution of Athens).
Dialogues.
On Monarchy.
Alexander.
The Customs of Barbarians.
Natural History.
Organon, or The Instrument of Correct Thinking.
On the Soul.
Rhetoric.
Logic.
Eudemian Ethics.
Nicomachean Ethics.
Physics.
Metaphysics.
Politics.
Poetics.

Aristotle wrote about four hundred volumes in all. These volumes covered practically every phase of human knowledge and of human activity.

✦✧✦

3

EPICURUS

342 B.C. – 270 B.C.

IN the first book of *Gargantua* Brother Rabelais tells us a fantastic story about the Abbey of Theleme. This fictitious abbey is the home of the religious order *Fais Ce Que Vouldras* (Do As You Like). The only rule to be observed in this abbey is to observe no rule at all. There are to be no clocks here to remind anyone of time for prayer or duty. Instead of taking the three vows of chastity, poverty and obedience, the monks and the nuns of this convent are to be allowed to marry, to make money and to live at liberty. The doors of this abbey are to be forever barred against "bigots, hypocrites, attorneys, magistrates, merchants, bankers, drunkards, liars, cowards, cheaters and thieves." On the other hand, this place is to be a congenial home for "all noble sparks in search of lively larks," men who love pleasure and women who are able to please — gay, witty, cheerful, spruce, jocund, sprightly, jovial, handsome, courteous, worthy, gentle, frolicsome blades and delicious, charming, mirthful, ingenious, lovely, magnetic, enticing, young, ripe, choice, dear, courtly, fine, comely, complete, clever, personable and ravishing ladies.

Such are the members who are to form the brotherhood and sisterhood of this religious order of "pious carelessness." Their sole business is to disregard the uncertain life of tomorrow and to concentrate upon the certain life of today.

This Rabelaisian Abbey of Theleme is a caricature of the Garden of Epicurus, that famous monastery of pleasure founded by the saddest of Athenian philosophers. The Garden of Epicurus, like the Abbey of Theleme, was a religious retreat. It was not, however, a hotbed of debauchery. On the contrary, it was a place of quiet meditation. The word *epicurean* is one of the most abused words in English language. An *epicurean* today is a devotee of selfish lust, a man who indulges in the appetites of his belly. He is far from being a disciple of Epicurus, the prophet who founded a religion based upon the pleasures of the mind. It is one of the practical jokes of destiny that the symbol of gluttony is associated with the name of the most famous ascetic in the ancient world. Epicurus was the least of the epicureans.

But let us look at the man.

II

HE was born on the island of Samos (342 B.C.) in the midst of the Macedonian aggression against the liberty of Greece. His father, an Athenian schoolmaster, implanted in his heart a contempt for tyranny. His mother was a quack doctor of the soul, a cunning peddler of prayers who offered to cure sickness by magic charms and incantations. As a child he was obliged to go with his mother from house to house, helping her in the dispensation of her pious frauds. In this way he acquired a healthy contempt for superstition.

He showed an early interest in the study of philosophy. One day, when he was about twelve years old, his teacher tried to explain the creation of the world. "Everything," said the teacher, "came from Chaos."

"Yes," replied Epicurus, "but what did Choas come from?"

"I don't know," said the teacher. "Nobody knows."

Right then and there Epicurus decided that it would be his business to know. He would make it his life's work to seek for the origin of Chaos which in turn was the origin of the world.

At eighteen he came to Athens. It was a period of turmoil. The ruler of Athens, appointed by Alexander, was the typical dictator of the ancient world (or of the modern world, too, for that matter). In his effort to break down the democratic spirit throughout the Greek states he "reshuffled" the population of the conquered territory, driving out the "rebellious" natives and replacing them with Macedonian colonists. Among the refugees who were thus dispossessed of their homes were the parents of Epicurus. They were obliged to flee to Asia Minor. Here Epicurus met them after a brief stay in Athens. He tried to forget the nightmare of life in the dream of philosophy. Added to his old quest for the origin of Chaos was a new impulse, a desire to find a way *out of* Chaos.

He never quite found it, either in the distractions of politics or in the abstractions of theology. He did, however, hit upon a few physical and metaphysical principles which enabled him to build for himself an oasis of peace amidst the whirling sands of existence. Enriched with this discovery, he returned to Athens, bought a house and garden in one of the suburbs and set up an outdoor academy for the teaching of philosophy.

The academy was co-educational. It was open to all classes, including even slaves and prostitutes. For, as Epicurus explained, there are no class distinctions in the realm of learning. The master and the disciples lived together in their academy on terms of equal sociability and mutual regard. As was to be expected, there was much idle gossip in Athens about the "sensual debauchery" and the "orgies of love" in the Garden of Epicurus. There was no foundation for any such gossip, however. Far from being gluttonous, the life of the academicians was simple to the point of abstemiousness. Barley bread and water with an occasional half pint of wine, was their daily fare. Cheese was a luxury reserved only for exceptional holidays. "Send me some preserved cheese," wrote Epicurus to a friend, "that our community may indulge in a festival." Rich food was taboo at the academy, for such food results not in pleasure but in pain - the pain of indigestion. "I am thrilled with my bread and water", wrote the master, "and I spit upon rich spices - not for their own sake but because of the inconveniences that follow them."

Bread and water and the wine of philosophy – this, to Epicurus, was the substance of the happy life. But what was this philosophy that enabled Epicurus and his disciples to find contentment in the midst of so much discontent? It was the negative philosophy of *ataraxia,* a Greek word which means *passionlessness. imperturbability, the tranquility, of a healthy mind.* Epicurus developed this philosophy in a series of three hundred books – the Greek philosophers not only had much to say but they had a long way of saying it. These books of Epicurus have all been lost. Fortunately we have a clear outline of his philosophy in the epic poem of Lucretius, *De Rerum Natura* (On the Nature of Things). Lucretius was an Epicurean philosopher who lived in Rome about two hundred and fifty years after Epicurus. His poem on the nature of things is one of the strangest compositions in the history of literature. It is a plea for cold logic, and yet it is written in a white heat of passion. It is the work of an infidel who denies the humanity of God but who asserts the divinity of Man. It has been called one of the great bibles of the world – a Bible for Unbelievers.

A brief survey of this Lucretian epic of profane scripture will usher us into the simple but fascinating Palace of Pleasure known as the philosophy of Epicurus.

III

THE purpose of living, according to Epicurus, is to enjoy life. But in order to enjoy life we must understand it. We must familiarize ourselves with the world that we inhabit and with the nature of its inhabitants. In other words we must find out *who* we are and *why* we are *what* we are.

First of all, then, let us distinctly understand who we are. We are not–asserts Epicurus–the children of a beneficent God, but the stepchildren of an indifferent Nature. Life is not the designed plan of a divine artist. It is merely an accident in a mechanical universe. But we can make it, if we will, a *happy* or at least an *interesting* accident.

And how can we do this? By driving out of our heads the two great terrors that beset mankind: the fear of the gods, and the fear of death.

We have nothing to fear from the gods–continues Epicurus – because we are not the slaves of the gods. They have no jurisdiction over us since they have not created us. Indeed, they haven't created anything. The universe is not the handiwork of God but the fortuitous outcome of the movement of atoms through infinite space.

And this brings us to the atomic theory of Epicurus– a theory which is a forerunner of the present-day mechanistic interpretation of the universe. Epicurus borrowed his atomic system from Democritus, one of those ancient Greek philosophers to whom the discovery of a scientific truth was more important than the subjugation of an empire.

Epicurus had found an answer to his old question about Chaos in the hypothesis of an atomic infinity of building material – infinitesimal bricks – out of which universes are made. For it more than explained to him the origin of Chaos–it did away with Chaos altogether. There can be no such thing as Chaos, or nothingness asserted Epicurus. And he gave three reasons for this assertion:

1. The world couldn't have come out of Chaos, for nothing can be created out of nothingness.
2. The world cannot he dissolved into Chaos, for nothing can disappear into nothingness.
3. Hence the sum total of matster–the collection of bricks out of which universes are built–remains always the same. There can be no addition to it out of nothingness, and there can be no diminution from it into nothingness.

The world, therefore, consists of an eternal infinity of *Somethingness* – that is, material atoms. (The Greek word for atom, *atomos* means a particle of matter that cannot be cut or divided into smaller particles. An atom, in the philosophy of Epicurus as well as in modern physics, is the smallest possible component of a material body.) The atoms that compose the structure of the world, said Epicurus, are birthless, deathless, immutable. They move eternally downward through *infinite* space. But now and then they swerve in their downward motion, like motes in a sunbeam or like raindrops whirled into eddies by a gust of wind. And as they are whirled together they collide and thus become kneaded into the substance of stars and earths and moons and suns and universes.

Now these atoms are of different weights and shapes and sizes. And these differences account for the infinite variety of things that go into the making of the world.

But our world, continues Epicurus, is not the only one in existence. There are others equally vast and equally wonderful. They, too, have their earths, with their mountains and oceans, and their races of men and generations of wild beasts. We are not the only pebble on the branch of the infinite sea; for the atoms come into the same kinds of combinations, under the same sorts of conditions, over and again as they whirl forever downward through the endless aisles of space.

And all this whirling movement is spontaneous. There is no hand to guide it. For even the gods are the mechanical creatures of the atomic flux. They are made of finer, more subtle sorts of atoms than those which go into the making of men. They live in their vast heavens, which are the cloudless spaces between the universes. Here they enjoy a blessed immortality which concerns itself not a whit over the joys and the sorrows and the struggles of mankind.

The gods have had nothing to do with our creation, and they are utterly indifferent to our fate. The life of man, believes Epicurus, is too crazy a farce to have originated in the mind of a sane Dramatist. No rational God would order a temple to be built in his honour and then strike it down with his own lightning. No merciful Providence would bring a young boy through a dangerous illness only to send him to a worse death on the battlefield.

The gods, therefore, enjoy their immortal felicity in their interspatial Paradise precisely because they are withdrawn from the cares and the obligations and the sufferings of mankind. "That which is blessed and immortal.... is equally exempt from favours or frowns, from compassion or wrath.... Untroubled themselves, they are infinitely removed from the troubles of men."

But if the gods do not trouble themselves about men, why should men trouble themselves about the gods? Because, replies Epicurus, if men try to become more divine they will succeed in becoming more human. By worshipping the gods – and Epicurus himself was always punctilious in his religious worship – we become more god like, more refined, more indifferent to the buffeting of fate and the vicissitudes of life. True religion, therefore, does not consist in sacrifice of superstition or fear. It consists rather in a pious imitation of the gods — that is, in "the contemplation of the nature of the world with a mind at rest."

IV

AND so we come once more to the Epicurean investigation into the nature of the world. This world of ours, maintains Epicurus, is self-generated as a result of the accidental whirling and collision of an infinity of atoms. But how does it happen that the gathering together of the unguided particles of matter should have combined into the making of trees and flowers, of birds and beasts and men? Through what process have atoms been able to produce a poet like Homer, a scientist like Democritus, a philosopher like Epicurus?; Through the process of trial and error, replies Epicurus: through the gradual development of matter from cruder to finer forms; through the elimination of the unfit and the survival of the fittest. In short, through the process of evolution.

Epicurus advanced the theory of evolution twenty-two hundred years before Darwin. In his poem *On the Nature of Things* Lucretius gives us an interesting picture of the world as represented in the Epicurean theory of the origin of species and the descent of man. The atoms in their eternal whirl, after many combinations and dissolutions, finally became united into what we call "the world." At first the earth was a lifeless lump of clay, but gradually it began to put forth grass and shrubs and flowers, just as animals and birds put forth hair and feathers. Life, came next. Birds began to fly and make music in the air, and beasts prowled over the forests and filled them with their bellowings. Some of these species were adapted to their environment and were thus enabled, either through their courage or their cunning, to survive. Others were born with insufficient sight or hearing or means of locomotion. They were the freaks of nature, the victims of a blind experiment in a planless world, and they were doomed to extinction. Man, the protagonist in this interesting play without a plot, was the last to arrive upon the scene. Hardy and savage and naked, he roamed over the earth like the other animals, living on herbs and fruits and acorns and sleeping in the open fields at night.

Attacked by the more ferocious beasts, he learned after a time to seek refuge in caves. The herding together of many beast-men into a single cave for mutual protection brought about the gradual development of speech and pity and the first crude feelings of friendship. The beast-men discovered the use of metal, and in this way they were able to produce better tools for their own protection and for the killing of others. One cave group began to exchange goods and ideas-and blows-with other cave groups, and thus little by little they acquired the arts of barter, commerce, navigation, agriculture, poetry, music, architecture, politics, diplomacy, litigation and war. In short, observes Epicurus, our civilization is nothing but a evolutionary process which enables man to adapt himself to an inhospitable world and to survive for a brief space in the eternal struggle for existence. For all life is a continual warfare, and there is no truce for any of us except in death.

And death, maintains Epicurus, is the end of our existence. The soul like the body, is mortal. For the soul, too, is a compound of atoms, a sort of liquid energy which fills the vessel of the body as water fills a pitcher. So long as the body lasts, the soul is held together. But when the body breaks, the liquid soul spills out and is dissolved into the isolated drops of its individual atoms. It was born with the birth of the body, and it dies with its death. Outside of the body, there is no thought, no feeling, no sensation, no memory, no life. "Dust thou art, to dust returnest" is equally true of the human body and of the human soul.

So much, then, for the scientific theory of Epicurus. This theory is very interesting, but it fails to convince the modern mind, as indeed it failed to convince many an ancient mind, because of two important omissions. In the first place, it does not explain how the movement of unconscious matter can produce Conscious thought. In the second place, it does not account for the principle of motion in the first place. What causes the atoms *to move?* And *who* causes them to move? And *why?* As a European scholar somewhat unfamiliar with English language has naively expressed it, "If the world revolves, where is the revolver?"

V

EPICURUS gives us a sad cold, bleak science-an intricate machine without a mechanic, a superhuman spectacle without a divine plan. And then he proceeds to give us an equally sad, cold bleak philosophy — a system or pleasure without joy, the negative tranquillity of death as an escape from the positive perplexities of life. The earth we live in, he reminds us, is rented to us for a little while, and when the time comes for us to move on we are dispossessed without a moment's notice. But if we cannot conquer death, let us at least overcome the *fear* of death. Let us not grieve over the brevity of human life. Instead let us accept it with a placid heart. For there is no consciousness after death, no pain and no punishment in hell for any mistakes that we may have made during our stay on earth. The white hand of Death soothes us into a sweet and dreamless sleep. For Death is the friendly warden who signs the papers of our release from the madhouse of the world. He is the gentle physician who cures us of the most dreadful of all diseases — Life.

But even if you have found life to be one continual feast of blessings, is it desirable to keep on gorging yourself indefinitely? Is it not much better to leave the table before you are overfilled and to retire smilingly, like a tired but happy banqueter, to a pleasant sleep? One fatal day, you lament, will rob you of all the prizes of life. But you forget to add that this same fatal day will free you from the desire to possess these prizes.

And so let us dismiss the fear of death and concentrate upon whatever blessings we may get out of life. Let us seek for a life of pleasure–a maximum of pleasure with a minimum of pain. At first, in his quest for the pleasant life, Epicurus adopted the idea of the Hedonists, the so-called "belly philosophers" who were concerned not so much with the quiet happiness of the mind as with the boisterous pleasures of the body. Like the Hedonists, he told his students to snatch at the golden moments of life. Later, however, as the appetites of his body lost their edge and the keenness of his mind increased he realized that the pleasure of the moment may sometimes result in the suffering of a lifetime. And then he conceived a negative rather than a positive theory of pleasure. The greatest pleasure, he said, is the complete absence of pain. Accordingly he began to teach a new kind of happiness — the happiness of an unruffled mind as it beholds from a distance the troubles and the turmoils of the world. Refrain from business. Stay out of politics. Watch the game of life from the sidelines. Avoid the storms that may wreck the barque of your happiness. Remain on the seashore as a spectator while the ships of your fellows are breaking up amidst the pounding of the waves.

A fine philosophy, this, for an old man's home but not for a practical world in which people must work and vote and help one another in order to get along. If everybody were to adopt this self-centred attitude of tranquil aloofness as advocated in the ethics of Epicurus, the world would come to a standstill. The pleasure–philosophy of Epicurus, if carried to the extreme, would reduce life to a supremely peaceful–and supremely unpalatable–foretaste of death.

There was, however, one positive aspect to Epicurus negative philosophy of pleasure. And this was his insistence upon the gospel of friendship. Epicurus had a genius for friendship. Though he lived on bread and water, he always tried to break his bread in the company of a friend. "It is more important to know with *whom* we are to eat," he said, "than *what* we are to eat."

His philosophy, to be sure, was self-centred, but it was a *shared* selfishness that he preached. The only way to be happy, he said, is to invite others to partake of your happiness–not because it is *noble* to do so, but because it is *expedient*. "It is not possible to live pleasantly without living wisely and justly and generously." Treat others as you want them to treat you. Inflict no injury in order that you may suffer no injury. Live and let live. For this life of ours is meant to be a festival of friends. Cultivate the genius of friendship. Make a religion of it. Worship it. For friendship is a sweet and beautiful and holy thing. The sympathy of true friendship is the only certain gift we possess in this world of doubtful worth. If the sufferings of life can reconcile us to death, then the holiness of friendship can reconcile us to life.

VI

THE sympathy of his friends reconciled Epicurus to his own sufferings. Poverty, bereavement and disease made his life indeed a thing of doubtful value. Yet we find him, on his very deatbed, writing the following letter to a friend: "And now, as I am passing this last and blessed day of my life, I write to you. Strangury (a painful disease of the bladder) has laid hold of me and wracking torments beyond which suffering cannot endure. But over against all this I set my joy in the memory of our thoughts and words together in the past."

Such was the last testament of this wise and gentle master whose name is now associated with so foolish and ungentle a creed. No philosopher has ever been more revered. No philosopher has even been less understood.

****

IMPORTANT WORKS BY EPICURUS

Epicurus wrote about three hundred books. These have all been lost with the exception of a few fragments on nature, about one hundred aphorisms and several letters in which he outlined the gist of his philosophy. The most important of these letters are the following:

To Herodotus, dealing with physics;

To Menoecus, on ethics and theology;

To Pythocles, on meteorology.

In addition to these sources we get an enthusiastic exposition of the entire Epicurean philosophy in *De Rerum Natura*, the famous epic of the Latin poet Lucretius.

4

MARCUS AURELIUS

121 – 180

WHEN Marcus Aurelius commenced his reign (in 161) the mighty Roman Empire had passed the vigour of its youth. It was rapidly approaching the decline of old age. Under the Caesars the Empire delighted in its conquests; now under the Antonines, it was ripe for philosophy.

For philosophy thrives in the sick chamber of civilization. When men have been struck a great bodily blow in their material fortunes they turn to the affairs of the mind. It is only through periodic illness that the world reflects, and it is only through reflection that the world is worthy of survival. When empires fall philosophy begins. In the case of Greek philosophy a great disaster, the destruction of the Athenian Empire, had set the stage for Plato, Aristotle, the Epicureans and the Stoics. These teachers tried to discover a path of moral conduct along which the individual might safely travel whilst the pillars of his national civilization lay in ruins.

Plato had dreamed of a new ideal state to rise above the ruins of the old. The ideal state was to be ruled by a philosopher-king. If ever a man was destined to remake the world and to raise its citizens to the stature of demigods, it would be such a ruler. With great material resources at his disposal and with great resources of the mind as well, with the armies of men to follow him and with the wisdom of God to lead him on, such a philosopher-king might bring the Utopian dream of Plato to a practical reality. But he must have good material to build with. There must be a great empire for the great emperor, a healthy body for the healthy mind.

Such was the dream of Plato. And it seemed as if the Rome of Marcus Aurelius might fulfil that dream. The Roman Empire, stretching from the northern tip of England to equatorial Africa and from the Atlantic Ocean to the Euphrates, had at long last, in Marcus Aurelius, received its philosopher-king. But Plato's dream was as far from fulfilment as ever. For Rome under the rule of Marcus Aurelius presented the spectacle of an unhealthy body with a healthy mind. Rome was powerful, but it was not sound. In its long and aggressive fight for victory this overambitious empire had bled itself dry.

II

At the age of eleven Marcus Aurelius decided he would be a philosopher. He adopted the shabby cloak of the Cynics, ate simple food and slept on a hard cot. His imagination was fired by the personalities of the gnarled old patriarchs from Athens who brought to Rome their schools of philosophy and their vermin. They walked with bowed heads and with hands folded behind their backs and lectured on the greatness of the universe and the littleness of man. And they practised what they preached, these Cynies who derided pleasure and these Stoics who ignored pain. They retired from the world of man and became voluntary prisoners behind the bars of their principles. But these men were no emperors. In renouncing the world they had nothing to lose but their sorrow. It was something new for a prince to be converted. A prince in the mightiest empire of the ancient world.

When Marcus Aurelius was eighteen, his uncle, the Emperor Pius Antonius, had adopted him as his son and successor to the vast realm. But meanwhile the precocious lad had discovered an even vaster realm-the realm of the spirit. He was annoyed that he couldn't devote the rest of his life to philosophy, but he resigned himself to his fate. Already he showed within him the makings of a Stoic.

His uncle spared no effort in educating Marcus to the throne. He gave him the foremost teachers in rhetoric and in history. He hardened him to the saddle of the war horse. He started him on a career of statesmanship. He bestowed upon him the title of Caesar. In the palace the young prince received the flattery of the courtiers; in the barracks he was drilled in army manoeuvres; in the quiet of his study he speculated on the "wherefore of empire, the whence of ambition and the whither of life." The conservative and practical-minded nobility would have been gravely shocked had they realized what was going on in the mind of their future emperor. The Romans were a nation who acted first and speculated afterwards. And irony of ironies, here was a royal philosopher in their midst!

He ascended the throne at the death of his foster father. The throne of the Caesars—founded in treachery, dedicated to oppression sustained with blodshed. As he donned the purple he made a mental reservation to himself: "Take care not to become Caesarified." Other idealists had renounced riches for poverty. Aurelius had been compelled to renounce poverty for riches. It was hard for a philosopher to content himself with a crown. It was distasteful for a scholar to plunge into a career of politics and battles. He had inherited an empire of snarling beasts. He must devote his life to the solution of quarrels not of his own making; he was tied to the crimes and follies of his ancestors. The barbarian hordes throughout the Empire, smarting under the lash of five centuries of Roman aggression, were ready to revolt. And when the philosopher Marcus Aurelius assumed the throne the storm broke. The barbarians had no respect for the meditations of an emperor; they respected only his armies.

He sent an army to put down the uprising of the Parthians east of the Tigris. The war was terminated successfully by Lucius Verus, an adopted brother of his whom Aurelius had made co-ruler of the Empire at his accession. He had hoped that Lucius would attend to the practical business of the state whilst he himself attended to his philosophy. But Lucius Verus died, and Marcus Aurelius was left alone with his kingdom-a dangerous toy for which he had no taste. His head was full of philosophy but his hands were full of trouble. The barbarians had flamed into a new revolt. The Quadi and the Marcomanni had swept into the provinces of the Danube. The races north of the Alps were feasting their eyes on Italy and their hearts on a desire for plunder. The mighty Roman structure was sagging. Marcus Aurelius rose to the occasion. He collected money for defence by selling the royal silver-ware and the palace jewellery at a public auction. He conscripted the gladiators from the Coliseum, the slaves from the markets, the thieves and the murderers from every corner of the Empire; and at the head of this nondescript army he placed himself and his books. He marched to the East, pitched his tent and sat down to await the onrush of the Quadi. At night, by the flicker of an oil lamp, as the wind whistled against the canvas flap and the wolves howled in the distance, he set down his thoughts on the sadness of fate and the savagery of war. Most of the remaining years of his life he spent in the warrior's tent at the battle front to safeguard the Empire that had been wished upon him. But every leisure moment that he could spare from the sword he devoted to his pen. Another warrior before him had divided his time between the sword and the pen. But Julius Caesar had exploited his literary talent to further the glory of his vanity. Marcus Aurelius undertook a more modest and more noble task — to demonstrate the vanity of his glory.

III

THE Roman Legions defeated the Quadi. Some of the soldiers believed it was the triumph of the doctrine of brotherhood that had turned the trick. For there were strange conscripts among the emperor's legions–men who professed to follow the teachings of a certain Nazarene. And they called up to their leader in heaven to stop the barbarians. The Quadi, with their greater numbers, had surrounded the Romans. They had cut them off from their water supply. Suddenly the great clouds in heaven burst open and the rain came down. The hard-pressed warriors of the emperor held out their helmets and drank to their hearts' content. And then another miracle happened. Lightning struck down with swift vengeance from the sky. The Quadi were engulfed in a hundred fires. But — so went the story — not a Roman was touched. It was a mightly victory for Marcus Aurelius. But the little band of Christians spread the news of this miracle throughout the world and hailed the battle as a victory for Christianity.

Marcus Aurelius and Christianity. Though a pagan in training, the emperor-philosopher was a Christian at heart. He rejected the miracle of the conquest. For he didn't believe in the God of battle. He did, however, believe in the God of love. He believed in the fatherhood of God and in the brotherhood of Man. He sympathised with his fellow men, his co-partners in the universal brotherhood of sorrow. "I cannot be angry with my brothers," he wrote, "or sever myself from them. For we are made by nature to help one another, like the feet, the hands, the eyelids, the upper and the lower rows of teeth."

Yet the Christian "brothers" of Marcus Aurelius were outlaws in the Roman state. Christianity was the religion of the dispossessed. It had descended "like the gentle rain from heaven" upon the hearts of the slaves, of the overburdened toilers, of the discouraged peasants who had been robbed of their freeholdings and herded by a class of wealthy exploiters into farm gangs on the soil. Society had failed the common man. And the common man, having lost his faith in this world, was passionately in search of a hope for the next world. Christianity supplied this hope.

The thinkers of the Roman world had also lost their faith. For they saw about them an aggressive monster the victorious Roman Empire — a power that knew how to divide and rule but not how to unite and govern. They saw a political and social and military system which implanted in the hearts of the people no allegiance but only hatred and cynicism and fear. Yet, unlike the Christians, they were unwilling to subscribe to a cult of emotional propaganda that placed revelation above reason. Instead they flocked to the schools of philosophy to find a way out. They remained indifferently loyal to the apparently indifferent old gods. Their chief concern was with the certain sorrows of this world rather than with the uncertain joys of the next. They didn't expect to control their own thoughts. They sneered at the Christian reformers who sought to remould the fellowship of the earth into something more akin to their dream of heaven. The Roman philosophers were not communists who believed in social equality; they were anarchists who had no social beliefs whatsoever. They divided themselves into two main groups; the Epicureans and the Stoics. The one group advocated, "Enjoy life while you can, for tomorrow you may be dead", the other, "Endure life while you can, for tomorrow you may still be alive to suffer."

Yet the Gentle Carpenter had gone a step beyond the Stoics. "Do not *accept* suffering," He had said: "*choose* it, Help one another to bear life's common cross, that in so doing you may lighten one another's burden."

IV

MARCUS AURELIUS was half Christian and half Stoic. And he and had good need for both of his Christian patience and of his Stoic indifference. For troubles were heaping themselves upon his head. Rumours had reached him that one of his most trusted generals, Avidius Cassius, was raising the standard of revolt in Syria. "Avidius," jested the punters, "is avid to be emperor." The ambitious soldier had gained a name for himself through his vigorous suppression of rebellions in Arabia and in Egypt. He dreamed, it was whispered that he was another Brutus whose mission it was to free Rome from the emperor–dictator. He was a restless soldier who chafed at his comparative inactivity under the military leadership of a philosopher. Born under the hot oriental sun, he was a dark-skinned man with a dark mind that could easily harbour disloyal thoughts. But Marcus Aurelius shrugged his shoulders at the rumours of disloyalty. "He is a good general strict and brave; the state cannot do without him." Besides, no one had stepped forward with a direct accusation. There was no concrete evidence for the whispered charges.

Confidently the emperor turned his mind to other matters. He must reject the human urge to indulge in petty recriminations against his friends. Life was too serious for that sort of thing. The philosophic soul must jump to no hasty decisions. "Do every deed, speak every word, think every thought in the knowledge that you may end your days at any moment," he confided to his books.

Meanwhile the treachery of Avidius, so the rumour went, had taken a more dangerous turn. The ambitious general, it was whispered, was now casting his eyes not only upon the emperor's kingdom but upon the emperor's wife. This new tidbit of gossip took on like wildfire. People began to hint that the marriage between the emperor and his cousin, Faustina, had never been sanctioned with the blessings of love. And yet there were many instances to convince the intimate friends of the royal family that Marcus Aurelius was a tender husband. Hand't he written numerous letters to his old tutor, Fronto, expressing his affection for Faustina? Hand't she borne him over a dozen children? Was she not always when her royal husband was at home, as solicitous, about his comfort as he was about hers? And now that he had pitched his tent on the field of battle, she was as faithful as Penelope–insisted their friends–weaving in the palace and waiting for his return.

But Avidius was not willing to wait. He suddenly spread a report that the emperor was dead. He rallied his legions to back him as the new emperor. The people of Antioch followed him to a man. The governor of Egypt joined him.

When the news of the rebellion reached Marcus he called his troops together. "Fellow soldiers" he addressed them, "my very best friend has plotted to overthrow me and has forced me against my will to take the field. I enter upon this campaign with the conviction that I have neither committed any act of injustice against Avidius nor left undone anything that I ought to have done for him." He had no indignation to express, no complaint to voice, he told his legions. "There is only one thing I am afraid of, fellow soldiers — for I shall speak the whole truth to you–and that is that Avidius Cassius may kill himself to avoid the shame of coming into my presence or that someone else, knowing that I am on the way to take the field against him, may do the deed. Then I shall be robbed of the greatest prize of the victor, such as no man ever had." And what was the prize? "To forgive the man who has done me wrong, to remain a friend to him who has broken his friendship with me."

The revolt lasted only a hundred days. As Marcus Aurelius had predicted, one of Avidius' own followers assassinated him. "I shall spare his wife and his children," announced the philosopher-warrior. He sent the senate a message in which he enjoined them from putting to death "any of the soldiers who had taken part in the rebellion. "Let the banished come home, let the proscribed take back their property. I wish I could recall from the dead the poor victims who have already suffered the penalty."

The hardened politicians of the Empire shuddered at

the mercy of their emperor. They wondered whether he was fair to his own family in thus sparing the family of the arch-traitor. But Marcus Aurelius quieted their fears with a shrug of the shoulders. For he was a stoic and a fatalist. "If my family deserves to be loved more than the family of Avidius, the gods will enable us and not them, to sit uopn the throne."

Having thus disposed of the conspirator's family, he set out, together with Faustina and with his son Commodus, to visit the cities that had joined the conspiracy. But he came with a message of forgiveness and not of revenge. When he reached the village of Halala, at the foot of Mount Taurus, Faustina fell ill and died. In spite of the scandalous stories he had heard about her behaviour, in spite of his own suspicions, he had never ceased to love his queen. Her death was a terrible blow. He built a golden image of Faustina to accompany him on his campaigns. He founded a home for destitute girls in her memory. He offered prayers and tears to her statue. And yet, though he sorrowed over death, he did not fear it. Nor did he fear life. He must live his life, as he would meet his death, bravely. He returned to the old front, for the barbarians had not yet ceased to make trouble. Existence was "a warfare and a journey in a strange land." He went back to his battles and his books, "victorious over pain and pleasure, independent of what others may do or may fail to do.... For the life of the body is but a river, and the life of the soul a misty dream."

Finally (in 179) he defeated the last of the rebellious

tribes. The Empire was secure–for a time. But the emperor had contracted a disease from his long exposure in camp, and he lay deathly ill.

V

THE Stoic Philosophy of Marcus Aurelius, like Christianity, was a product of the East. The founder of Stoicism, the Semitic Zeno, was a spiritual brother of the old Hebrew prophets. His people were Phoenician. He had come to Greece from the island of Cyprus and had set up a school of philosophy at Athens. A swarthy Isaiah, careless of the opinions and the conventions of society. A sunburnt rebel with a passion for justice. A hardened cynic with gentle eyes; a citizen of the universe, looking upon the mortals of the earth and the immortal stars in the heavens as his fellow citizens. Like his brother dreamers in Judea, he was inspired with the conviction that God is One. "God is ether. God is air. God is the spirit of ethereal fire... God goeth to and fro throughout all that is. God is mind. God is soul. God is nature." The Hebrews called Him Jehovah. The adopted son of Athens identified him with Zeus. One God, one human family, one law. "Ye shall all have one law and one custom–like a flock, herded under one crook, that feedeth together."

This Stoic philosophy of Zeno, like the other schools of Athenian thought, had emigrated to the Imperial City when Greece came under the conquering orbit of Rome. The Romans appropriated these alien schools of philosophy, as they appropriated their alien captives, and pressed them into the service of their practical life. They rejected the metaphysics of the various philosophies and accepted their ethics. For they cared little about the mysteries of the heavens. They were concerned mainly with the realities of the earth.

The realistic philosophers of Rome found Stoicism especially to their liking. For the Stoics taught that if man couldn't banish the sorrows and the evils of the world he could at least discipline his own will to endure them courageously. And furthermore, by a process of intellectual acrobatics the Stoic could even become optimistic about the imperfections of the world. For actually — he maintained — there was nothing evil in experience. Only popular credence made is so. The world was good, for it was governed in accordance with the laws of nature. "All events are merely natural processes and have no intrinsic moral values, whether good or bad." If we feel that Providence has struck us too keen a blow, we must remember that we are in no position to judge the workings of the entire universe from our own mortal — and moral — vantage spot. There is nothing good and nothing bad but thinking makes it so. We suffer from our opinions from our limited vision. It is possible for us to make ourselves misfortune-proof by adopting a simple formula. If unfulfilled desires are the bane of our existence let us limit our desires to the scope of our ability to fulfil them. Since the material goods of life are so fleeting and rare, let us be content with our spiritual goods — a good mind and a good character. Call these the positive virtues. Fix them as the ultimate meaning of life. And consider that everything else is indifferent. Health, illness, pleasure, pain, riches, poverty — all these have no meaning. Even death, though it destroys the mind as well as the body, the good character as well as the good fortune, must not be regarded as a negative event. For death may destroy the philosopher but not his philosophy. It kills the mind of the individual, but it does not disturb the majesty of the world. The majestic order of nature is bound to outlast all the little minds of those who seek to define it. Learn, therefore, to be indifferent to your fate. For all of us are subject to the same fate in the end. All of us alike, from the highest to the lowest, are the equally helpless puppets of an inevitable and impartial destiny.

This creed denied all the artificial criteria whereby men were divided into classes of master and slave, king and commoner, rich and poor. It struck the very knynote of democracy. All events are to be faced with equanimity; all men are equal. Interestingly enough, it was the slave, Epictetus, who converted the emperor, Marcus Aurelius, to the democratic gospel of Stoic philosophy. Men are born to different stations in life, wrote Epictetus but at the moment of death the destitute are amply compensated. For death serves to take away more from those who have more or less from those who have less. And if the rich, sobered by this levelling of human fortune, had their lives to live all over again, they wouldn't take a penny less. Nor the poor a penny more. For nature has too great sense of humour to let man profit by his experience. Nothing changes; no human nature ever grows better or worse, more human or less human. Indeed, there is no yardstick for human progress. Man is forever stepping gingerly on a treadmill that churns the vast infinite waters of the past and the future. He has nothing to lose but his footing, nothing to gain but a few more moments in a struggle to keep his balance before he topples over. Why should he try to moralize and classify things into the beautiful and the ugly, the good and the bad, when all he can observe around him is the stretch of the earth and the heavens? They are neither beautiful nor ugly, neither good nor evil, but vast overwhelming, eternal. They are nature. And nature is the only true reality. Let us adapt ourselves to this reality. Let us live in accordance with the laws of nature.

It is the irony of man's foolishness — observes Marcus Aurelius — that in the midst of his impotence he should be spured on by an ambition for glory! "Camillus, Caeso, Volesus, Leonnatus; after them Scipio and Cato, Augustus, Hedrian and Antoninus — all are forgotten. All things hasten to an end, shall speedily seem old fables, to be mouthed for an instant and then to be buried in oblivion." Rome too! The grandeur and the glory of an empire is but the report of gossipy narrators, a handful of pebbles and dust to be dug up by archacologists groping among the ruins.

Is there, then, no hope for mankind? Yes, replies Marcus Aurelius, there is the ultimate hope of renouncing all hope. In thus renouncing hope, man can free himself from his greatest enemy — disappointment. Indeed, he can become a mirthless apotheosis of jubiliation, decked out in sackcloth and ashes. All he must do is to drink deep with his mind into the intoxication of complete apathy. Let us be like the gods, indifferent to the buffetings of fate. "Take me up and cast me where you will. I shall have serene within me my own divinity." Here is the achievement of supreme triumph through supreme abnegation. Yet even the stoic reaches the limit of self-denial. There is a margin beyond which humility pays no dividents. When all is said and done, there is an active as well as a passive side to the philosophy of Marcus Aurelius. He is indifferent to his fortune, but he is not indifferent to his duty. And this duty is — to govern his own soul and his Roman subjects firmly but fairly. Live in accordance with nature — that is, in accordance with the laws of reason. For there is a ruling reason in the universe whose ultimate purpose is co-ordination, interdependence, reciprocity–in a word, justice.

Justic to his fellows and indifference to his fate — this was the highest virtue in the philosophy of Marcus Aurelius. This, and fearlessness in the face of death. "Banish the fear of death by regarding it not with superstition or awe but merely as one of the natural functions in the cycle of life, such as eating and drinking, sleep and sex."

Like Epicurus, Marcus Aurelius argues that death is nothing more than the dissolution of the elements of which every human being is compounded. Does not the conservation of energy preserve every atom in the universe? "And if in their successive interchanges no harm befalls the elements, why should one suspect any harm in the change and the dissolution of the whole? Death is natural, and nothing natural can be evil."

This is the very summit of self-conquest. For where there is no evil there need be no fear. "If in death all sense be extinguished, there can be no sense of loss. But if a different sort of sense be acquired, you become a different creature and do not cease to live."

The Stoic philosophers did not trouble themselves about the problems of an after–life. And this is the reason for their equanimity. For if there is no individual immortality the evils of life are forever stilled, and the individual cannot even realize that he has been charged out of his hope of eternity. If, on the other hand, there is immortality for the individual, well and good. Unlike the Christians, the Stoics did not believe in a last judgment either of damnation or of salvation. But they did believe in a future eternity either of conscious or of unconscious peace. Free from fear of hell, they were able to a great extent to free themselves from the fear of death. Hence their supreme sense of self-conquest. The Stoics felt that they could afford the luxury of self-annihilation. But they won this earthly victory at a tremendous price — the sacrifice of their heavenly hope.

VI

IT was the winter of 180 A.D. Marcus Aurelius lay dying in his tent. He was only fifty-nine years old. A strange, paradoxical, dicontented failure of a man, this emperor–soldier-philosopher who had preached contentment all his life. The Dr. Jekyll and Mr. Hyde of the ancient world. At night, in the quiet of his study, he had been the ardent scholar and sensitive poet who was searching his own heart and weaving the substance of his thought into the plan of a better world for happier men. But in the daytime, amidst the clash of arms he had become the perfect commander who swept to victory by the Roman formula of no surrender and no mercy. His convictions had been greater than his courage. "My city and country, so far as I am Marcus Aurelius," he had written in his *Meditations,* "is Rome; but so far as I am a man, it is the world." Yet in actual life he had forgotten that he was a man; he had merely remembered that he was a Roman. He had taught magnanimity to his fellow men. "If you cannot maintain a true magnanimous character, go courageously into some corner where you *can* maintain it; or if even there you fail depart at once from life." Yet in his treatment of the Christians he had been the direct opposite of magnanimous. Regarding their gentleness as a menace to the imperialistic dreams of the Roman Empire, he had ordered their leaders to be crucified. He was a good man in bad company. Living in Rome, he had been compelled to do as the Romans.

And now as he lay dying in his tent he thought of his miscast role in the fitful drama of life. His mind had been fashioned "for nobler times and calmer hearts." He had aimed at contentment and he had won glory instead. Yet "glory is nothing but a vapour and after fame is oblivion."

Vanity of vanities. The life of Marcus Aurelius, his pomp, his ambitions, his wars, his victories, his triumphs — all vanity!

The Romans were glad to see him go. They wanted a leader who was less of a philosopher and more of a warrior. His son Commodus and his other heir were anxious, foolish little men, to come into their worldy inheritance. The dying emperor clasped his mantle tightly about him. "I am leaving a life from which my very partners, for whom I toiled and prayed and planned, are wishing me to depart. Why, then strive for a longer life?"

VII

THERE is a story that when Marcus Aurelius died the Olympian gods held a banquet is his honour. At his right sat the Emperors Augustus, Tiberius and Vespasian. At his left sat the other great Roman emperors — Nerva, Trajan, Hadrian and his own foster father, Antoninus Pius. Nero and Caligula, however, had been refused admittance at the door. Jupiter announced a contest to decide as to which of the emperors had been the greatest Roman. Each candidate stood up in turn and made a short address in his own behalf. Most of them boasted of their conquests. But when the time came for Marcus Aurelius to speak he merely said: "I, a humble philosopher, have cherished the ambition never to give pain to another."

Marcus Aurelius, concludes the story, was thereupon crowned the greatest of Romans. But not the greatest of men. For Marcus Aurelius the philosopher was thwarted in his ambition by Marcus Aurelius the king.

****

Chief Work Of Marcus Aurelius

Meditations. These meditations do not represent a systematized outline of Stoicism. They are rather disconnected fragments of Stoic thought jotted down at odd moments — in the midst of administrative duties or in the intervals between battles. Hence their philosophic incompleteness and their dramatic charm.

Among the best English versions of the *Meditations* are those of George Long (1862, revised and reissued in 1900), G.H. Rendall (1898) and J. Jackson (1906).

✦✧✦

5

SAINT THOMAS AQUINAS

1225 – 1274

THE count of Aquino lived in a castle high up in the mountains of Italy. He was a military man, descendant of the Lombard kings, and nephew to the Holy Roman emperor. He was a man of the world. And six of his seven sons were men of the world. But his seventh son, Thomas, "disgraced" him. He preferred thinking to fighting, in spite of the fact that he was named after his grandfather, who had been the commander of the imperial forces.

Thomas Aquino was a sturdy lad. He had huge oxlike eyes. There was a cavern of understanding in them. And behind them was a head full of common sense. He left his brothers to their warlike games and joined his elders to hear the stories of the mendicant friars who stopped at his father's house. Most of the time he would deposit his large body — for it *was* large — in a corner, away from the rest of his family and ponder about the most inexplicable things. On stormy nights, as he lay a bed and listened to the rolling of the thunder over the crags of Rocca Secca, he would ask himself questions about God, that misinterpreted and abused and maligned Father of men. In His name legions of His Children were sentenced to a life of hard labour on the soil for the benefit of the lords and ladies of the land. In His name armies of "believers" were butchering the "unbelievers" who ventured to love Him in their own unorthodox way. There was something wrong about all this, thought Thomas. Perhaps, when he grew to be a man, he would learn how to right this wrong.

He went to study at Naples. He spent seven years mastering the sciences and the rhetoric and the theology of the school curriculum. When he returned home he was eighteen — an age at which his brothers had taken the lance and joined their father's military force. Here was the finest physical specimen of them all. What a soldier he would make for his country and his king! It was a severe blow to the count when Thomas flatly refused to become a soldier. Why, fighting was as natural an instinct to the sons of a nobleman as mating. The well-born Italian of those days had a threefold duty in life–to breed, to lead, to bleed.

But then if Thomas didn't choose to fight, he could at least take a degree in theology and become a bishop. The Church, too, was a great career. Social prestige and money and all kinds of honour accrued to the bishopric. The Aquino family, that had sprung from kings, could do worse than exchange the sceptre for the keys of St. Peter. Indeed, the most powerful men in this theocratic world of theirs were not the kings but the bishops. For they had the ear of God.

But at school in Naples Thomas had looked long and

steadfastly out over the bay. He had feasted his eyes for many years on the solitary vastitude of the sea. And he had beheld the vision of a lean and gentle beggar, Francis of Assisi, the patron of the poor. Francis, too, like Thomas Aquino, had been born of wealthy parents. But he had laughed at the silly little accident of his birth and had given up his riches.....

"Father," said Thomas now that he was home again, "I wish to be a friar."

"A *what*? A ragged, barefooted friar?"

"Yes Father."

"And take the vows of poverty? And give up your career? And go hungry and beg for alms? An Aquino of Rocca Secca Impossible!"

"It was possible for Francis of Assisi."

"He was a madman!" cried the Count.

"He was a saint," corrected Thomas.

II

HIS mother sent a letter to the Pope, urging His Holiness to "rescue her son from his madness" The archbishop of Naples promised to do what he could to prevent the Dominican order from accepting Thomas. The young man, indignant at his family's interference with his chosen career left home. He set out for Paris with a group of friars who had become his friends. But one day, as he was resting on his journey by the roadside, several horsemen galloped up to him and tried to carry him off. He recognized his brothers among his assailants.

He drew back. "What in the Lord's name are you trying to do?"

"In the Lord's name we are going to bring you back to your senses. Come along, we have our family honour to uphold."

"I belong to a greater family than yours," countered Thomas. He tried with all his prodigious strength to fight them off. But in vain. They overpowered him and carried him to a tower in the vicinity of Rocca Secca. Here they made him prisoner. His father came to plead with him.

"Give me back my hood," demanded the young man.

"Keep your hood," said the count wearily "Adopt the monastic life if you will. Only I beg of you to accept the position of abbot at Monte Casino for my sake."

But Thomas Aquinas was obstinate. "I do not care to be a leader. I wish to spend my life as a humble follower of the Lord."

His mother came to him with tears in her eyes. "Remember, my son, you are descended from princes, Frederick Hohenstaufen is your cousin."

"He is an infidel."

Relenting somewhat, his family brought him books to read. They could not bear to see him suffer unduly. Surely Aristotle's *Metaphysics* and Peter Lombard's *Sentences* couldn't defeat their purpose. And they brought him something more lovely than books — a female companion. They hoped the sight of a beautiful face could convert him to common sense. The woman was a gentle symbol of what the outside world might offer to a young man who would recant.

It was a cold day when the young woman was brought to him. Thomas was busily stirring the fire in the hearth, and it was across the flames that he beheld her face. To whom could it belong but to salamander, a magic spirit of lust who would bring only evil in its embrace? He drew a fagot from the hearth and shook it at the visitor. She withdrew in haste. And Thomas, in a wild ecstasy, traced a symbol on the wall of his prison cell. Tradition has it that it was the sign of the cross.

Another woman visited Aquinas — his sister Marietta. "I will help you to escape from the tower. I have softened the hearts of our brothers. We admire your courage."

They came with a basket and a rope. And they lowered him to the ground in the pitch of the night. Then they wished him Godspeed.

III

HE took his breviary, tied together a bundle of bread and cheese and fruit and set out once more over the dusty road to Paris. Groups of pilgrims passed along in silent meditation. Cavalcades of noblemen rode by in arrogant splendour. Beggars sat on the roadside and held out their hands for scraps of food. The young friar who was escaping from his fortune crossed the plains of Lombardy, footsore, sharing his bread with the hungry and sleeping in barns. Finally he reached Paris after a journey of fifteen hundred miles. But when he arrived at the great university city he learned that the famous professor Albertus Magnus, from whose fountain of scholarship he wished to drink, was lecturing at Cologne. So he crossed the Rhine and continued on his way to Cologne. He entered the crowded lecture hall and sat at the feet of Albertus.

Seldom in history does the head of one man contain so great a proportion of the knowledge of his time. Albertus was a walking and talking summary of medieval culture. He continued the great tradition of Aristotle, scanning the heavens for the constellations, the sea for fish, the air for fowl. But he was not interested, like Aristotle, in scanning human nature for the true and the false. There was no need of doing that, he said. He had been born a Christian; therefore he took the teaching of Christ for granted. Students from all over Europe flocked to his lectures. They were fascinated by him. Thomas Aquinas, it was to be expected, would be no exception.

And yet to his fellow students he did seem to be an exception. He sat quietly for hours listening, taking no part in the general discussion of the students, offering no suggestions or comments on the subjects discussed. All the other students paraded their knowledge. But Thomas was the least star in this firmament of culture. He hung aloft in his solitude and flickered ever so faintly whilst the lesser lights blazed shamelessly far below him. His fellow students were unable to get a word out of him. They marvelled at his huge head and ponderous frame. He was as big as on ox. Indeed, they called him "the dumb ox." One day a student who prided himself on being a wag looked out of the window during a recess between lectures and cried, "Look, look there is a bull flying overhead!" Thomas Aquinas stuck his head out of the window, only to be greeted by a howl of derisive laughter. He faced the company solemnly. There was contempt written across his face. "I'm not fool enough to believe that a bull can fly through the air", he said. "But on the other hand, I couldn't believe that a man of God would stoop to tell a lie."

Albertus became courious about the silent young man. One day he called him into his study and asked him a few questions. He discussed theology with him and grammar and metaphysics and logic. At his next lecture he announced to the crowded assemblage: "You call our brother Thomas a dumb ox, you? I tell you that someday the whole world will listen to his bellowing."

IV

THOMAS and Albertus became close friends. When Albertus was transferred to the University of Paris, Aquinas followed him. Here he continued his studies until he received a bachelor's degree in theology. For it was his purpose to combine the humility of St. Francis with the scholarship of St. Augustine. He had taken the black friar's garb as a vow to God. But he was not interested merely in living a life of the good heart. He was anxious to dedicate himself also to a life of the good mind. St. Francis had inspired men with the *drama* of Christianity; Thomas Aquinas wanted to enlighten them with the *philosophy* of Christianity.

At the age of thirty–three he was appointed professor of religion at the University of Paris. Here he found himself entrenched in the theological atmosphere of the day — the powerful fortress of logic which had been raised to protect the gentle spirit of faith. The Catholic religion was upheld by an intricate system of syllogisms and subtleties of reason that had transformed theology from a philosophy into a science. The Gospels had been given the sanction of Aristotle, that great "Christian metaphysician" who had never heard of Christ. Aristotle had defined the world as a product of substance and form. The substance is the stuff out of which the world is made. The form is the potential energy which has put the world into a state of ever becoming, of ever striving for higher and higher modes of expression. The form or energy of the world was prior to the substance. When the form entered the substance the world began.

The Aristotelian philosophy was now imported from the pagan into the Christian world to prove the central doctrine of Catholic theology — the Word made Flesh in Christ. Aristotle's form is the divinity of Christ; Aristotle's substance is His flesh. Satisfied with this Christian interpretation of Aristotle's philosophy, the scholastic professors of the day restricted themselves to a sort of logical parrying. They merely attempted to defend Aristotle's system from attack. They interpreted, paraphrased and repeated his ideas, but they made no original contribution to them. They were excellent teachers but mediocre thinkers, these scholastic philosophers of the thirteenth century.

Thomas Aquinas, however, had too original a mind

to submit to the scholastic convictions of his duty. He was meant for something better than a mere interpretation of Aristotle. He tried his best to employ his powerful intellect within the limits of his profession. He began to express individual and, to some of his contemporaries revolutionary, convictions. Yet he attracted crowds of students to him. They recognized his massive dignity. They remarked that he was rightly called Thomas — the word Thomas means *depth* — for this man was deep beyond all other teachers of his day.

Deep mentally, huge physically. When thoughtless people laughed at his immense stomach he replied philosophically. "The cucumber also grows without food." For he who looked like "a full-bellied wine cask" led an austere life. He just happened to be built on a larger scale than his fellow men — larger in bulk, larger in thought, larger in sympathy. He should have been into the land of Paul Bunyan, with the Rocky Mountains for his altar, the Grand Canyon for his chapel and freedom for his text. He was a strong pioneer ready to strike beyond the boundaries of contemporary thought — a stout–hearted Gulliver setting out on a spiritual adventure among the Lilliputians of his day.

V

ONCE he was invited to dine, together with hundreds of other guests, at the palace of the French king. In the course of the banquet, as the king was waxing eloquent in conversation, a robust individual in the middle of the hall suddenly brought his fist down on the table with the force of a giant oak and muttered in his beard, loudly enough for all to hear, "*That* will settle the infidels!" Instantly the great hall was silent. Who had dared to interrupt the king? Louis looked down from his mighty seat, awaiting an explanation from Aquinas.

"I was dreaming, your majesty." remarked the intrepid friar. "For a time I had forgotten where I was. I was thinking of arguments I could use to sustain my philosophy against the unbelievers."

Louis smiled benevolently. "I shall order my secretaries to jot down your arguments for future reference, in the event that you forget them. I trust they are valuable."

VI

"O CREATOR beyond human utterance," Aquinas prayed to his God in the solitude of his cell. "Thou who art called the fountain-head of life, and of wisdom, bestow upon me the keenness of wit to understand, the power of a retentive memory, the method and ease of learning, the ability to impart information, the gift of fluent speech." Constantly he paced the floor, his hands behind his back and an air of abstraction in his eyes. He was fighting out great battles in his mind. And when he spoke from the lecture platform his head was turned upward, his eyes were closed.

He had long used every source at his command to defend the faith. He had wielded his pen like a lightning flash to illuminate the skies of knowledge. And now he was troubled, sorely troubled. For as he looked around he could scarcely recognize that faith. He watched the great processions of the bishops in their scarlet robes and he heard the pompous titles by which they addressed one another. Was this the humble religion of Christ? He felt that the entire ceremonial of the Church, with its relics and its symbols, had become a mere external show. The Church had been transformed from a spiritual into an ecclesiastical power. Was this what the Fathers of the early Christian community had envisaged?

"Poor, unwilling blunderers, indeed, are the men who undermine and pervert the very principles of their Gospel!" The Christian eyes had become so eager to behold Jesus in the flesh that the Christian heart had forgotten to see Christ in the spirit. Men blessed the dead bones of the saints, but they failed to understand their living souls. It was time to bring men back to the true ethics of Christianity. Some voices had called in accents of love, others in tones of wisdom. And now Thomas Aquinas came forward to combine the two. He decided to weave the sayings of the Holy Fathers and the scriptures into one vast philosophical system to embrace the intellectual and moral and theological life of the Catholic world. Had not Saint Socrates and Saint Plato and Saint Buddha and Saint Confucius done the same for their own pagan world?

So he composed his *Summa Theologica*, the monumental hand–book on ethics, religion and metaphysics. The existence of God is affirmed not as an act of faith but as a fact of reason. The entire social and moral philosophy of the Scripture is expounded in a series of logical propositions that remind one of the treatment of that later philosophy of faith, Spinoza's *Ethics.* The handiwork of the Lord is *Sensible fact.* Who else but the Lord could have taken the nameless chaos of substance and moulded into a meaning and a form?

The universe is His instrument. And we are the keyboard, touched into tone by the fingers of the Divine Musician, the mighty Virtuoso who plays the flaming concerto of Existence in the music hall of Eternity packed with angelic hosts. And we men of the world below, do we not feel the music vibrate through each and every one of us? Have we not hearts to tremble at its cadences and minds to understand its harmonies?

And Thomas Aquinas analyses these harmonies in his mighty book. He discusses everything pertaining to God and life and conduct and mind. To give an idea of the scope of the work, let us mention a few of the chapter headings. He considers the question of, states his proof for and answers the objections to the "Existence of God," the "Simplicity of God", the "Supreme and Eternal Goodness of God", the "Knowledge and Will and Love of God." He then discusses the "Creation of the World," the "Problem of Evil," the "Needs of Human Conduct" and the "Nature of Happiness." From these general investigations he narrows his discussions down to the field of human ethics and considers wherein man's happiness exists — whether in riches, honour, fame, glory, power or pleasure, or in a combination of all these factors. He discusses in particular the problem of human passion, notably the passions of love, of hatred, of desire, of pain and sorrow, of fear and of anger. Then he passes on to a systematic study of human habits, of civil and moral law, of war and peace, of sedition and homicide, of theft and robbery, of usury, of fraudulent dealing in buying and selling, of hope and despair, of flattery, hypocrisy, pusillanimity, courage, nobility, martyrdom, charity, compassion and faith. And finally, having thus in the cold light of analysis reviewed every branch of human activity he concludes with a stirring recapitulation of the good life and of the humble path which men must travel on earth if they are to find their way to the kingdom of Heaven.

Summa Theologica. The summary of the Word of God through the mouth of a philosopher!

VII

SOFT, Thomas, you are nearing the end. It is the season of Lent, the year of His Divinity twelve hundred and seventy–four. Outside the bare walls of the Cistercian monastery it is snowing. The heart of the world is cold. The monks bring fagots to the hearth and stir up a fire. Scarce fifty, Thomas, but your day is done.

The perspiration comes too easily to your cheeks. Come, Thomas, you are weak. Surely you'll not abstain from food. Would you like the delicacy of a herring? It is a rare dish from France.

A tallow candle throws out its gleam to chase the scampering shadows. Thomas is dreaming fitfully. He grasps in his hand the warming torch of light. Take it away from his trembling hand! It will slip to the floor and send the whole monastery into flames!

Around him gather pious, sombre men. Friar Reginald, his closest friend, is holding Thomas in his arms. Now they chant, "*Adoramus to devote qui adoras deitatem......*" Like a river of limpid knowledge this saintly philosopher has irrigated the entire Holy Church. He has travelled on a mule through Italy, defending the faith by the force of his scholary arguments. Has given away his life in lecturing and writing. *Summa Contra Gentiles, Articles of Questions, Compendium of Theology, Quodlibets*... logic, logic and more logic!

He cries out from his bed, "Whence comes this honour that holy men should carry faggots for my fire?" Hush, Thomas, it is cold. "Nay, but God's servants must not stir the fire for me. See, the sun is so bright." Ridiculous, Thomas. It is winter now, and there is nothing but the snow outside. He tosses about fitfully. "Spring," he murmurs. "Spring!"

And his eyes close as the winter shadows fall. But in his heart there is a clear voice: "Of course it is spring, my beloved! Come, let us go into the fields."

****

Important Works By Aquinas

Summa Theologica.
Summa Contra Gentiles.
Disputed Questions.
Commentaries on *Boethics,*
On Divine Names.
On the Book of Causes.
Commentaries on Aristotle's *Physics, Metaphysics, Ethics, Politics, etc.*

One of the best modern editions of the works of Thomas Aquinas is the Leo XIII Edition (Rome, 1882).

6

FRANCIS BACON

1561 – 1626

ENGLAND under good Queen Bess was a land of merry mortals and easy morals. The court and the aristocracy lived through a brilliant midsummer's night. A thousand aspiring politicians wore asses' heads for power and played Bottom to the Fairy Queen. Never did literary men write more slavishly for court advancement. In every cowslip lurked a poet to toss a fragrant rhyme. It was the age of Puck, a buoyant, mischief-making elf age that courted wickedness with malicious grace, practised deceit in the midst of beauty, concealed poison in the scent of the musk rose, talked treachery in a refined whisper and girdled the world with a belt of pirate ships. It was an age of vicious intrigue that lay like a roast crab in the gossip bowl of history.

Into this world, this age, this forest of exquisite dreams and evil enchantments a man of science was born.

II

FRANCIS BACON'S father was a politician — the Keeper of the Great Seal; and his mother was a scholar — the preserver of the Greek and Latin tradition. While Sir

Nicholas upheld the laws of the modern world Lady Anne translated the manuscripts of the ancient world. Under the influence of such parents it is no wonder that young Francis developed into a politician and a scholar — and a snob. At the age of twelve he entered Trinity College, Cambridge, where he immediately tilted the nose of his intelligence at the established scholarship of fifteen hundred years. At sixteen he declared openly that the Cambridge professors who based their teaching on Aristotle were in error. They suffered, he said, from a naive science that was grounded on a crude and scanty observation of nature.

Francis Bacon felt that he had a "mission" in life. He would free the world from this... "Aristotelian theology" which everybody regarded as an authoritative science. But more immediately he was concerned with another mission — to free Francis Bacon from debt. For Sir Nicholas, who had apportioned his estate among all his sons with the exception of Francis, died just as he was preparing to make provision for his sixth son. And thus Francis found himself almost penniless at the age of nineteen.

This was a hard blow for a young man who had emptied wine bottles with princes and who had played with the hearts of the great court ladies. He petitioned for a post in the royal palace. And he chose his uncle, Sir William Cecil, prime minister of England, to plead his cause. But Cecil had a son of his own whom he wished to advance. He did nothing for his nephew.

Francis was faced with a practical problem, and he

was not the young man to avoid it. He could choose philosophy and face destitution or he could take up law and carve out a career for himself. He decided upon a combination of the two. He would depend upon law to fill his purse and upon philosophy to feed his soul.

He entered Gray's Inn and graduated to the bar. He was blessed with a forceful voice and brilliant forensic style, and it was not long before he gained a seat in Parliament. Yet rapid as was his progress, his imagination was always several laps ahead of his achievement. Already he saw himself swept into the woolsack of the chancellery and beyond it into the council chamber of the queen.

To be sure, he was the son of his scholarly mother as well as of his political father. The problems of theoretical knowledge continued to bother him. Did he not see the light in the realm of science? Could he not bring humanity back to truth? Ah, but the light from the palace chandeliers and from the eye of a dainty duchess were far more pleasing to him... "Whereas I believe myself born for the service of mankind and could bring the truth to shine upon every nook and cranny of nature," nevertheless, as he confessed, "political power is what I want, power over men and affairs," with the Great Seal of England in his hand and a hundred servants. Away with the contemplative life! "Men ought to know that in the theatre of human affairs it is only for gods and angels to be spectators."

III

FOR twelve long years he sought a foothold at court-

unsuccessfully. Time and again he threatened his uncle who at a word could have secured him the coveted position — that he would leave his legal profession and retire to the scholarly seclusion of Cambridge University. Such threats failed to put Cecil out of countenance. He answered his nephew coldly and turned to other affairs.

But there was at court a faction whose power rivalled that of his uncle. It was headed by the dashing Lord Essex, the queen's favourite. To this powerful and affable nobleman Bacon addressed himself. And with his elaborate manners and his gift of eloquence he won the heart of Essex.

Bacon looked upon his friendship with Essex, as he looked upon everything else, with a practical eye. "There is little friendship in the world," he reasoned, "and least of all between equals..." But there is a *kind* of friendship to an end, "between a superior and his inferior, for mutual advantage." The wise master has thus obtained a faithful servant, and the crafty servant has found a master who can be used as a stepping-stone to higher things.

Bacon had great need of a stepping-stone just then. He was constantly falling into debt. He loved to dine well and to put on a fine appearance. Lord Essex made him frequent gifts of money, and this lessened the dunning of his creditors. Philosophy had earldom enthralled. But as yet no political office for Francis Bacon. He wrote speeches flattering the vanity of the queen. He published political treatises glorifying her reign. "Mr. Bacon is beginning to frame well up to our desires," remarked Her Majesty. But when the office of Master of the Rolls became vacant she passed Bacon over for someone else in spite of the remonstrances of Essex. A grave disappointment. "I must bear the yoke," sighed the philosopher. Essex lessened the burden of the yoke. He presented Bacon with a large estate.

One good turn deserves another thought Bacon. Now that Essex had given him a rich house, someone ought to give him a rich wife. A judicious marriage might present him with a fine opportunity to reimburse himself. His eye had chanced upon a widow of ample means and noble blood. Instantly he presented himself as a suitor and enlisted Essex in the cause. But in spite of Essex's recommendation the lady refused him. She accepted instead Sir Edward Coke, a rival lawyer who had been appointed over him to the office of Queen's Attorney. Bacon shrugged his shoulders philosophically, though he could not understand how the affluent widow could prefer the elderly gentleman against whom, as the gossip went, there were seven objections — "his six children and him-self."

To unburden himself of his bitterness Bacon wrote an essay on injustice, plunged into an orgy of spending and landed in a debtor's prison. As usual, Essex came to the rescue.

And still he sought to free the human spirit from the prison of its Aristotelian scholasticism. The whole system of theological metaphysics must be down. There must be a new liberal education for the sons of a new dawn. The horizons of knowledge must be widened. The medical sciences must be reconstructed; disease must be tracked down. "The betterment of man is my province; the foundation of a new civilization of the intellect is my duty.....

This is what I ought to do if only I had the time, the leisure, the financial security." He must teach man to become the *architect of his own success.*

IV

SLOWLY ESSEX was losing favour with his queen. There had been violent quarrels between them. Essex had been sent against his wishes to command the army in Ireland. He feared that in his absence his rivals might supplant him in the queen's graces. The smile of the court was as unsubstantial as it was dazzling. The fortunes of Essex hung on the dizzy pinnacle of the royal caprice, ready to fall at the slightest contrary wind. The earl rushed home from Ireland without the queen's leave. Elizabeth had him imprisoned. Although she released him before long, she never took him back into her favour. Clerarly the nobleman was no longer the architect of his own success. Powerful enemies were plotting against him. He began to lose his reason, and there was imminent danger that he would shortly lose his head.

Where was his friend Bacon? What counsel did Bacon give him? What consolation? The queen's heart had been set relentlessly against Essex, and it was whispered in the court circles that "Mr. Bacon is thought to be the man who moves Her Majesty thus..."

For he found a good policy to side with the queen now that Essex could no longer be of any use to him. Francis Bacon had wrung Essex dry, and it was time for him to look elsewhere for new revenue. Few people at first believed these rumours. Even Lord Robert Cecil, the son of the former prime minister and the foremost political enemy of Essex, was shocked at the story. He wrote a letter to Bacon. "Cousin, I hear it, but I believe it not, that you should do some ill service to my Lord of Essex!" But it was true. It was also so scientifically sound.

As the state prepared to try Essex on a charge of disloyalty to the queen, Bacon pleaded to be allowed a part in the prosecution. But this would greatly enhance his legal career. But common decency forbade Elizabeth from granting this heartless request.

It seemed evident that the only crime of which Essex was guilty was a hot temper. He had gathered his kinsmen around him to "teach a lesson" to those men who had banished him from the "sunlight of her Majesty's smile." Knowledge of the gatherings at his house had come to the ears of the government. His plot was thwarted. He was arrested and confined to the tower. The question immediately resolved itself as to whether Essex was guilty of a rash impulse against his political opponents or of more serious attempts against the life of his sovereign queen. There was little doubt in anyone's mind that the former was the case. He had lost his head. No charge of deliberate treason was thought likely to be entered against him.

Essex was brought before the bar. And Francis Bacon rose to his feet. The court looked at him inquiringly. He was not officially a member of the prosecution. What was he going to say and in what capacity? The court soon discovered that he would speak as a voluntary witness for the state, especially as a man who had been an intimate friend of the accused and who therefore possessed a thorough knowledge of his ambitions and his motives. Here would be weighty testimony indeed. The court was hushed. A brilliant orator, a suave advocate this. What a charming manner be had!

Brushing aside the theory that Essex was responsible for nothing more than a rash impulse, Francis Bacon charged the earl with the deliberate conspiracy to usurp the throne – a crime punishable by death. With great and learned oratory, with all the resources of his mind at his command, Bacon stated the case. He spoke, he said, not before a provincial jury of ignorant men who could be swayed by emotion, but before a bench of learned and impartial judges, and he begged them to look at the facts with the utmost objectivity. Could Essex deny that he had intended treachery to the person of the queen? "My lords, even Cain, our first murderer, feigned impudency to out — shame the facts of his crime." And then Bacon brought forth an imposing array of parallel cases from his great wealth of historical knowledge. Had not the traitor Pisistratus lanced himself and rushed into the city bleeding with wounds and calling on the people for pity at the very moment his kinsmen were seizing the power of the state at his command? "I speak not as learned counsel of the prosecution but as a friend of the accused," he said in a voice that sounded husky with emotion. And it was as a friend, he insisted, that he was obliged to confess — although against his will; Essex had planned to murder the queen and to seize her throne. He could therefore be subject to no extenuating circumstances. Bacon scoffed at the idea that the earl had temporarily lost his sanity and that he could not have known what he was doing. Essex was a traitor, he concluded, and he must pay for his treachery with his life.

This testimony, given against Essex by the man to whom Essex had given an estate, convinced the judges. They condemned the unfortunate nobleman to the block.

What had been Bacon's motive in sending his best friend to his death? In return for "services rendered" he received twelve hundred pounds from the state. "Ah well," he remarked sadly as he pocketed the money, "the queen has done something for me, but not so much as I had hoped for."

Then he sat down to write a medical treatise on the methods for the prolongation of human life.

V

BACON had a fertile, versatile intelligence. He could employ it for good as well as for evil. If he found it expedient to resort to treachery in order to make his way in the world, he found it fascinating to plunge more deeply into philosophy than anyone before him when the mood seized him... "I possess a passion for research unequalled by any man... I know more legal precedent than any Englishman. Can anyone compete with me in my knowledge of Latin and Greek?... I am an encyclopedia of learning... I have understood what is wrong with all the science of man since Aristotle." The trouble with the Greeks was that they confused moral ends and purposes with purely mechanical functions. Thus they described a rainstorm not only in terms of atmospheric conditions but also in terms of theology. Water evaporates into air and falls on earth, they said, because God wishes to feed the crops and to make the world fruitful for man. This sort of naive and unsceientific reasoning, declared Bacon, has got to stop. We must separate our ideas about God from the physical universe and we must judge things in terms of their natural functions. We must become modest in our aims and specialized in our investigations. We must begin not with certainties but with doubts. We must organise large armies of men from all the leading universities of the world, each of them to investigate thoroughly his own special field of learning. And thus only, through the common co-operation of countless nameless workers, will the sum total of truth be attained. "Already I have drawn up the plans for this great Restoration of knowledge. I shall classify the different branches of natural science, allocating to my workers the investigation of the unsolved problems in each field. We shall put Nature on the rack and compel her to bear witness. The very thought makes me *dizzy.* But when shall I find the time to organise all this?"

Once more he was thrust into prison for debt, and once more he was released through the intercession of the royal court. But within two years after the death of the Earl of Essex, Queen Elizabeth passed away and the Scottish King James ascended the English throne. James had been very friendly to Essex. What an embarrassment to those who had condemned the unfortunate earl to death! But Bacon was unperturbed. Time to change face! He was a master analyst of the human heart. Having ascertained that the new king prided himself on being a classical scholar, Bacon sent him a message of greeting commencing with a line from the Vulgate and closing with a line from Ovid. And in the body of the message he declared, "There is no subject of Your Majesty's who could more desire to sacrifice himself as a burnt offering to Your Majesty's service." He had his eye on the office of the King's Attorney.

When the king ignored his petition Bacon turned to Robert Cecil, his wealthy cousin. He informed him that he was in debt again and he begged him for a little credit. He assured him that he had bidden farewell to politics for good, that his thirst for office had been entirely quenched and that he now intended to devote his energy to a search for an "affluent bride" so that he might settle down to a life of comfortable tranquillity. Parenthetically he suggested that as a means to assuage his disappointment at his failure in his petition for a court office he could bring himself to accept the "almost prostituted" title of knighthod, provided Robert Cecil interceded in his behalf. But he added that he deprecated the vulgar custom of conferring the title on large groups of people assembled at the same time. He would prefer to be knighted all by himself, as befitted his dignity. A week later, at the coronation of King James

I, Sir Francis Bacon rose to his feet a knight — together with three hundred other people.

But he intended at all costs to wid personal recognition at the court. King James was extremely vulnerable to flattery. Bacon showered him with letters in which he compared this rather ordinary mortal "to the Lord God, the Prime Mover of the Universe." Moreover, as a member of Parliament, he took every occasion to defend the king's illiberal policies, his arbitrary dispensation of justice without regard for the advocates of the people or for the common law, and his illegal taxes which bulged his revenue and made him independent of the people's representatives. Bacon was lavish with his advice for "better scientific methods" of suppressing popular government. And in the meantime he married the daughter of an alderman. Upon being congratulated on the happy occasion, he replied dryly that his "finances had been somewhat improved by his match." As for love, this sort of emotion never entered his mind. "Great men," he wrote in one of his Essays, "always keep away from this weak passion."

At last his practical and opportunist mind brought him recognition from the king. He was appointed solicitor general of England. What especially recommended him in the eyes of King James was his ingenious suggestion that a foreign war could always serve to kill off the excess population of a country. Bacon was a man after the king's own heart.

Bacon's split personality was an amazing manifestation of that greatest of all mysteries — the human mind.

He increased the number of scholarships at Oxford and Cambridge, so as to give the masses of England a greater opportunity for education, and he presided at the King's Star Chamber of torture. He wrote a glowing essay on charity, he published a magnificent work *On the Advancement of Learning,* and he pointed out to his public in little essay how a man might "work" his friends by discovering his "weaknesses and disadvantages." And then without a blush he penned a treatise on the virtue of goodness and truth. "There is no vice that so covers a man with shame as to be found false and perfidious," he said.

He always found an excuse for his unscrupulous ambition. He depended upon it, he said, to provide him with material security so that he might be free to offer his gift of philosophy to mankind. "I will liberate my fellows from false thinking," he reasoned. "I will show men the true nature of heart, the laws of motion, the principles of diet. But first I must gather wealth so that I may have leisure for my experiments. You will suspend judgment on me until you see the results. Let me reach the height of power; and then, when I retire, I shall found new universities and endow new chairs. I shall write and search and benefit mankind. Are my ends unworthy? He who would reach these ends must not shudder at the means."

VI

As he grew older his mind became more powerful. He wrote the famous prose work of the age, *Novum Organum* (The new Organon). Philosophy had long been in need of a new method of scientific inquiry. And here it was.

Before we can investigate the truth — said Bacon — we must destroy a number of fallacies, or *Idols* that have hampered the human mind. First there are the *Idols of the Tribe*. This class of idols represents the tribal or universal fallacy that man is the measure of all things. Man analyses the universe as if it had been created and ordered for his convenience. "The human understanding from its peculiar nature, easily supposes a greather degree of order and regularity in things than it really finds...although most cogent and abundant instances may exist to the contrary..."

A second class of idols consists of the *Idols of the Cave*. "For everyone has a cave or den of his own, which refracts and discolours the light of nature." Some minds are analytical — they tend to divide the world into its differences; other minds are synthetic — they try to organise the world into a coherent structure. To the first group belongs the scientist, to the second the artist. But all of us must realise that the truth lies independently of them both.

Thirdly, there are the *Idols of the Market Place*, emanating "from the commerce and association of men with one another." "There arises, from a bad and inept formation of words, a wonderful obstruction to the mind." Scholars as well as laymen talk about the universe in glib generalities of which we should beware. We must expurgate from the language of science such vague and misleading expressions as *First cause, uncaused the absolute, prime substance, infinity.* We must be merciless with our definitions. We must make a fresh start with rigorous exactitude.

The fourth and the last class comprises *the Idols of the Theatre.* These spring from the dogmas of the philosophers. All our accepted systems of philosophy "are but so many stage plays, representing worlds of their own creation after an unreal and scenic fashion." The worlds constructed in the fancies of the thinkers are "more as we should wish them to be than true stories.... out of history."

Now that we have cleared a path through the forest of ignorance, we are ready to build our new highway to knowledge. What is the new method? It is the method of doubt, of trial and error, of classification and reclassification. It is the method of *simple experiment.* "The true method of experience first lights the candle and then, by means of the candle, shows the way." First we must collect by diligent research the available data; then we must arrange these data of our experience into a well–digested order from which we may formulate axioms. From these axioms we may then proceed to new experiments, and from these new experiments we may finally deduce facts. This method is therefore one of hypothesis, experiment and deduction.

The process of deduction from hypothesis through experimentation to fact is not easy. And in order to facilitate this process Bacon proposed a convenient *modus operandi.* He constructed a "table of more or less." By means of this table all data may be classified and eliminated one by one until the essential facts pertaining to the cast stand out in the clear. Bacon illustrates his method by examining the nature of heart. He looks for some phenomenon that invariably increases with the increase of heat and invariably decreases with the decrease of heat. One by one he examines the various physical phenomena that react to heat until he chaces upon the one factor which is so correlated to the expansion of heat that it eliminates heat itself upon its own elimination. This factor is motion. Whereupon Bacon concludes that heat is a form of motion.

Unfortunately his ingenious table proved in the end impracticable, owing to unforeseen difficulties. And yet *Novum Organum* is the scientific Declaration of Independence. For its general method of elimination through experimentation has become the common usage of science to the present day. The "laboratory plan" has opened a new path to knowledge. "No man has better known than Bacon the cause (and the cure) of human error."

VII

IN the meantime the king wasn't advancing him rapidly enough to suit his political ambitions. Other people were being promoted. Why not he? "My love must creep where it cannot go," he reflected unblushingly. Few men had ever descended to such lengths to obtain office. He fairly grovelled at His Majesty's feet.

"If it please Your Majesty to perceive how some people are being favoured above me and some below me..."God preserve Your Majesty....." "Accept my sacrifice of thanksgiving for your gracious favour...." "Ah, sire, do not my words require a place very near you from which to praise you everlastingly?" "My sovereign, do not permit me to waste to nothingness for want of your favour.... " "I crave leave to make at this time a humble offering of myself..." "I shall be a ready chessman to be wherever Your Majesty's royal hand shall set me...." These and many similar petitions.

Finally His Majesty raised Sir Francis from his knees and made him attorney general at a goodly salary. More servants, more comfort, more power–and more ambition. When the Lord Chancellor, the highest political officer in the kingdom, fell ill Bacon rushed to his beside with a silent prayer that the obsequies might be soon forthcoming. He watched over the sick man with great display of solicitude and sent to the king daily reports of the dying man's condition. Finally he wrote with assumed sadness, "Your worthy Chancellor. I fear, goes his last day.... Now I beseech Your Majesty, let me put the present case truly...If you appoint my Lord Coke (his great rival) to the Lord Chancellery, nothing but misfortune will follow you... If you take my Lord Hubbard, your royal prerogative shall be broken... But if *I* were the man... It would be the *least* of my duties to act as an impartial judge in equity between parties. I would be a faithful overseer for you, a zealous disciple among your peoples, the machinery through which you may ever advance your divine right."

But the Lord Chancellor refused to die. "I was with

him yesterday," Bacon wrote, "almost half an hour. He used me with wonderful tokens of kindness. I wept, which I do not often." The Lord Chancellor resumed his position, and Bacon looked around for another office.

But at last death took the Chancellor, and Francis Bacon received his reward. He was made the new Lord Chancellor of England.

He was inducted into the office with great pomp. He was given the title of Baron Verulam and Viscount St. Albans. "Crafty men *condemn* studies," he had written in one of his essays; "wise men *use* them." Knowledge put to the right use meant power. "Happy the man who has learned the causes of things ...." He had learned the causes of fame, the mainsprings of political influence. He had reached the very pinnaele of fortune. And he was about to learn the effects.

For tragedy struck quickly. Within three years after his installation into the chancellery the House of Commons brought sensational charges against him. Francis Bacon was accused of taking bribes in court! The country was stunned. His past political record was well known. So, too, were his philosophical achievements. Who was this man of dual personality — the devil incarnate?

A large number of witnesses came forward and testified to the chancellor's habit of "gift taking." The Commons drew up a formal indictment. When the messengers brought the indictment to Bacon they found him sick in bed. How did he answer to the charges? "My lords," he said, casting his eyes to heaven, "I have withdrawn my mind from wordly matters. I am thinking of my account and my answers in a higher court...."

The whole country is aroused. Speeches everywhere, from the pulpits, in the streets, demanding the punishment of the Lord Chancellor. Can he deny the accusation? What is his defence? All his philosophy is now unavailable to save him.

The "sick" man takes up his learned pen. "There are three degrees of bribery. First, the least degree: bribery to prevent justice while the case is still pending; second when the judge conceives the case to be at an end; third..." Stop this verbal hairsplitting, this crass hypocrisy! You are not analysing chemical elements. Answer the question, "Were you bribed?".... "Of the first type of bribery I have mentioned," he goes on, "I am as innocent in my heart as any babe born upon St. Innocent's day. Of the second...." Loudly they demand a categorical answer. Whereupon he replies with much erudition. "I do ingenuously confess and acknowledge that, having understood the particulars of the charge, not formally for the House but enough to inform my conscience and memory, I find the matter sufficient and full, both to move me to desert the defence and to move your lordships to condemn and censure me." But he adds slyly that a moderate rebuke will be just as effectual to deter him from taking further bribes as a severe punishment. He reminds his judges that the times are generally immoral and that some day perchance any one of them may be brought before the bar on the same charge — in which event they will have reason not to regret their former leniency. Finally he writes jestingly to the king that a "man who has taken bribes is apt to give bribes" and that therefore he will present His Majesty with a history glorifying his reign for all future time.

By his refusal to reply to the specific counts in the indictment Francis Bacon had confessed nothing in particular. The judges, however, were not to be put off by his bland acknowledgment of his general guilt. They demanded his signature to a full and specific confession. And Francis Bacon was finally compelled to submit.

Twelve lords of the realm visited him and received the confession from him. "Is this your handwriting?" they asked.

"My lords, it is my act, my hand, my heart..."

"Then return to us the Great Seal of your office."

He bowed his head. "By the king's great fovour I have received the Seal; by my own great fault I have lost it."

As he sat in the Tower, a humble, broken prisoner, the scholar in him asserted that at least he had never handed down a wrong decision through ignorance of the law. And in the light of his own strange reason he was absolved. "I was the justest judge that was in England these fifty years. But," he added wryly, "It was the justest sentence in Parliament these two hundred years."

VIII

FIVE years passed. He had been released from prison almost immediately upon his confinement, with the injunction that he must forever stay away from Parliament and the courts of England and that in the future he would be debarred from any office in the land. But the incorrigible optimist did not renounce his political ambitions even then! He sent a flood of letters to the king — flattering him, wheedling him, and beseeching him with every argument at his command. But to no avail. His day was done. He could not flatter his old age into a second youth and vigour. He could not wheedle the burden of a disgraceful reputation away from his shoulders.

And one day, as he rode on horseback, he pondered the problem of preserving the human body after death. He dismounted and killed a fowl. Then he stuffed it with snow and was about to bring it home for observation when a sudden chill seized him. He stopped at a house nearby and sent a note to one of his friends. "I am likely to have the fortune of Caius Plinius the elder, who lost his life by trying an experiment..." Then he took to his bed and looked forward to the last great experiment of them all.

He was confident and calm. He knew that when he put to sea there would await him, undisturbed by the tides of time, a great Island of Utopia, his own *New Atlantis* one of the dreams of his philosophical system — glittering in the sunlight of Enternity. Here was a promised land with a happy and flourishing population under a government of wise and enlightened men. Here were no politicians, no office seekers, no king's favourites harassed by ambition, but an administration of scientists, chemists and biologists, physicians and architects, sociologists and philosophers and astronomers. They were not engaged in campaign speeches, or in gathering factions of followers by political promises, but rather they observed the stars and harnessed the water power for industry and studied anatomy and developed healing balms to combat disease. They constructed ships to fly in the air and vessels to speed underneath the waves. They traded not for gold and silver or silk and spices, "but only for God's first creature"-light!

And death approached so humbly it brought a tear to his eye.

****

Important Works By Francis Bacon

The Advancement of Learning

Introduction to the Interpretation of Nature

Novum Organum (New Organon)

New Atlantis

Natural History.

Essays.

The Wisdom of the Ancients

Colours of Good and Evil.

Sacred Meditations.

Apothegms

The History of Henry VII.

Confession of faith

Things Thought and Things Seen

Description of the Intelletual Globe.

History of the Winds.

History of Life and Death

Silva Silvarum (a collection of facts and observations)

Maxims of Law.

7

RENE DESCARTES

1596 – 1650

RENE'S mother died of tuberculosis a few days after his birth. Rene, too the doctors warned his father, was destined to an early grave. For he had inherited his mother's pale complexion and dry cough. His father, a country official of Poitiers, gave him into the keeping of a nurse who shielded him against the sports of the other children of the village. As a result of this coddling he grew up with a "feminine" mind — delicate, introspective, aloof. His father laughingly called him "my little philosopher."

At eight he entered the Jesuit school of La Fleche, where his teachers continued to encourage him in the quiescence of his body and the exercise of his mind. They allowed him to stay in bed till a late hour, where he could "meditate" his studies whilst the other youngsters were obliged to recite their lessons in the classroom. As a result of his extra leisure he not only kept up with his prescribed studies but managed to absorb a great deal of additional information. He was especially fond of reading the classics, "to take mental journeys," as he expressed it, "into the past and to hold converse with the noblest men of other ages."

He left the Jesuit school at sixteen, and then he took a physical journey into the present. He went to Paris, where he fell in with some of the frivolous youngsters of his own age. He learned to dine, to wine and to gamble. In his gambling he was especially lucky, since he based his guesses — as his friends remarked — "on his uncanny knowledge of mathematics rather on the laws of chance."

He had outgrown his tubercular taint, and he was pleasantly surprised to find himself in the possession of a healthy body as well as a brilliant mind. So delighted, indeed, was he with his newly discovered health that for some time he neglected his mental for his physical activities. In the spring of 1617 (at the age of twenty-one) he enlisted in the army of Prince Maurice of Orange in the Netherlands.

Yet he was not a soldier by instinct. He enjoyed the army as a school for exercise, but he had no liking for it as an instrument of war — "My military impulses," he said, "were due to a temporary heating of the liver which passed away with time." He refused to receive a soldier's pay, and therefore he was excused from a soldier's duties. He avoided active fighting whenever possible. Throughout his life, indeed, he avoided a fight-whether on the physical battlefield or on the battlefield of thought. Courage was not one of Descartes' Virtues.

For two years he kept up his amateur interest in the military life, joining in turn the Dutch, the Bavarian and the Hungarian armies — and then he turned back from his militarism to his meditation. For "a sudden flood of light" had burst upon him in 1619. "That year I was visited by a dream that came from above..... I heard a clap of thunder.... It was the Spirit of Truth descending to take possession of me." The following morning he prayed to God to give him light. For his life thenceforth was to be dedicated to the search for Truth.

He sought it for ten years, travelling from country to country, studying people, reading books, snatching at the broken threads of infinity and trying to trace them to their source and jotting down the results of his studies in his notebooks. And then, at the age of thirty-three, he retired into Holland, "there in silence and solitude to arrange his thoughts into a consistent whole." He shut himself completely away from the world, concealing the place of his residence even from his friends.

He had found, he believed, a fragment of the truth. He confided it to the pages of first book. *La Monde* (The World) — and then refrained from publishing it. For he was afraid. He had advanced in that book the revolutionary theory that the earth was in motion, and he remembered the persecution of those philosophers and scientists — Bruno, Campanella, Vanini, Galileo — men who had dared to proclaim similar revolutionary theories. As a safeguard against any temptation to publish the manuscript he sent it away to a distant part of the country. It was not until after his death that this book was issued, and then only in part. Then truth had made Descartes wise. But it had failed to make him free.

II

YET in spite of his moral timidity — a timidity due, perhaps to the excessive coddling he had experienced in his early life — Descartes was destined to revolutionise the thought of the world. A sceptic by nature and a conformist by training, he developed a new kind of philosophy, a temple of faith constructed out of the material of doubt. In order that we may understand this paradoxical nature of his philosophy let us glance at two of the ethical maxims which Descartes had set down for the guidance of his own life:

1. "To follow my thoughts wherever they might lead.... In this I should be doing like the travellers who, finding themselves lost in a forest, know that they should continue to walk as straight as they can in one direction, not diverging to the right or to the left... By this means, if they do not go exactly where they wish, they will at least arrive somewhere at the end, where probably they will be better off than in the middle of the forest."
2. "To obey the laws of my country, to adhere to the religion of my fathers and to follow the customs of the most judicious men with whom I might come into contact."

These two maxims are, as you will note, somewhat irreconcilable. A man can hardly follow his footsteps "wheresoever they may lead" if he has determined in advance that they are to lead him only in the paths of orthodoxy. Yet, starting with this paradoxical handicap, Descartes succeeded in evolving a system of thought which has distinguished him as "the father of modern philosophy."

For this philosophy — as developed in his *Discourse on Method* and his *Meditations* — is based upon the principle of science. (Descartes himself called it the method of mathematics as applied to philosophy.) It starts with the scientific assumption that we must accept nothing as true. We enter into the realm of physics and of metaphysics with a questioning mind. We neither believe nor disbelieve. We are just neutral. We want to be shown. We come through the door of scepticism into the treasure house of mystery. And what do we find in this treasure house?

At first nothing. All is dark. We are like people lost in a forest. But let us not hesitate. Let us go straight ahead doubting, examining, verifying, seeking the truth.

Above all, we must doubt everything. "Because I wished to give myself entirely to the search after Truth, I thought that it was necessary for me.... to reject as absolutely false anything as to which I could imagine the least ground of uncertainty... And since all the same thoughts and imaginations which we have while awake may also come to us in sleep, without any of them being at the same time true, I resolve to assume that everything that ever entered into my mind was no more true than the illusions of my dreams."

Yet this very dreaming brings Descartes to this first reality. For dreaming requires a dreamer. "The fact of my thinking reveals to me something that thinks." What is this something? It is I. *Cogito, ergo sum. I think, therefore I am.* My very doubt proves my existence as a doubter. Otherwise doubt itself could not exit,

And so scepticism leads to once certainty. *I am.*

But who am I? What am I? To this question Descartes gives a simple and logical answer. I am that thing which does the doubting. In other words, I am a *thinking* thing, or a *Mind*. I may doubt that I am a body or that there is a material world in which I live. But I cannot doubt away my doubt or the existence of my thought. "Hence I know that I am a substance whose entire nature it is to think and for whose existence there is no need of any place, nor does it depend on any material thing: so that this 'me', that is to say, the soul by which I am what I am, is entirely distinct from my body and is even more easy to know than is the latter; and even if the body were not, the soul would not cease to be what it is."

And thus, by the simple process of questioning everything, including the existence of the body, Descartes succeeds (at least to his own satisfaction) in establishing one thing — the existence of the soul.

Let us now pause to catch our breath. Descartes has led us into the treasure house of mystery through the door of scepticism. But this has been a revolving door. It has turned us around in a dizzy whirl, giving us but a hasty glimpse into our own nature as mirrored in the murky glass of his metaphysics and whisking us out again before we have had a chance to step inside.

For such is the nature of metaphysics, the study of the "ultimate realities." It is an attempt to paint a concrete picture of an abstract thought to search through the dark with "a blind understanding" for the lamp of truth. "There was a veil," writes Omar Khayyam, "past which I could not see. Some little talk awhile of me and thee there was — and then no more of thee and me."

But now having recovered somewhat from our first spell of metaphysical dizziness let us rejoin Descartes in his "little talk of me and thee." I am a thinking thing, he tells us. But in order to think, it is necessary to be. Hence I am being a living soul. This is the first thing that I, who started as a doubter, can conceive clearly and distinctly as true. This, then, is the first established fact — my living soul.

Are there other established facts — that is, things that I can conceive clearly and distinctly as true? Yes, replies Descartes. There are two such facts: the presence of my body and the existence of God.

My body as I can clearly see, is a substance. It is a *material* substance, just as my soul is a *thinking* substance. The thing called *me*, therefore, consists of two distinct parts — the machine that moves, or body and the mechanic that thinks, or soul.

This philosophy of machine and mechanic is known as the *dualistic* system — that is, the system which divides the world into two *separate entities*, body and mind. It therefore serves as a basis for the two divergent philosophical theories of modern times — materialism and idealism. The materialists, like Thomas Huxley, maintain that the mind is part of the body and that therefore the mechanic is but one of the wheels in the machine. "I hold with Descartes," writes Huxley, "that the human body, like all living bodies, is a machine, whose every (physical and mental) operation will sooner or later be explained on mechanical principles." The world, therefore, has no soul. The idealists, on the other hand, insist that the body is part of the mind. Berkeley, for example, denies the existence of matter. "No object," he asserts, "exits, outside of the mind perceiving it.. The table I write on, I say exists, because I see it and feel it... As to what is said about the existence of things without any relation to their being perceived, that is to me perfectly unintelligible. Their very existence *(esse)* depends upon their being perceived *(percipi).*" The world, therefore, has no body.

Poor Descartes, to have been the father of two such inharmonious offsprings as the Esau of modern materialism and the Jacob of modern idealism!

But let us return to Descartes' search for the oasis of faith through the desert of doubt. He has now established to his own satisfaction, the reality of his mind and the presence of his body. He next proceeds to establish the existence of God. "Whatever I conceive very clearly and distinctly," asserts Descartes, "is true." Bearing this in mind, and reflecting on the fact that I am assailed with doubt, I realize that my existence is not quite perfect. "For I see clearly that it is a greater perfection to know than to doubt." But whence have I learned to think of anything more perfect than myself? Obviously from some nature which really *is* more perfect than myself — a nature which has within itself all the perfections of which I can form an idea — in a word, God. Only that which is perfect can be attributed to God. There can be no imperfection in Him. Doubt, inconstancy, sadness, anger, hatred — these are not the attributes of God, since they are qualities whose absence would make us happier. That is, they are *imperfect* qualities, the badge of humanity and not of divinity. God is perfect, which means infinite, eternal immutable independent, omniscient, omnipotent, divine. This fact of the existence of a perfect God, asserts Descartes, "equals and even surpasses in certitude the demonstrated facts of geometry." God is the perfection that leads our imperfect footsteps instinctively toward that light.

This, then, is Descartes' picture of humanity — a mechanical body, a living soul within and the spirit of God above, guiding and sustaining us all.

III

IT was a comparatively easy task for Descartes to allow his footsteps to be guided towards the light through the path of tranquil contemplation. For he was free from the distractions of the economic struggle for existence. At his father's death he inherited a sufficient income to maintain him in comfort if not in luxury. He never married. The stream of his life flowed along in a lazy, uneventful current. He ate well, slept well — he still rose very late in the morning — and lived well. Occasionally he took a trip abroad, but for the most part he stayed at home and "conversed" with his friends through the medium of his correspondence. He told them of his philosophical discoveries, of the "pleasure he experienced in the solitude of his abode," of his good fortune in escaping from the various maladies which were afflicting "the majority of mankind" and of the contempt in which he held Beaugrand, Petit, Roberval, Campanella, Galileo and the other "contrary-minded" philosophers and scientists of his day. He referred to them as those "little yelping dogs of whom no notice should be taken." Descartes apparently believed that all's fair in the love of disputation and the war of wits.

And thus he spent his indolent, meditative, yet somewhat cantankerous days in the pursuit of truth — "loving life," to quote his own words, "yet not fearing death." Indeed, he considered himself now (at the age of forty four) "really further from death than when still young." His health and his teeth, he wrote to his friends, were excellent. Not for thirty years had he "suffered anything worth calling an illness."

And then he met with the first real blow of his life. He had become the father of an illegitimate child, Francine. He adored her above everything else in the world. He was planning to take her to France, where she might be brought up to the position of "a fine lady," when suddenly she died. In the presence of her death Descartes might have added a new proof of the reality of his existence: "I suffer, therefore I am." His biographer, Baillet, tells us that "he wept for the child with a tenderness which showed that the thought of eternity may sometimes be extinguished by the grief of the moment."

But after his momentary grief he returned to the citadel of his thought. He bought a beautiful country estate not far from Leyden and only "two little hours" from the sea. Here, attended by "a suffciency of well-selected servants," he sat in his octagonal study, looking out upon a picturesque old garden and dreaming his dreams of sceptical orthodoxy. A dapper little figure of a philosopher — small, slight body, big head, black hair growing down almost to his eyebrows, pale complexion, prominent wart on the upper lip, lower lip projecting somewhat through the malformation of the teeth, dark brown beard cut after the French fashion, black silk scarf to protect his throat against cold, black coat and knee breeches, black silk stockings — a metaphysical statuette with an enigmatic smile on the lips and a mysterious light in the eyes. When he went outdoors he put on a wig and drew woollen stockings over his hose. For he dreaded the effect of the slightest change in temperature upon "the inherited weakness" of his chest.

Owing to his fear of his pulmonary weakness he remained more and more at home as he grew older. It was therefore with mixed emotions that he received a letter from Queen Christina of Sweden, inviting him to take up his residence in her country and to become her teacher in philosophy. The climate of Sweden was ever so much more severe than that of Holland. It might prove too dangerous for his health. But, on the other hand, the favour of a queen was not to be scouted, even by a philosopher. And Queen Christina was a woman who generally managed to have her way. Having lost her father, Gustavus Adolphus, at the age of six, she had been brought up with the training of a man. For Gustavus Adolphus had expressed the dying wish that his country might be ruled by a female king rather than by a male queen. And a female king indeed she was — every inch of her stocky five feet. She disdained the effeminacies of the boudoir and the niceties of dress. And tousled head without a crown, short petticoats and skirts and flat shoes with low heels — such was her court attire. But her character was firm as steel, and her body was as strong as her character. She ate little, slept little and exercised like a soldier training for a fight. She could gallop ten hours on a horseback without tiring. She could endure heat and cold with equal indifference. She could shoot with deadly accuracy whether on foot or on horseback.

In addition to her physical prowess she displayed a mind of unusual versatility. She was an expert linguist, able to converse fluently in Swedish, French, Italian, Spanish and German — to say nothing of Latin and Greek. She enjoyed more than a smattering of the sciences, and she possessed a genuine love for philosophy. And binding together this remarkable combination of sinew and muscle and brain was an indomitable will. Again and again Descartes refused to accept her invitation. He sent her letters of fulsome flattery, assuring her that "Her Royal Highness is created in the image of God to a greater degree than the rest of mankind." But he begged to be excused from the privilege of "basking in the sunlight of her Gracious Presence." The honour of being summoned by the queen was, he assured her, overwhelming. Yet "after twenty years of solitude, and being no longer young. I pray that Her Royal Highness will spare me the unnecessary fatigue of the journey."

But Her Royal Highness had no intention to spare him. She had made up her mind to bring the celebrated philosopher to her "land of bears between rocks and ice." And she succeeded. In September 1649 he set out for Sweden.

And his death. For on his arrival in Stockholm Descartes had not only the severity of the Swedish climate to contend with but the stubbornness of Christina's will. The queen, believing that her mind would be most receptive to pholosophy in the early hours of the morning, insisted upon his arriving at the palace everyday before sun-up. This early rising in the rigorous frosts of the northern winter proved too much for a philosopher accustomed to the luxury of protracted morning meditations in a warm bed. "In this country," he complained, "a man's blood freezes just like the water in the rivers."

He was able to stand this sort of life a few weeks.

One morning in midwinter, as he was on his way to the palace, he suffered a severe chill. Two days later pneumonia set in. The queen sent him a German doctor, but Descartes distrusted him. When the doctor offered to bleed him he objected. "You shall not shed a drop of French blood!" he exclaimed. When finally he submitted to the bleeding it was too late.

February 11, 1650. Descartes opens his eyes. "What time is it?" he asks in a voice scarcely audible.

"Four o'clock in the morning."

He makes an effort to rise. "Time to get up. The queen is waiting." And then is a whisper, as he falls back, "Time for the *soul* to get up."

"I am a living soul," he had said "in quest of Truth." And now he was rising to meet Truth face to face.

****

Important Works By Descartes

Rules for the Direction of the mind.

The Search after Truth.

Discourse on the Method of Rightly Conducting the Reason.

Principles of Philosophy.

Meditations on the First Philosophy.

The World.

Treatise on Man.

Dioptric.

Geometry.

8

BARUCH SPINOZA

1632 – 1677

SPINOZA'S fate was unparalleled in the history of philosophy. As a rationalist he was severed from the Jews. As a Jew he was isolated from the world. Never was a man so lonely as Spinoza. Yet this loneliness was necessary for the development of his unique system of thought.

His father was a successful merchant, and he hoped that his son would be a successful rabbi. But Baruch-this Hebrew name means *blessed* — was more interested in truth than he was in success. And his quest for the truth led him into unorthodox channels that were far removed from the world of dollars and dogmas. As a child he had stood at the grave of Uriel Acosta, a Jewish sceptic who had been publicly banned from the society of his fellows for his heresies and who had killed himself as a result of this public disgrace. The scene had made a profound impression upon Spinoza. He wondered what it was that caused people to hold divergent views and to torture one another for these divergencies in their views. On that day, without being quite aware of the fact, the little Jewish boy of Amsterdam had consecrated himself to a life of investigation.

As he grew older he plunged into the study of the Bible and Talmud, the poetry of the classics and the science of the moderns. And he steeped himself especially in the great philosophical thoughts of the ages. He distilled through the alembic of his analytical mind not only the ethical metaphysics of the Jewish philosophers, Philo, Maimonides, Levi ben Gerson, Ibn Babirol and Hasdai Crescas, but the metaphysical ethics of the Gentile philosophers, Plato, Aristotle, Epicurus, Giordano Bruno and Descartes. In order to extend his horizon in the Gentile world he took up the study of Latin under the Dutch scholar, Van den Ende, a brilliant philosogist and rebellious sceptic who several years later incurred the displeasure of Louis XIV and was honoured with a public hanging.

Van den Ende had a daughter who assisted him in his teaching. Under her guidance Spinoza studied not only Latin but love. Forgetting for the moment that he was a poor man and a Jew, he asked her to marry him. But she reminded him of his forgetfulness and gave her hand to another of her pupils, a fellow by the name of Kerkering, who in her eyes enjoyed a double advantage over Spinoza — he was a Gentile and he was rich.

Spinoza was now completely transformed from a lover into a philosopher.

In the meantime his heterodox ideas had reached the ears of the elders int the Synagogue. They summoned him for a cross-examination and then, when their suspicions about his "dangerous doctrines" had been confirmed, they offered him an annual income of $ 500 in return for his official silence and his external adherence to the orthodox faith. He refused the offer; and on July 27, 1656, he was excommunicated from the Synagogue. From that day on this "moral leper" was, "in accordance with the judgment of the angels and the sentence of the saints, to be anathemized, execrated, cursed and cast out from the tribes of Israel." No one was "to hold converse with him," no one was "to do him any service, to live under the same roof with him or to read any document dictated by him or written by his hand."

Harsh as were the terms of this excommunication, the elders of the Synagogue believed themselves desperately in the right. For the Jews, persecuted on every side, found their only fortress in their faith. Any Jew who dared to attack this fortress was, in their eyes, a traitor to his people. But Spinoza felt that had he *failed* to attack the dogmas of orthodoxy he would have been a traitor to the truth. It was therefore inevitable that his people should exile Spinoza from everyday world into the lonely kingdom of philosophy. Spinoza was twenty-four years old at the time.

II

AS a result of his excommunication his father disowned him. Later when his father died, Spinoza's sister tried to deprive him of his inheritance. Spinoza contested the case in court, won the decision — and then turned the money over to his sister. What Spinoza had been after was not the possession of the money but the establishment of justice. His personal advantage was but of little moment in the epic drama of life whose plot he was trying to ascertain.

And in this effort to ascertain the meaning of life's drama he withdrew to an attic in the Outerdek suburb of Amsterdam. He changed his name from Baruch to Benedict — the Latin word for *blessed* — and he took up the avocation of lens grinding as a means for a livelihood and the vocation of philosophy as the business of his life. This was quite in keeping with the tradition of his ancestors. The ancient Hebrew teachers had recommended a manual trade as a prerequisite for a scholarly life. Learning, they maintained, is too precious a thing to be exchanged for cash. "Use your hands," they said, "for worldly goods, your head for heavenly thoughts." Like these ancient teachers, Spinoza was a devotee of the aristocratic creed of amateur sportsmanship. But it was a sportsmanship of brains rather than of brawn.

And so he lived in his attic and polished his lenses and devoted his spare time to thinking and writing about the mystery of God and the meaning of life. At the age of twenty-eight he moved, together with his hosts, to Rhynsburg, near the city of Leyden. Here he shut himself "like a silkworm in his cocoon," rarely going out except for a walk or to buy his simple food of milk and corn meal and an occasional handful for raisins. His chief amusement, next to conversing with his hosts, was to watch the antics of spiders just as some angel might be watching the antics of men. The sight of their battles would sometimes send the tears rolling down his cheeks with laughter. If ever he came near to losing his temper, it was when his landlady would carelessly sweep away the cobwebs from his room.

All the time that he sat watching the spider's web he was spinning out the threads of his own philosophy. First he wrote a theological book, *A Treatise on Religion,* in which he criticized the orthodox interpretation of the Bible. And then having rejected the conventional God of the Old Testament, he adopted a more merciful God in a New Testament of his own. This New Testament of Spinoza, his famous book of *Ethics*, is one of the strangest books ever written. Composed in Latin, it is geometric in its form, Greek in its idealism, Italian in its content (it is based upon the pantheism of Giordano Burno), French in its foundation (it develops the mehanistic theory of Descartes) and Hebrew in its faith ("at bottom," writes Spinoza, "my belief is the same as that entertained by the Hebrew prophets of old") Was there ever a man so universal as Spinoza?

Let us take a brief excursion into the universal mentality of this "God-intoxicated" philosopher.

III

SPINOZA like the rest of us, was vitally interested in the questions:

1. *What sort of world do we live in?*
2. *Who put us here?*
3. *Why?*

In order to find an answer to these questions he set out to examine (1) the structure of the world, (2) the nature of God and (3) the life of man.

The world, observed Spinoza, is infinite. It has no beginning in space. Suppose for argument's sake, the world did have a beginning. Let us then in imagination project ourselves to that beginning and look beyond it. What do we behold? Nothingness? But nothingness is inconceivable. Hence here is something beyond our imagined beginning — an infinite stretch of the world that extends past the furthest imaginable horizon of human thought. In like manner we can establish the fact — asserts Spinoza — that the world has no end in space.

Furthermore, the world is eternal. It has no beginning and no end in time. For nothingness in time is just as unthinkable as nothingness in space. Individual objects within the world have their physical boundaries, their growth and decay, their beginning and end; but the world itself is all — pervading, everlasting, complete.

In this infinite and eternal world the earth and the planets, indeed all the marching hosts of suns and stars, are nothing but a few grains of sand swept together into an obscure little corner of the universe. And what we call our universe is but a microscopic atom in the infinite body of the whole. The number of universes in this extended world which we call the *whole* is infinite in number, just as the world itself is infinite in space and time.

This infinity and eternity of the world — in a word, its *wholeness* or *perfection* — Spinoza characterised as the *substance* of the world. And by the term *substance* he meant *essence, being, existence.* The world everlastingly *exists, is.* And this little word of two letters, in the language of Spinoza, means not only *is* but *was will be.* It is to Spinoza perhaps the most important word in the dictionary. The world never was created, never will be destroyed. It just simply and profoundly and etternally *is.*

So much, then for the structure of the world. And now for our next question — *who put us here?* The answer is — *God.* And who is God? To this question Spinoza gives a unique and, at first glance, surprising, answer. God, asserts Spinoza, *is the world.* He is all — pervading, everlasting, complete. He *is.* Every object in the world is a momentary idea or attitude of God. Each of us is a definite part of Him, a cell in His body, a thought in His mind, a syllable in His epic poem of life. Yet each of us, with our scanty five senses and our limited intelligence, can understand but a small segment of this truth. It is as if we were looking at the sea or the sky through a narrow chink in a prison wall. We suffer from insufficient vision in the prison cell of our body. A half-blind person can distinguish only a few drab colours. Our senses are colour-blind to the multifold attributes of God. A worm, crawling on the ground, can have but a infinitesimal glimpse of the vast world of which he is a part. We are nothing but grovelling worms when we try to understand God of whom we are a part. The greatest philosopher has but an infantile conception of the true nature — that true is, the character — of God.

Yet even this infantile conception, declares Spinoza, prompts us to conceive that God is in everything and that everything is in God. He is the Intelligence that guides the world and the world that is guided by that Intelligence. He is the eternal artist who weaves, "on the roaring loom of time," the garment of planets and stars that we see Him by. The visible universe is the body of God, and the energy that moves the universe is His mind. And here Spinoza departs from Descartes. The French philosopher had maintained that life consists of there entities — a mechanical body, a thinking mind and the spirt of God above. Spinoza, however, combines the three entities into one. God is not *above* us but *within* us. Body, mind and spirit are but three aspects of a single reality. The visible world is the body of God, the thought that contemplates it is his mind, and the energy that moves it is His spirit. God, in other words, is the infinite substance, idea and motion of the world. He *is* the world. Every blade of grass, every clod of earth, every unfolding flower, every living creature, however lowly, partakes alike of His divine essence. The most magnificent constellation in the Heavens and the meanest beggar on earth are equally important syllables in the poem of life.

Every human body, therefore, is a part of God's body and every human thought is part of God's mind. Let us not, however, confuse our own puny intelligence with the infinite intelligence of God. The world is governed not in accordance with our individual desires but in accordance with God's all–embracing and all–comprehending plan. The story which He has woven into the drama of life is beyond our understanding. It is not for us to pass judgment upon it, since it has not been made for our benefit. It is as logical to believe that the world was made for man to enjoy as it would be to believe that hands and feet were made for mosquitoes to bite or that noses were made for spectacles to rest upon. The human individual, the human race, is but a small part in the infinite plan of God. The entire earth is but a microscopic cell in His body.

But we must be careful, in speaking of God, not to ascribe to Him a human form or human emotions. God is not a capricious overseer with a long beard who sits in heaven and who is swayed by our prayers to help us or by the prayers of our enemies to injure us. What seems good or bad to us as individuals is no concern to Him. For though our mind is a part of God's mind, it is only a microscopic part. All things, to be sure, partake of the intelligence of God. But in this world there are different grades of intelligence. The mind of a tree, for example, has very little in common with the mind of a dog; the mind of a dog has very little in common with the mind of the average human; and the mind of the average human has very little in common with the mind of a Socrates or a Shakespeare or a Descartes. But even the mind of Descartes as compared to God is like the mind of a tree as compared to

Descartes. Together with Emerson, Spinoza might have said as he looked upon our human hatreds and rages and ambitions, "Why so hot, my little fellow?"

Yet — and here comes the hopeful phase of Spinoza's philosophy — our destiny is greater than we think. Each of us, though but a small part of God, is an *equally important* part. Our present sojourn on earth, as the Spinozist Walt Whitman has hinted, is but a stage in our ultimate development. You, I, the peasant at the plough, the workman in the factory, the artist before his canvas, the poet at his desk, the vagabond in the gutter — all of us are realed pupils in the selfsame school of eternity. We happen to be in different grades, depending upon our state of mental and spiritual development, at this particular moment. But in the long run, whatever our present grade or station, we shall all alike reach the senior class of the elect. This, in the philosophy of Spinoza as interpreted in the poetry of Walt Whitman, is the true essence of Democracy.

We may use another illustration in order to clarify Spinoza's idea as to the part that each one of us plays in the divine scheme of life. The world may be compared to a symphony, of which every one of us is a note. Taken by itself, each note is nothing; but as a contributing part of the symphony, it is everything. Even the so-called 'failures" in life are important in the summary of the whole. Suppose, to return to our symphony, the composer puts in a note and then strikes it out again in order to insert something which will be more harmonious in that particular passage. The note which has been written down and then rubbed out has been *necessary* and *important* in the development of the composer's thought as he kept on perfecting his symphony.

To use still another figure — painting. Every stroke of the brush, whether it remains in the final picture or is erased, has played its necessary part in the development of the artist's thought. No line or colour that has ever come into being has been in vain.

In like manner no human life, however short or unhappy, has been in vain. Each of us is an essential thread in the infinite tapestry of life, a significant note in the symphony of God, a contributory stroke of the brush in the painting of God — in a word, an intimate *part* of God.

God, then, is the universe. The stars, the planets, the trees, the flowers, the oceans, the mountains, the clouds — these are the body of God. The spirit that gives them shape and colour and motion and beauty is the *mind* of God. Every human body is part of God's body, and every human mind is part of God's mind. This philosophical doctrine is called *Pantheism*, from the Greek words *pan* (the whole or everything) and *theos* (God).

This doctrine of Pantheism is more than a mere theory. It has tremendous practical and ethical implications. For if all humanity is one body and one soul, it follows that no individual can hurt others without hurting himself.

To do an injury to your neighbour is to cut off your own finger or to pluck out your own eye. The happiness of each of us depends upon the well-being of the whole body of mankind. For the human race, like every human being, is a united living organism. We are more than brothers of a single human family under the fatherhood of God. We are members of a single human entity which in turn is an integral part of the divine essence of God.

And now Spinoza has told us what sort of world we live in and who put us here. There still remains the third question, *why has God put us into this world?* The answer to this question, according to Spinoza, Is that we have been born into this world in order to be happy.

But what is happiness? The presence of pleasure and the absence of pain. It is our business in life to seek pleasure and to avoid pain. In order that we may be able to do this most effectively, advises Spinoza, we must first try to understand our limitations. We are cogs in a cosmic machine. The will that moves this machine is the infinite and eternal mind of God. And the mind of God is the law of nature. Light travels from star to star and man traces a path of consciousness between a sleep and a sleep because they both follow the will of God — that is, the necessary law of light and of life. As for our human will, it also follows the laws of necessity. There is no such thing as free will.

We are the creatures of circumstance, the product of our environment. "There is in the mind," writes

Spinoza, "no absolute or free will; but the mind is determined to will this or that by a cause which in its turn is determined by another cause, and this by another, and so on to infinity." In other words, all our actions, just like the features of our face and the muscles of our body, are dependent upon natural forces which have been operating as far back as the human imagination can reach. In accordance with the fixed laws of nature it has been destined from time immemorial that a Shakespeare should be born to write divine dramas and that a Socrates should arise to die for his fellow men. Our acts are no more free and they have no more to do with the will than the falling of the rain from the sky or the flight of an arrow that has been shot out of a bow. The only difference between the flight of an arrow and the act of a human being is that the human being is *conscious of* his act and mistakes his *consciousness* for *will power.*

We know what we do, but we have no freedom or power to do otherwise. We are chained to our destiny. We are permitted to be interested spectators in the little drama of our life, but we have no voice in its direction. We have the ability to *Watch* our acts and we mistake it for the ability to *will* them. Our decisions are the result not only of our own past life but of the past lives of all our ancestors.

Let us, therefore, understand our limitations. Let us realize that we are not free agents but parts of a divine machine which thinks and acts in accordance with the eternal laws of nature. And, understanding this, let us now return to the purpose for which we live. This purpose, as we have seen, is to be happy, to seek pleasure and to avoid pain. *Our chief interest in life is to love ourselves.* 'Each man," writes Spinoza, "must love himself and seek what is useful to him."

This sounds like the height of egoism. But Spinoza goes on to prove that it is the height of altruism. For, as Spinoza points out, in order to love yourself you must love others. Love, pleasure, happiness — these treasures of the soul are best enjoyed when most generally shared. We have already met this doctrine of enlightened selfishness in the philosophy of Aristotle. Spinoza amplifies the idea and applies it to modern life. The wise man, declares Spinoza, knows that he can help himself only by helping others. He realizes that *individual* happiness is *mutual* happiness. He avoids envy because envy produces not happiness but pain. He avoids hatred because hatred begets hatred. he avoids hurting others because he knows that injury is repaid with injury, that he who takes up the sword is destined to perish by the sword. He avoids conquest because he realizes that every military victory sows the seeds for a future war of revenge. "Our greatest victories," writes Spinoza, "are won not by arms but by greatness of soul."

The truly good man, therefore, the truly *happy* man, will be the truly wise man. He will be generous to others because he *knows* that is this way he will be most generous to himself. And so our ultimate object in life is to seek happiness through knowledge, through the acquisition of wisdom, through the enlightened understanding of the vital interrelationship that exists between man and man. He who understands will hate nothing, despise nothing, injure nothing and fear nothing. He will live a life not of individual ambition but of mutual co–operation. He will adhere to the teaching of the ancient prophets and to the principle of the Golden Rule. He will "desire nothing for himself which he will not also desire for the rest of the mankind."

For all men are equally important parts of God. And so, asserts Spinoza, in order to be happy you must love yourself. But to love yourself is to love mankind, and to love mankind is to love God. And *this* is the reason for which we have come into the world.

IV

LOVE, declares Spinoza, is that which transforms our temporal life into an eternal ecstasy. It is the supreme emotion which gives a real meaning to our existence. In the presence of love the pain of death disappears. For "he who loves his fellow men is untouched by the fear of death." Death is but an incident, a transitional moment, a passage from mortal life to immortality. The body dies but the soul lives on. For the soul of man is part of the soul of God. Each human life is like the reflection of the sun in a pool of water. The water dries up. You no longer see the light of the sun reflected in it. But the sun has not been lost. It still glitters in all its splendour among the stars. In like manner the individual body dies but the universal soul lives on. "The human soul," writes Spinoza "is not destroyed with the body, but something of it remains which is eternal."

And what is that eternal something? It is the divine essence which lives in the body but is not *of* the body. It is the visible thought of God's divine poem printed upon the page of time, just as the visible thought of a Homeric poem is printed upon the page of a book. When the book is cast away and the page is destroyed it is not the poem but the printed copy of it that has perished. The thought of Homer is imprinted upon many pages. You may tear up the pages but you cannot tear up the thought. To change the metaphor, each of us is a bit of coloured glass in the kaleidoscope of life. When the glass is broken the colour is not lost but melts into the white rediance of immortality.

Each human being, therefore, is a related part of a divine unit. When the individual dies his soul is like a drop of water returning to the ocean, a single note melting into the splendour of a symphony, a sublime thought taken out of its temporal context and put into the framework of eternity.

And it is only in this framework of eternity, *sub specie aeternitatis,* that we can understand the true dimensions of our own existence. Let us, remembering our united destiny, learn to be satisfied with little, to return love for hatred and to accept with a smiling courage whatever our individual fate may have to offer. This is the sum and substance of the happy life, "the whole method," as Spinoza would say, of the superior man's wisdom. Above all, he urges, learn to take joy in your intimate relationship with the rest of the world. Bear constantly in mind the fact that your own and your neighbour's existence, however insignificant they may appear to you, are necessary threads in the weaving of the tapestry of universal life. "The greatest good is the knowledge of the union which the mind has with the whole of nature." If the world has not been made for you, be happy in the thought that you have been made for the world. You are an important page in the book of life. Without you the book would have been incomplete.

V

THE page of Spinoza's own life was beautiful but to his contemporaries unimpressive — a noble manuscript published in a cheap edition. In appearance he was anything but striking — small body, dark skin, black curly hair, long black eyebrows, eyes feverish with the unhealthy lustre of consumption. He was careless about his clothes. "A mediocre article," he said, "should not be put into a costly envelope." And he was indifferent about his temporary valuation because he was so certain of his eternal worth.

He went through life in obscurity. Yet a few discerning souls were able to recognize his greatness. At the request of these appreciative friends he moved to The Hague where he remained for the rest of his life. He lived, as before, in a single room. This was his shop, his lodging place and his reception hall for the few visitors who came to pay their respects to his greatness. Among those who thus honoured him with their visits were the German inventor, Von Tschirnaus; the secretary of the British Royal Society, Henry Oldenburg; the Dutch scientist. Huygens; the philosopher, Gottfried Leibniz;

and the wealthy Amsterdam merchant, Simon de Vries. These men tried to extricate him from his obscurity and to protect him against his poverty. But in vain, for he did nothing to help them. When De Vries offered him a gift of $1000 Spinoza refused the offer. Later, when De Vries proposed to will his entire fortune to Spinoza, the "foolish wise man" refused a second time. And finally when this merchant at his death bequeathed to Spinoza an annuity of $250, Spinoza insisted upon reducing the sum to $150. At about this time he declined a much greater gift — a pension from Louis XIV with the proviso that Spinoza should dedicate his next book to His Glittering Highness. Spinoza, in refusing the pension, quietly observed that he couldn't honestly flatter a man whom he didn't admire.

At last there came to him an opportunity for "honourable" recognition. He was offered the chair of philosophy at Heidelberg University. Here, he was assured, he would be allowed to exercise "the most perfect freedom in philosophizing" if only he would promise not to abuse this freedom by "calling in question the established religion of the state." Again Spinoza rejected the offer with thanks. He preferred to starve and to speak the truth as he saw it.

For the petty offers and honours of life meant less than nothing to this man whose eyes were centered upon eternity. Anchored in the peaceful harbour of his thoughts, he was quite indifferent to the tempests that agitated the minds of his less philosophical contemporaries. Holland and France were in the midst of a war. But Spinoza took no interest in the conflict. It was a foolish battle of spiders. The end of this war, whatever the outcome, would be merely the beginning of the preparation for another war. He had nothing to do with the ambitions and the rivalries and the hatreds that brought death to the bodies of men. He was interested only in their deathless souls. Foe and friend were alike to him. One day he was almost lynched because, with the innocence of a child — or of a sage — he went to the enemy's camp at the invitation of their commander, Prince Conde, in order to have a philosophic chat with him!

Fortunately he succeeded in convincing his compatriots that he was not a traitor to their cause but only a harmless lover of wisdom. He escaped with his life.

But not for long. For he, too, was engaged in a war a war — against his disease. It was a losing battle: and, like all the other battles of life, it left him indifferent. For "the human soul is not destroyed with the body. but something of it remains which is eternal."

And that part of him which was eternal looked on courageously as that fragile body of his wasted rapidly away. The winter of 1677 was too much for his shattered wings. He died on Sunday, the twenty–second of February, while his host and his hostess were in church. The only one present was his physician, who seized the money that he found on the table, together with a silver–handled knife, and then left the body unceremoniously. How Spinoza would have laughed to see this!

VI

SPINOZA had not only one of the most universal minds of modern times but one of the most sympathetic hearts. In 1882, when his statue was unveiled at The Hague, Ernest Renan concluded the dedicatory exercises with these words: "Here came perhaps the truest vision ever had of God." He might have added the words, "because here came perhaps the noblest affection ever entertained for Man."

****

Important Works By Spinoza

Ethics.

Treatise on the Improvement of the understanding.

Short Treatise on God. Man and His Well-Being.

Treatice on Religion and Politics.

Metaphysical Thoughts.

Essay on the Rainbow.

The Calculation of Chances.

The Principles of the Cartesian Philosophy.

9

JOHN LOCKE

1632 – 1704

"I NO sooner perceived myself in the world than I found myself in a storm," wrote John Locke of his birth. The "storm" took place in the little town of Wrington, north of Somerstshire. It was in fact a tempest, a tornado of political unrest that had swept upon the sunny British countryside from Whitehall. King Charles the First — first in bigotry and arrogance and tyranny — had dismissed the English Parliament and had attempted to rule alone. The great struggle between the divine right of royalty and the divine royalty of right had left the realm of political theory. It was a time to try hearts and to break heads.

John Locke's father was a country lawyer who believed in freedom. He took up arms against the king and joined the cavalry. The revolutionists swept over England. They unseated Charles from the throne and relieved him of his head. The thud of the royal crown as it fell from the scaffold was heard round the world. A few people had dared to rise up and to challenge the sanctity of the law invested in the person of the king.

They had summoned him to judgment: they had accused him of a crime against their sovereignty, and they had made him answer for the crime, for the wilful transgression of the one against the prerogatives of the many. The bluebloods all over Europe were shocked out of their high-heeled boots. They felt of their necks tenderly. In a huge expanse of wilderness many thousands of miles away bands of Puritan pioneers who had been hounded out of their homes for their religious beliefs, under the regime of Charles, rubbed their cold hands over their New England firesides and felt that they were vindicated.

Such were the restless times in John Locke's boyhood. Everywhere about him there was contention and bloodshed. When Charles was dishonourably dismissed from the ranks of life Oliver Cromwell merely replaced one tyranny with another. For eleven years England was a military dictatorship. John Locke's schooldays were miserable. He was drilled in Puritan dogma. The chiefs of the state, "divinely elect" but not popularly elected, suppressed all freedom of instinct in education. Student life was just one lugubrious sermon after another. All over England the divines administered spiritual spankings to the students for their failure to regard their salvation with the proper funereal attitude.

Everywhere in the country dogma was eating dogma. Intolerance was the order of the day. But in his own household John found the proper tolerance. The Locke family lived a life of free and equal co-operation. When Locke was a young man his father called him into his study and said, "My boy I owe you an apology."

"Why, father?"

"I believe I lost my temper and thrashed you on one occasion many years ago."

II

AT twenty Locke entered Christ's Church, Oxford. He felt no pleasure in studying. His education was little better than a self-imposed exile. The curriculum had as much soul as his old schoolmaster's rod. And the teaching reached a hardly more susceptible part of the anatomy. "I found very little light brought to my understanding," remarked Locke, speaking of his university course several years later. He suspected that he was getting nowhere in college. But he was wrong. He was developing a healthy contempt for dogmatic scholarship, and he reacted so violently that, without knowing it, he was laying the foundation for a new system of knowledge. Such is the beneficent effect of bad schooling upon the mind of a thinker.

Shortly after his graduation he was appointed teacher of Greek at Christ's Church. In addition to his academic duties he became interested in practical politics and in medical research — not a bad start for a young man who had despised his studies in his schooldays.

In his middle twenties he found himself bereft of his entire family. His mother had died in his childhood. His father had succumbed to a lung disease soon after John's graduation from college. His only brother followed his father within a short time. The young philosopher had good need of his philosophy.

But the gods had blessed him with a splendid

gift — the power of making friends. His numerous friendships transformed his life into a "protracted festival of joy."

And of mutual and practical good will. One of his most intimate friends was Lord Ashley, an influential peer of the realm. Locke had met him while a student at Oxford (in 1666), a few years after Cromwell and his stiff-necked Puritans had been overthrown. The Stuart regime had been brought back under the jaunty leadership of Charles II. The pleasures of a repressed society were restored, and with a vengeance. Obscenity became a fine art. Debauchery was systematized by order of the court. The old maid, Tudor Bess, had never in her most unmaidenly moments dreamt of *this*. And her dreams had not been above suspicion.

Charles resorted to licentiousness as a means of restoring the unlicensed government of his fathers. The old serpent of absolutism was gliding under the tree of knowledge and urging the populace to pluck the fruits of sin. It was harvest time in Merry England. But the winter wouldn't be long in coming.

Lord Ashley, Locke's new-found friend, was one of the foremost political opponents of the king and his debaucheries and his divine "rights." He stood for the decencies of parliamentary government. Another clash between the king and the middle classes was in the offing. And Locke was destined to have an excellent observation point in the great political drama that was about to begin.

But Locke was not inclined to be a spectator. By nature

he was an actor. Though he had by this time developed a most remarkable proficiency in his studies, he was no mere academician. He was, in a true sense, a doctor of learning, *a practitioner of knowledge.* Most people, when they acquire learning, lose their common sense — that is, their sense of the common interests of mankind. They become exclusive, aristocratic, aloof. They regard their knowledge as a rare and volatile perfume which they must keep carefully sealed up lest it escape and evaporate into thin air. But Locke admitted everybody into the open space of his thought. He invited all those who were blessed with a healthy pair of nostrils to take a liberal breath of good clean air. Let us all partake of the fragrance of knowledge. Let us all benefit by it.

Among those who were the first to derive benefit from Locke's extraordinary knowledge were Lord Ashley and his family. Locke became an adviser to Lord and Lady Ashley; a tutor to their children and a physician to them all. When Lord Ashley's oldest son arrived at a marriageable age Locke found him a wife. And when the young Lady Ashley was about to become a mother he offered his services as her obstetrician. At this time he had not received a medical degree nor had he ever practised medicine. His entire medical knowledge was theoretical. But he felt no hesitation in undertaking the delivery of the child — and he succeeded. Shortly after the birth of the child he performed a difficult operation on the grandfather, Lord Ashley, removing a tumor from his breast. And, miracle of miracles, the operation too was successful. Such proceedings would today shock the medical fraternity. But Locke, like Bacon was a universal scholar and therefore a universal practitioner. All branches of knowledge came within his theoretical province and whenever possible he put his theories to practical use. Together with the Latin poet Terence he might have said "I am a man and nothing human is beyond the scope of my activity."

As for his medical activity, one of the foremost physicians of the age Dr. Sydenham, wrote to a friend that Locke had not only the greatest judgment but the greatest skill as well. He even referred to Locke as an authority with regard to his own skill. "You know how thoroughly my method of curing fevers is approved by John Locke."

Locke's interests were almost as versatile as the interests of Francis Bacon. And he possessed one quality which the Elizabethan philosopher lacked — a sense of honour. Like Bacon, he became active in politics. But, unlike Bacon, he was an *honest* politician. Through Lord Ashley he was appointed to the administratitve board of the crown colony of Carolina. He helped to draft the constitution of the colony, emphasizing a programme of political, social and religious tolerance. A constitution of this sort was as badly needed in England as it was in the colonies.

Thus far Locke had lived on the sunny side of fate. His friends were influential, his mind was vigorous, his reputation solid. But now, in his late thirties, he developed a disease of the lungs. To the end of his life he was racked with a cough that gradually sapped his strength. But he was cheerful in spite of his illness.

And this was fortunate. For the political career of Lord Ashley and his own fortunes were about to be sorely tested.

Lord Ashley, in spite of his well-known liberalism, had been elevated to the highest office in the kingdom — that of Lord Chancellor. From now on he was to be known to history as the Earl of Shaftesbury. He had become the first great leader of the mercantile classes in England. Owing to the rise of these mercantile classes British politics was undergoing an evolution from authocracy in the direction of democracy. The kingdom of one party consisting of the absolute monarch and his nobles, was giving way to a kingdom of two parties-the party of the nobles and the party of the merchants. Shaftesbury was head of the mercantile party called the Whigs as against the supporting party of the king, known as the Tories.

Shaftesbury's career was like the rise and fall of a stormy sea. After his elevation to the chancellorship the king suddenly grew suspicious of him, discharged him from his office and sent him to the Tower. Locke, who was likely to share in his master's fortune, bad or good, thought it advisable to seek a warmer climate for his political as well as for his physical health. He travelled to the south of France, and upon his return to England he found Lord Ashley not only restored to the favour of the king but ensconced as the presiding officer of the royal council. Within two years, however, Shaftesbury was again committed to the Tower on a charge of high treason.

Shaftesbury's life was just one prison term after another and Locke's one trip to the Continent after another. But the earl benefited even more than the philosopher from this strange routine. For if Locke, upon his return from exile, found himself free to speculate upon the vicissitudes of life, Shaftesbury, upon his release from the Tower, was to find himself freed even from the necessity of speculation. For he retired from one prison cell to another — the grave.

Whatever we may say of Shaftesbury's retirement, we know that Locke's was well spent. Greatness develops out of loneliness. And the greatest glory is often shed upon a country by the sons she has cast from her bosom. The human family has frequently been saved by its "black sheep." The spiritual lawbreakers of history are a veritable rogues' gallery — of saints.

Shaftesbury had died in disgrace, and Locke was a marked man. For he had been Shaftesbury's intimate companion. It was rumoured that he was the author of a pamphlet advocating rebellion against tyranny. He was looked upon as a dangerous radical. The government had set spies upon him at Oxford. They watched his every movement. The college authorities, when questioned, reported that they knew nothing of his "Whig" intrigues. Whereupon the spies engaged him in conversation in the hope that he would let fall some suspicious words. To no avail. "Not a word ever drops from his mouth that discovers anything of his plottings within."

But the king, to be on the safe side, ordered his dismissal from the Oxford faculty. Realizing his precarious position, Locke departed for Holland, the haven of all liberal refugees. The king sent agents after him to "ferret him out." Proceedings of extradition were issued against him. The king's court was prepared to try him. But one obstacle stood in the way of the king's triumph. Locke was nowhere to be found. "He had vanished into thin air." Actually he had found a hiding place in the house of a friendly physician at Amsterdam.

Locke had now the good opportunity to weigh the merits of the liberal government in the Netherlands as against the defects of the coercive government in England. He felt that the world needed a new philosophy, a new code of ethics, a new religion of tolerance. Man must be tolerant — that must be his only dogma.

III

Sic cogitavit de intellectu humano Johannes Locke, anno 1671. "Thus pondered John Locke on the problems of human understanding, 1671." Locke had made this entry in his notebook a decade earlier, when the discussion at his club had turned upon the mystery of the human intelligence. This philosophical problem had always fascinated Locke. But the more he learned about the operations of the human mind the more he despaired of its sanity. In France the great masses of the people were sweating and starving for the greater glory of a few indolent nobles. — In England religious tolerance was out of fashion, and those who tried to revive the style had good reason to fear for their lives. All over the European continent the sheeplike millions, fed by a few cunning shepherds in the pasture lands of prejudice, were allowing themselves to be fleeced of their possessions. Society was a "divinely ordained" system of castes — with the majority of men belonging to the outcasts. Yet a little common sense might have changed all this.

In Holland alone, it seemed, there was a measure of common sense. The Dutch middle classes were alive. They were the bankers and the traders who applied their shrewd business scepticism to the affairs of the government. They were used to weighing their politics as they weighed their merchandise. The traffic of goods was a matter of give and take. So, too, they reasoned, should be the traffic of government. Business was based upon contracts between the seller and the buyer. In like manner government must be based upon contracts between the ruler and the ruled. The king has no divine right to force his authority upon the people. He merely has a commercial right to sell it, at a price that is satisfactory to the customer. The king, in short, must enter into a mutually acceptable contract with his people. In the commercial philosophy of the rising middle classes, Locke saw the keynote to a greater philosophy — the philosophy of a sounder basis for human relationships, the conquest of prejudice through common sense.

While Locke was preparing his notes on the all-important question of human prejudice, one prejudice in the world of men was set aside forever — the Stuart prejudice. By a lucky turn in the wheel of fortune the

Dutch King, William of Orange, had come to the English throne. The British liberals and the growing mercantile class had pleaded secretly with him to overthrow the bigoted Stuart and to become their king in his stead. The Great Revolution of 1688 was middle-class revolution. William landed on the English shore and effected a bloodless uprising on the part of the bourgeoisie. They installed him on the throne after they had bound him to a contract like the good businessmen that they were.

Locke was now able to return to his native land. He published his *Essay on Human Understanding,* the greater part of which he had compiled during the excile. "Essay" is a modest term. The book is a monumental work, quite in keeping with the monumental events that were taking place.

For some time Locke had known what was wrong with the philosophy of the world. Men were unwilling to put their moral ideas to the test as they had done with their commercial and their political ideas. They had begun to doubt the divine right of kings but they still believed implicitly in the divine right of predudice. Sectarian teachers and dogmatic philosophers were stressing the unlimited capacity of the human mind to arrive at certain "infallible truths." Man was supposed to be born with preconceived ideas about God and men — ideas subject to no revision, liable to no dispute. Those who refused to subscribe to these ideas, whether in the realm of religion or of social relationship, were doomed to persecution. Such was the foundation of the mighty structure of intolerance and bigotry and malevolence that enslaved the human mind.

IV

WHAT was the *actual* truth with regard to the so-called "infallible" truths of mankind? Locke's answer to this question descended upon the world like a bombshell.

"Our minds are not made as large as truth nor suited to the whole extent of things." Let us be honest with ourselves and admit as much. "It will become us better to consider well our own weakness and exigencies what we are made for, what we are capable of." Such must be our modest beginning. Far from having any innate knowledge of things tucked away in the crevices of the mind, we must face the one fact that we can conceive no true ideas beyond our experience.

The human mind has no ideas of its own. It is only a mirror that reflects whatever is held up to it through the medium of our senses. Or perhaps we can look upon it as a layer of wax that if moulded into the shape of the ideas which it receives. The mind has no creative power of its own. It cannot even create the idea of God. God exists independently of the human intelligence, just as the sensory world exists outside of the human intelligence. But the idea of God is grasped in a different manner from the ideas of the outside world. In fact there are two ways in which the mind receives its ideas. The first is by means of simple *sensation,* by the perception of the objects of the external world. The second is by means of *reflection,* by the assimilation and the classification of the ideas which the mind receives from the senses. The mind has a way of *combining* and *repeating* sensory impressions. When the mind thus combines and repeats its sensory impressions — that is, when it reflects upon its own operations — it gives rise to the ideas known as doubting, willing, thinking and believing.

The only way in which the mind can tell whether it is assimilating its ideas into true or into false propositions is through its power of intuition. Intuition is indeed the basis of all our fundamental knowledge. "It is irresistible and, like bright sunshine, forces itself immediately to be perceived." It is through intuition alone that we know ourselves. And it is through the knowledge of ourselves that we perceive our Creator.

There are, then, two kinds of ideas, observes Locke. Our simple ideas of heat and cold spring entirely from our experience; our simple ideas of will and doubt spring from our reflection upon our experience. These simple ideas are the materials over which we have no power, "either to make or destroy." All that we can do is to "unite them together" or to set them by one another, as the builder does with his bricks. Whence, however, come the complex ideas that we have of *beauty* and *resignation* and *justice* and *love?* From experience also. For these complex ideas are made up of combinations of the simple ideas of sensation and reflection. For example, we receive the simple idea of an object that gives us an aesthetic pleasure. In the course of our experience we receive other ideas of a similar nature. The mind assimilates and combines all these ideas into a co-ordinated unity which upon reflection we call "beauty." However we have never *seen* "beauty." It becomes an abstraction with us. The simple experiences of certain beautiful objects or sensations are real, but then the mind upon reflection takes the isolated realities and transforms them into a general abstraction. And this is how we receive the most complicated of all the conceptions — the conceptions of eternity and of infinity. In our daily life we experience definite limits of time. Taking these definite limits of time — seconds, minutes, hours, days, years, centuries — as a measure, we extend them in both directions into the indefinite, or infinite, duration of the past and the future. The same is true of our conception of space. The mind has a quirk for adding concrete units of experience into endless abstractions — seconds into eternity, inches into infinity, individual affection into universal love.

All knowledge, therefore, is based upon our experience. Our knowledge of God is based upon experience of ourselves. The brain cannot transcend its environment. For the brain comes to birth only through the forces of environment. It is *an integral Part* of its environment. The brain is doomed to failure when it tries to theorize beyond its own immediate limits. It feeds upon itself as a toad feeds upon its own skin.

And so let us stop speculating about impossible abstractions, "infallible." truths and inconceivable states of perfection. We can no more experience infallibility or perfection in this life than we can experience infinity or timelessness. It is indeed a logical conclusion that just as God exists as an eternal truth and as an eternal testimony to the laws of reason so too must absolute morality, which is dependent upon the will of God, exist as a *reasonable* truth. And yet it is a fact that the human eye has never seen an act of ideal justice or of perfect goodness. Conduct in this world of ours is a relative matter. Experience teaches us that men will seek good and avoid evil for the most utilitarian of motives. That which brings man the greatest pleasure he calls good. That which brings him the greatest pain he calls evil.

Since, then, the human mind is incapable of experiencing absolute truth, concludes Locke, it behoves us in the name of common sense to allow every man his right to square himself with the Lord in his own way. Society must not attempt to impose standards upon the private conscience of the individual, so long as the actions of the individual do not interfere with the public welfare. Let each man do good in his own way. The conduct of the community as a whole should be based upon its common usefulness. What contributes to the pleasure of the greatest number, that must be esteemed greatest good. Leave every man to his own conscience and his own religion. Protestant, Catholic and Jew, all of them alike are trying to do God's will. For what the eye is unable to measure, the heart is able to feel. And the human heart has a capacity for goodness and piety that comes tolerably close to perfection.

V

HERE, then, in the word of Locke, is the first crude architectural plan upon which the whole mighty edifice of modern thought and of modern tolerance is based — a thought confined within modest limits, tolerance and a mutual respect among all minds struggling weakly for little light. Mutual respect breeds mutual freedom. Freedom of religion and freedom of conscience. "Tolerance, after all, is merely a matter of common sense" — the intuitive common sense of the average man.

It is true that Locke was more sound in his philosophy than he was in his psychology. The modern psychologists have rejected Locke's theory that the mind is a sickly, homeless and helpless waif in an alien world. They are inclined to give it more plumpness, more boldness in the shaping of its destiny. Today we are aware that the human mind is more than a mere receptacle for helter-skelter ideas. It is an active and creative personality. Yet in spite of its psychological shortcomings Locke's *Essay on Human Understanding* remains a great declaration of independence in the annals of thought. It is the opening chapter in the epic of modern democracy.

Locke's was a great century in human progress. A trinity of tolerant scepties — three Englishmen — were introducing to mankind the ways of "sweet reasonableness." They were simple, healthy men without pretence, without illusions without a sense of martyrdom or messianic complex of any kind. But they were blessed with the grace of greatness. And all three of them were intimate friends. The first was William Penn, who brought light to the New World. The second was Isaac Newton, who defined the laws of the universe. The third was

John Locke, who paved the way of understanding between man and man.

To the very last summer of his life John Locke remained an ardent soldier on the battlefield of goodwill. With the accession of William and Mary he resumed his active role in public life. He sat on the Board of Trade and helped to develop the industries of Great Britain. He wrote pamphlets defending the rights of labour to an equitable share in the production of wealth. He interested himself in the education of the masses. He defended with all his vigour a bill to insure the freedom of the press, in order that any man might have "the right to print whatever he would speak."

And in his waning years, when his political sun had set and he felt that the "dissolution of the cottage was not far off," he called his friends to him and told them to be of good cheer. For now at last he was finding his way to the understanding that lay beyond all differences and doubts — the *infallible truth.*

****

Important Works By Locke

Letters on Toleration.

Two Treatises on Government.

Essay Concerning the Human Understanding.

Thoughts on Education.

The Reasonableness of Christianity.

10

DAVID HUME

1711 – 1776

DAVIE was an uncommonly good boy. He was the third child of the Laird of Ninewells. The "mansion" of the Home family — David later changed the name to Hume — was one of the landmarks of the countryside, nine miles west of Berwick near the slopes of the Lammermuirs, in the land called the Merse, by the Lower Tweed.

It was shabby enough dwelling, to sure. No paper on the walls, no carpets for the floors and scarcely any furniture — just a few tables and chairs hewed out of oak and beds boxed into the walls. Contrary winds whistled through the cracks in the window — panes and blew down the chimney. There were a couple of cows on the ground floor and a few frozen hens. Lady Home of Ninewells, dressed in a gray woollen wrapper and heavy stockings, helped her barefooted servants with the house cleaning. The children rose at seven and trudged to a neighbour's barn for their lessons. The laird collected his rents, the maids wove the linen. And at night the entire family crowded into the one comfortable bedroom to seek refuge under the stuffy blankets. The blankets alone kept the class alive and warm. And it was a bleak and pinching kind of warmth. But they were happy folk, these prelates of parsimony. And no less happy were the poorer people.

Such, the writers of the period tell us, was the life in Scotland in the year of our Lord 1725.

It is night. Davie studies his homework in the bedroom. A portrait of his blessed father, but lately deceased, stares down at him from the unwashed wall. And by his side sits his young widowed mother humming a Scottish tune and knitting a comforter for one of the children. There is a strong odour from the wick of a candle that sheds light and weaves shadows. Davie rests his elbows on a damp and warped table and nods over a beastly Latin passage written by that unaccommodating fellow Ovid. And facing him is brother John, learning the rules of grammar. And cheery Uncle Home, the parish minister, sits over his two–penny mug and quotes the Gospel. In the corner lie several handly volumes, the *Saint's Recreation,* a book of ***Palmistry,*** a hymnal — and, of course, the Bible and Shakespeare.

"Come ye'll be wanting some halesome barley, uncle Home," says our hostess, Davie's mother. "And we have some agreeable claret to wash it down for you." 'Twas a night to make the stomach freeze on one. The wind slithered in through a crevice in the wall and tickled the ankles. In the bunk the youngest child was asleep.

Up came the claret from the cellar, and an honest loaf of white bread which was a luxury to be had only rarely. "Get along to bed, Davie, tomorrow is church....."

Tomorrow and tomorrow, stern tomorrows! The children rose early and put on their shoes. Six days a week they went around barefoot. But this was the Lord's day. Ha, there is Jennie on the stool for all the congregation to see! No one pays any attention to the sermon. Just look at her swellling figure. What a deligthful scandal to brigten up this dull Sunday! Jennie stares at the ground. There are tears in her eyes. Her lips are trembling. Just wait untll Mr. Home finishes his discourse on the "Cedars of Lebanon." Then he will denounce her in a voice to make the heart grow cold. The women squint up from their prayers in anticipation. The sermon is over. And now at last, with a sombre gesture toward the penitent, the Reverend Mr. Home beseeches the Lord to punishh Jennie for her sin. Let her die in her labour pains as an example for all the other young women of the parish. No mercy. She has broken the sacred covenant. Amen....

Church is out. The children return home. There is a fine hill to climb not far away from their house. But Davie mustn't let Mother and Uncle George know that he intends to play on Sunday. So he slips quietly out of the house during tea. Then he runs like the wind. He throws himself on his hands and knees. There, at the top of the slope, is a cave — his *cave*, "Lordy," he thought, "but the world *is* a beautiful place to live in!" Even on Sunday.

II

HE walked jauntily through the busy streets of Edinburgh, the capital of the Scots. He was a young man of thirty-three with an agreeable face. His mother had meant him for the law, and for a time he had submitted to her wishes. For his own part, however, he would rather dream than study. Dream of the high-heeled young ladies with their crimson shoes who flounced through the smoky streets or rode horseback in the parks, swearing like grenadiers and tickling their nostrils with snuff. As he passed by the garbage-littered house landings, nudging shoulders with tradesmen and shoppers and scribblers and lawyers and clerks, busy thoughts were running through his head. Canny merchants were amassing material fortunes. Canny churchmen were amassing credit with God. Canny women of pleasure were amassing lovers. And David Hume was troubled. Where was he headed? What was he going to do?

He knew. Nothing like wetting your head with a drink. He would go and have a glass with Mitchell in his picturesque cavern on the West Bow. There, now, over a chopin of claret. A damp cellar. And here was Mitchell, the crazy tinker who fancied he was a messiah, looking at him from under ardent lashes.

"How now, Davie, be you writing essays or be you slipping out of Bristol harbour in a merchant brig, leaving lassies with full hearts behind?"

David laughed. The "professor-pewterer" was referring to certain indiscretions of his which had lately stirred the world of his friends.

"No, my good Doctor Mitchell. I have not published any writings since last year when I was foolhardy enough to try my arrogant immaturity on the booksellers and critics of London. I do not fancy myself a scribbler any more."

"Dod, man. Never was literary attempt more unfortunate than your *Treatise on Human Nature.* I ken, people don't take much to your philosophy. You should have stayed to the law, as becomes an honourable Scot. Here is a busy city, man. Can you not find your rightful place in it?"

David finished his drink before he spoke. "This city, this country of ours....is hard and narrow and bigoted and frightfully efficient. Once I was a part of it. I was brought up by the side of the kirk, in the company of thrifty folk who were marvellously sure of their world. Hadn't Adam signed a contract with the Lord God for the eternal salvation of Scotland? What could be better business? God was thrifty like the best of us. He didn't scatter salvation around in the streets. He hoarded it for the chosen few Scot Covenanters like ourselves. That's what our ministers taught us. So I decided to go the whole way. Since I owed my very existence to a business deal, might I not at least acquit myself with good humour in the part assigned to me? I gave up the law and shipped from Bristol as a merchant's apprentice. Then I returned and wrote an inquiry on human nature. Human nature indeed! I soon perceived that the world of my fathers is no longer *my* world,

Mitchell. I began to see a certain truth that lay beyond this Edinburgh. And do you know what that truth is?"

"What, my lad?"

"The truth that there is no truth."

"I ken you not."

"Very few people understand me, Mitchell. But see here, I have a letter from the third Marquis of Annandale. He wants to engage me as his instructor in philosophy at three hundred pounds."

"An excellent thing, Davie!"

"He has taken a liking to my essays on morals and politics, Mitchell. He is my one admier. And he is hopelessly insane."

III

WINTER at Weldehall. A madman and a philosopher in a lonely mansion. The Marquis George was a man with a powerful fortune and a feeble mind. The courts had declared him mad. Three persons were appointed trustees — as motley a group as ever strode the stage of melodrama. One was the solicitor general of England, the other a thick–witted country squire and the last a tough-minded, hard–drinking captain of the king's navy who was out to swindle the marquis of his estate. The philosopher had been hired to humour the marquis. They hoped that Annandale would die during the winter. If he died of Hume's philosophy, so much the better.

The marquis' moods were unpredictable. One day he pressed Hume to his breast and wept in his face for friendship. The next day he ordered him out of the room. He ranted and raved and cooed like a dove. He became suddenly studious and sat up nights doing research work. He locked himself in his library and took to writing fiction. No one could come near him for days at a stretch. Plainly his condition was becoming worse all the time.

Hume wrote to the trustees, suggesting that the marquis be removed from his country home into the city, especially since winter was approaching and Weldehall Mansion would become more lonely than ever. The trustees would not hear of this. The winter came on — an unusually cold winter. The rooms at Weldehall were heavy with drapings and empty of sunlight. The servants were all in the pay of the naval captain who had made it his business to see that George didn't survive. They tiptoed along the grey corridors day and night with secret messages. The doctors attending the marquis prescribed diets that sent the fever raging to his head and made his poor brain more confused than ever. But if his mind was feeble, his body was strong and agile. He leaped over the sofas and scrambled down the banisters. He crept with the cunning of a tiger over the carpets and sprang upon people with a ghostly laugh. He scratched at the eyes of his servants and cracked their heads with logs. Finally they locked him up. He begged to see David Hume and discoursed on morals and politics with him. At times like this he would display toward David the faith of a little child in the presence of his father.

Far away in Dumfriesshire the stately dowager mother of the marquis had washed her hands for the entire business. She wrote endearing letters to her "beloved son," but she made no effort to help him. The solicitor general of England was busy with his soliciting, the country squire was busy collecting his. The scattered wits, and the captain of the king's navy was busy — indeed too busy — collecting the marquis' money for himself. Life at Weldehall had become excruciating for Hume. He did his best to comfort the marquis and to indulge him in his whims. Finally he could stand it no longer. It was a relief when the naval captain dismissed him from the job.

And now to London — the Strand and Holborn, guttersnipes and gutter satirists, Covent Garden, National Gallery, fireworks — and St. Clair, the periwigged general of the king, with sword at his side and snuff stains on his military coat.

"Will you come with me and lead the life of a soldier. Davie? I am going to Canada with a battalion of right good Englishmen to smoke out the French."

"I am a philosopher, General." said David Hume, "and it's high time I settled down."

"Fiddlesticks! A military expedition will do your Scotch blood good. Learn how brave men live and die, David. Smell the powder of battle and look death in the eye. I want you for my secretary."

David thought awhile. He was preparing to write a history of England. What could be better experience than a military campaign?

They never arrived in America to join the eight thousand colonial troops in the march on Quebec. The British War Office dallied in supplying the funds for the expedition. The War Office was a notoriously inefficient branch of the government. Some years later a fellow by the name of George Washington would find that out.

The summer wore on. The ships remained anchored in the harbour. The men were huddled abroad. Of the war secretary it was a common saying, "He lost half an hour every morning and spent the day searching for it." "Well, well," said the secretary when the summer had passed and it was too late to set out for Canada. "We'll have our little expedition yet. I've got to send these boys in their bright red uniforms and shiny buttons somewhere. If they can't drive the French out of America, they can at least drive them out of France." Then came the order from His Majesty's War Office. "Sail with the first fair wind to the coast of France and make an attempt on La Rochelle, or sail up the river to Paris, or sail anywhere on the western coast."

"But your lordship," ventured poor General St. Clair, "can you not give me more precise orders than these?"

"I don't care a fig where the ships go, General, so long as they get out of sight."

"There isn't a man in the contingent who knows the

French coast. Indeed, we've supplied ourselves with Indian scouts for the New England wilderness."

"Too bad, but it can't be helped."

"May we at least, in the interest of our expedition, be presented with a map of France?"

"It's right across the channel. You can't miss it."

One patriot managed to pick up a small map in a bookstore. It was entirely adequate for a grammar–school lesson in geography. Hume and his companions set sail from Plymouth. They put in timidly at the French L' Orient, made a mouselike and unsuccessful attempt to penetrate inland and then boldly set sail again for another port. A storm scattered the fleet. But the philosopher and the general arrived at Quiberon Bay with the majority of the soldiers, many of whom were suffering from cramped muscles as a result of their protracted huddling in the narrow quarters of the ship. Finally there was a battle — in which not even a bloody nose was recorded. One of Hume's companions committed suicide out of disgust.

Within a year Hume was back in England in civilian clothes. Now he was well equipped to write his monumental history.

IV

HE sat as Sir Librarian to the Faculty of Advocates at Edinburgh. It was a good position. Not much salary but plenty of books to read and plenty of leisure to write. He was hard at work on his *History of the Stuart*

Reign. He had grown very fat at his sedentary job. He had invested his money shrewdly and speculated himself into a tidy sum. And he had become a social lion — a most gentle lion, a most amiable, corpulent, gout-ridden epicure of a lion. Every time he travelled in a coach that lurched to the side he imprinted his corpulency upon his fellow travellers and rendered them black and blue. When, on the occasion of a diplomatic visit to France, he made his debut at the royal court he was excused from the customary procedure of bowing himself backward out of the room. "Ah monsieur, never mind the etiquette. You are not accustomed to this movement and the floor is slippery."

But in return for all this kindness he treated the world most cavalierly. For this mountain of a man laboured — and brought forth a swarm of theories that swept like locusts over the harvest of men's most cherished ideals. "For all his good nature, David loves to shock," said Hume's friends. It was whispered that he was an unbeliever. Once he came to dinner at the house of a pious friend and started up from the table insisting that he woundn't eat because there was an enemy present. "An enemy?" "Yes," he insisted, and he pointed to a Bible that lay on the table. "Take it away."

"But, David, you used to be such a good Scotch moderate. A mild and temperate man."

"I still am a mild and temperate man," answered David. "A sober, discreet, virtuous, frugal, regular, quiet good – natured man with a bad character."

He finished his *History of the Stuart Reign.* It was quite unorthodox. Indeed, no history like it had ever been written. He irritated all the different classes of people who might be likely to read it — Whigs and Tories, Royalists and Revolutionists, the sane, the insane and the vain. "I decided to neglect the cry of popular prejudices!"

The industrialist classes who had overthrown Charles and James Stuart were made the villiains of the peace. The tyrant kings were made the heroes. He attacked the Protestant Reformation and the English Civil War. "I scarcely, indeed, heard of one man in the three kingdoms — England, Scotland, Ireland — who could endure the book," he wrote gleefully. Never had a work created so adverse a sensation. He was greatly encouraged. He continued with an excursion into the Elizabethan age of England — a dissertation in which he offended the liberals by attacking the British constitution and the Jacobites by attacking Mary, Queen of Scots.

And now a number of people remembered him as the canny Scot who some years previously had written a treatise on human nature in which he denied the possibility of proving that there was anything natural or human in the world. At that time the book had attracted but little attention. But since then he had persisted with his essays until he had collected quite a following of enemies and a few incautious friends. "I can't make English of him", muttered some of his well-wishers. "Why should he wave a red flag in the face of the public? All the learned detest him." "Symptoms of a rising literary reputation," remarked Hume cheerfully. After all, what else could they expect from a Scot who had attended a madman for a year at Weldehall?

He had written two works of an unusually devastating nature — an essay defending suicide and another essay denying the immortality of the soul. His friends begged him not to publish these essays. He complied with their request. Instead he published a long treatise *On the Natural History of Religion* in which, far more elaborately than ever before, he reviewed all the arguments for immortality and annihilated them one by one. "The whole world," he declared, "presents nothing but the idea of a blind Nature.... pouring forth from her lap, without discernment or parental care, her maimed and abortive children." In this book as usual, he showed no respect for Christianity. The best way to become a Christian, he averred, is to be a sceptic. As for our Lord — if we have any — remarked this cheerful pessimist, it is inconsistent to expect any favours from Him. For if He has human interests, He must also have human weaknesses. And the chief of these weaknesses would be, "a complete disregard for inferior creatures." The English public was aghast at these words. "I think a wickeder mind, and more obstinately bent on public mischief, I never knew!" exclaimed a bishop.

V

BUT if England abhorred Hume, the French took an instant fancy to him. They looked upon him as the

English Voltaire, and they were delighted to hear that he had accepted an office on the staff of the English ambassador to France. The giant unbeliever, with the soil of Scotland clinging to his nails, was storming the Citadel of Unbelief. Said Mr. Hume grandly, "I carry only four books along with me: a Virgil, a Horace, a Tasso and a Tacitus." "So much the better for his reputation," remarked the French rationalists. "A lesser man would have carried the Bible."

The famous "mountain of scepticism" was introduced to the royal family. In some of the letters Hume wrote from Paris we get an interesting picture of his reception at the royal court. The king's oldest grandchild, the Duc de Berry, aged ten, said very prettily, "Monsieur, you have a great reputation in this country. Your name is very well known. It is with pleasure that I meet you." Then the second child, the Comte de Provence, aged eight, bowed and said, "Monsieur, we have awaited your arrival in this country with a great deal of impatience. I look forward with pleasure to the day when I shall be able to read your fine *History of England*." Next the Comte d' Artois, aged five, advanced and bowed and mumbled something very politely about Hume's history. He was followed by his sister, an infant who merely bowed but said nothing. She was too young to memorize her speech.

As he helps himself to the dainty desserts and the ladies' smiles at the Salon des Quatres Glaces, while the great nobles gamble behind the screens, he must repeat his fundamental truths over and over again.

"Ah, *mon maitre de philosophie* –"

"-*et mon maitre de morale,* you say we have no minds, nothing with which to think. How horrible!"

"Madame," replies David sternly, "I say nothing of the kind."

"He frowns," observes De Beauveau, "upon our silly belief that things and people must have a *necessary* cause for their existence. How can there be a cause for the world when there is absolutely no reason–"

"Pardon, but there is a reason for one thing — love!" declares a gallant as he bows low over his lady's hand.

"And if the lover is caught by her husband," whispers one mademoiselle into the ear of another, "there will be a reason for the sword marks on his entrails."

"Custom, just sheer silly custom," said Madame de Boufflers blandly. "As Monsieur Hume has observed, there would be no logic to such a procedure."

"According to Monsieur Hume," buzzed the Prince de Conti, "there is no logic in anything."

"Certainly not in his own conduct," insinuated a young man in low voice.

And indeed, Hume's conduct was hardly befitting the dignity of a philosopher. He had fallen recklessly in love with the mistress of the most powerful nobleman in France. "You may cut me to pieces, limb by limb," he cried to her with the ardour of a schoolboy, "but I shall expire still attached to you."

And the great sceptic entered into another attachment which was even more outrageous. Crying, *"Je tiens Jean Jacques,"* he embraced Rousseau, the most notorious philosopher-madman of the century, and he brought the prophet in his Armenian coat back to London together with his mistress and his dog. Almost immediately the "happy atheist" quarrelled with his "honest savage" and the reverberations were heard around the world.

Such were the fruits of Hume's trips to Paris.

VI

IN the spring of 1776, when the philosopher had attained his sixty-fifth year, he wrote the story of his life. It was the life of a man sorely perplexed by life. His autobiography was the last testament of a believer reviewing the progress of what people chose to call his unbelief. He had been born pious. In the course of events, however, he had lost his piety and gained his religion. His keen mind could never accept the rigid orthodoxy of his church. Yet to the very end he clung to a philosophy of faith compared to which the conventional theology of the day had been dwarfed into insignificance.

He was misunderstood by those who worshipped as well as by those who attacked him; for he had not only assailed the unreasonableness of superstition but he had exploded the very foundations of reason.

Why do men look for causes and effects? Is there any necessary correlation in the world of things? Actually we experience a sequence of impressions which we link together by a propensity of memory and habit into what we are pleased to regard as laws of cause and effect. When we observe one particular species of events always following another, we begin to assume a secret and necessary tie between them. But try as we may, we can never see the hidden tie. If we assume that "such and such a thing" is the effect of some previous cause, then we must assume that the previous cause is the effect of some still earlier cause, and so on to infinity. Hence we shall struggle backwards in an endless chain of mystery if we try to understand the cause of anything.

Actually no experience can cause another experience, argued Hume, any more than one fact can produce another and entirely different fact. For example, how can it be argued that if B follows A it is therefore the immediate and necessary result of A? What about the intermediary steps between A and B — A^1, A^2, A^3, A^4 and so on and on? How do we know that his endless intermediary sequence of events between A and B is an inevitably linked chain of cause and effect? The so-called laws of causation, therefore, explain absolutely nothing.

Experience is composed of random sensations. We apprehend each sensation as it comes to us. It is the eccentricity of the human mind that imposes a fictitious union upon the outward phenomena which impinge upon our senses.

Indeed, we assume that the world as we have known it yesterday will exist tomorrow. We assume that since we have seen a rubber ball return to us every time it was thrown into the air in the past it will do the same in the future. We have framed in our minds a general law about the ball. However, there is no relationship between a necessary law of timelessness and the actual experience of the moment. We experience particular things in temporary relationships; we do not experience abstract ideas in permanent relationships.

Whence, then, come our general propositions? Our propositions indeed are tools for classifying and analyzing experience in terms of greater or less coherence and of greater or less probability. The so-called laws of necessity are, in fact, propositions of probability. The world as we apprehend it is not a chain of unmistakable past causes and unavoidable future effects but a succession of past and future probabilities.

This philosophy of Hume's naturally created a sensation in Europe. This "exposure" of reason drew irrational applause and equally irrational attacks. If "reason is but the effect of custom," and if there is no necessary connection in things themselves, what becomes of all our "certain" knowledge? There can, in fact be no "certain" knowledge of anything, but only endless inference. The only "certainties" are the passing, random, disconnected sensations of experience.

Locke had declared that all our knowledge comes to us through the experience of our senses. "There is nothing in the mind except what was first in the senses."

Hume goes a step further. Our knowledge of ourselves, *of our own minds,* comes also through the experience of our senses. What, indeed, *is* the mind, the ego, the personality called I? It is a bundle of moods and feelings and emotions which are by inference grouped around a persistent identity. Each mood is forever followed by a new mood. Each sensation is perpetually succeeded by a new sensation. One moment the self is anger, the next contentment, the next sorrow. We perceive these separate ideas, memories, feelings. But we do not perceive an entity called the mind. We infer, with the highest degree of probability, that there is a permanent relationship between the moods and feelings, a permanent "I" underlying the temporary and ever-changing manifestations of "self." Probability but not certainty.

Subtract all the forms and colours of our so — alled "certain" beliefs, and what remains? A heap of empty, random sensations whirling around endlessly like unsubstantial soap bubbles in the wash-bowl of nothingness.

Hume's "abolition of the human reason" threw everybody into a turmoil of excitement. "Who am I?" the whole world of philosophers gasped. Like disappointed children they turned angrily upon the man who had robbed them of their sweet illusions. They branded him as a "traitor, atheist, scoundrel." And they refused to hear him out.

But if mankind lost faith in Hume, Hume was far

too gallant to lose faith in mankind. He was determined "to save the world from its illusions."

Yet he was not always sure of himself. "I dine, I play a game of backgammon, I converse and am merry with my friends; and when after three of four hours of amusement I would return to my speculations they appear so cold and strained and ridiculous that I cannot find it in my heart to enter into them any further."

For at bottom he was a true believer. He well knew that he had killed not a substance but a shadow. Reason at best is but a negative function. It merely reveals to us the limits of our knowledge and of our experience. It can never reveal their depths. Had Hume destroyed anything really essential to men? Nothing but the foolishness of the "little" thinkers of the world who believed that their powers of reason could lead them to positive truths. Hume denied no more than he affirmed. For to deny, as well as to affirm, implied a sense of knowledge. Hume remained intellectually in a state of suspended judgment. But morally he retained his belief. And in the quiet of his heart he whispered, "I ask what is the cause of this belief? I care not; I know not; that doesn't concern me. But I do know that there is a God."

In his heart he was one of the profoundest believers of the age. He believed in the dignity of the individual, the freedom of man. In 1774, when asked to comment on the struggle of the thirteen stubborn little colonies on the coast of North America for their independence from King George, he replied,; "I am an American. I believe in America's destiny."

VII

"IN the spring of 1775," writes this "believing unbeliever" in his autobiography, "I was struck with a disorder in my bowels, which.... has become incurable. I now reckon upon a speedy dissolution." Thus he calmly awaited his end. It was difficult for a man to be more detached from life. "To conclude historically with my own character," he tells us, "I am or rather was (for that is the style I must now use in speaking of myself)... a man of mild disposition, of command of temper... I cannot say there is no vanity in making this funeral oration of myself, but I hope it is not a misplaced one."

When his friends learned that he was about to leave the world they flocked to pay their last respects to him. Most of them were secretly curious to see how reasonably this man who discounted reason would prepare for the end. If they expected a change in Hume they were doomed to disappointment. They found the ghostly emaciated ruins of what had once been a person of huge bulk. But the old humorous twinkle remained in the philosopher's eye.

"I am wondering," he told them, "how I can meet Charon who ferries the souls of the dead over river Styx. What excuse can I make for having remained just a little longer on this bank of life? 'If you please, good Charon,' I shall implore, 'have a little patience,

Let me stay awhile. For years I have been trying to open the eyes of the public. If I live a few years longer I may have satisfaction of seeing the downfall of the superstitions I have fought against.' But Charo would certainly lose his temper and burst out in a rage, 'You incurable dreamer, that *will* not happen in a thousand years. Do you think I will grant you a new lease of life for so long a term as that? Get into my boat this instant, you lazy, loitering, foolish optimist of a rogue!"

****

Important Works By Hume

Treatise of Human Nature.

An Inquiry Concerning Human Understanding.

Political Discourses.

Inquiry Concerning the Principles of Morals

Dialogues Concerning Natural Religion.

History of England, five Volumes.

Four Dissertations: The Natural History of Religion. Of the Passions, Of Tragedy, Of the Standard of Taste.

Letters.

Essays.

11

VOLTAIRE

Francois Marie Arouet

1694 – 1778

VOLTAIRE was the jester at the court of the philosopher kings of the world. He began with a jest. He was born half dead, and the nurses had to slap him into life. They gave him not more than four days to live. But he fooled them all and lived eighty-four years. And he ended with a jest. As he lay on his death-bed and the priest came to shrive him he asked, "Who sent you here, Monsieur l' Abbe?" "God Himself, Monsieur Voltaire," replied the priest. "Ah, my dear sir," came back from Voltaire, "and where are your credentials?"

For more than half a century Voltaire made it his business to shatter with his laughter the pretensions and the hypocracies of the world. He tore away the veils of diplomacy that convered the political and the social institutions of his day and left exposed — the bitter truth. "I laugh," he said, "in order to keep myself from going mad."

II

HIS entire life was a paradox. He despised mankind and yet he was passionately fond of men. He ridiculed the clergy and dedicated one of his books to the Pope. He made fun of royalty and he accepted a pension from King Frederick the Great. He hated bigotry and he was bigoted in his attitude towards the Jews. He sneered at the vanity of riches and he acquired a vast fortune (by means that were not always not honest). He disbelieved in God and he tried all his life to find Him. He had no respect for religion and he created a new religion of laughter. When he gave way to his anger he could be as merciless as a tiger. Yet when his sympathies were aroused, especially at the sight of injustice, he would cast aside his own interest and plunge for years at a time into the dangerous business of helping the weak against the strong.

Thin as a skeleton, long-nosed, pock-marked, beady-eyed and sarcastic, he was perhaps the ugliest man in Paris. And the most popular. The women idolized him. Sickly throughout his life, he was a very dynamo of energy. Once, at a rehearsal of his play *Merope,* he tried to inspire an actress to speedier movement. "To act as you require," she complained, "I should have to have the devil in me." "That's just it," retorted Voltaire. "You've got to have the devil in you to succeed in any of the arts."

And this was secret of his own success. *Voltaire avait le diable au corps,* as Sainte-Beuve has observed. Indeed, he was a combination of the devil, Aristophanes and Rabelais — with not a little of Saint Francis thrown in.

His father was a Jansenist, which in itself was a paradox. For the Jansenists were a sect of "Protestant Catholics." They protested against the dogmatic strictness of the established church and they insisted upon a personal study and a personal interpretation of the Bible. Like the Puritans of England, they despised the pleasures of the earth and preached an other-worldly doctrine. It was their business, in the words of one of their pious historians, "to depopulate the earth and to bring new citizens to heaven."

This was the atmosphere in which Voltaire — his real name was Francois Marie Arouet — spent the early years of his childhood. He had lost his mother in his infancy. His father imposed his doctrine of abstract mysticism so vigorously upon him that Voltaire grew up with a rebellious thirst for concrete reality. He cordially hated Jansenism.

But he grew up with another hatred — hatred against the persecution of the Jansenists. Against any kind of persecution. To despise an idea was one thing. To punish people who held that idea was quite another thing. Voltaire was fifteen years old when Louis XIV destroyed the Jansenist college at Port Royal and ordered a plough to be driven through the cemetery "of their saintly dead." Voltaire disliked the saints but he was indignant at the sinners who oppressed them. He had now discovered his role in life. He would devote it to the persecution of the persecutors. He would become a soldier of the pen.

His father, however was a practical lawyer in spite of his being a Jansenist — another of the strange paradoxes of this strange family. He tried to discourage his son from being a writer. "A literary career," he said, "is useless. It leads only to starvation." He sent Voltaire to a law school immediately upon his graduation (at the age of sixteen) from the Jesuit college of Louis le Grand. Voltaire neglected his legal studies and devoted his time to poetry, gambling and love. His father, in a final effort to bring his prodigal son to his senses, secured for him a position in the employ of the Marquis de Saint-Ange. This man, a veteran politician, knew all the "right" people. Besides, he had an entree into the palace of Louis XIV — a back-door entree, so to speak. He boasted that he had an intimate knowledge of the entire life, both public and private, of the illustrious Sun King. He loved to gossip about the discretions as well as the indiscretions of his royal master — and as he gossiped Voltaire took notes. He was laying the foundations for his future historical work.

The marquis warned his young protege to watch his steps as he treaded his way through the ambitions and the rivalries and the jealousies of the court. He undertook to protect Voltaire against all outside interference. But he was unable to protect him against one thing — Voltaire's own sharp tongue. Louis XIV had just died (1715), and the regent, Philip of Orleans, became the target of all the cynicism that had been put up during the oppressive reign of the Sun King. Voltaire, joining in the sport, wrote a lampoon on the regent and was rewarded with an eleven months' lodging at the Bastille.

it was during this prison sentence that he adopted the pen name of Voltaire and produced the first of his literary works — an epic poem on the life of King Henry of Navarre.

His prison sentence was followed by a further punishment, a year's exile from Paris. During this exile he wrote his first tragedy, *Oedipe*. It enjoyed a run of forty-five nights — a record which not even the tragedies of Corneille and Racine had attained. Nothing succeeds like success. The regent not only pardoned Voltaire but gave him a medal and a pension in recognition of his dramatic skill. Voltaire thanked the rengent for taking care of his board and begged him thereafter not to concern himself about his lodging. He preferred the discomfort of his home, he said, to the "comforts" of the Bastille.

He followed *Oedipe* with a number of other successful tragedies which netted him a tidy sum of money. This money he invested with the skill — and with the luck — of a Wall Street broker. Once, when the government was conducting a lottery, he outwitted the managers, bought up all the tickets at wholesale and carried off every one of the prizes.

More plays, more success, more wealth — and then he found himself once more in the Bastile. Here is how it happened: One evening at the opera, as he was entertaining a group of friends with his customary wit, an aristocrat walked up to him and drawled out insultingly, "Arouet, Voltaire, what's your real name?" The Speaker was the Chevalier de Rohan, a man who bore one of the noblest names in France but who personally had never done anything to distinguish it. Voltaire glanced at the chevalier and returned to his conversation without answering him. But Rohan was not to be put off like that. "Did you hear what I asked?" he cried insolently. "I want to know your name!" This time Voltaire was ready with his answer. "The name I bear, my lord, is obscure. But *I*, at least, have brought honour to it."

The chevalier flushed and then turned on his heel and walked out. The following night Voltaire was attacked and severely drubbed by a band of Rohan's hired thugs. Voltaire challenged Rohan to a duel; but the chevalier, fearing that his rival's sword might be as nimble as his tongue, appealed for protection to the chief of police, who happened to be his cousin. Voltaire was arrested and sent to the Bastille for his 'treasonable talk and disorderly conduct."

Upon his release from Bastille (1726) he left Paris with its titles and its thugs and took refuge in England. He arrived in London on the king's birthday, which was celebrated by a water festival on the Thames. The royal barge, to the accompaniment of the "water music", passed in procession down the river between "six miles of ships in full sail." Voltaire was thrilled at this spectacle of "a free island perched upon the threshold of an enslaved continent". His receptive genius found itself perfectly at home in the new sorroundings. He learned the English language with his usual facility. Within a year he had mastered all of its literature — with the exception of Shakespeare. The laughing

French philosopher was never able to understand the English mind at its best, just as the serious English philosophers were never able to understand the French mind at its best. Voltaire regarded Shakespeare as a savage; and Carlyle retaliated a century later, by calling Voltaire a madman.

But if Voltaire was unable to appreciate the greatest Englishman of the past, he found many congenial spirits among the Englishmen of his own day. He relished the freedom of their thoughts and the courage with which they expressed them. He became acquainted with the Quakers, and he admired their attempt "to convert the Christian countries to Chiristianity." He even thought of taking up his permanent residence in England. "In this country," he wrote to a Parisian friend, "it is possible to use one's mind freely without fear of cringing. If I followed my own inclination I should stay here if only to learn how to think."

Indeed, he atcually came to "think in English." He acquired a scientific background for his philosophical speculations; he conceived a passion for constitutional government as against absolute monarchy; and under the influence of Jonathan Swift, he developed from an adolescent cynic into a mature satirist.

It must have been a feast for the gods to hear the two greatest satirists of the century engage in a duel of tongues. One of the most charming of Voltaire's romances, his *Micromegas* (Little-big), was inspired by *Gulliver's Travels.* Voltaire lacked the bitter pungency of Swift's satire — his pen tickled while Swift's pen stabbed — but his imagination was richer. The book pokes gentle fun at our vanity in believing that we play an important part in the scheme of things. Micromegas, an inhabitant from Sirius who is half a million feet tall, meets a Saturnian, a little shrimp of a fellow who stands only fifteen thousand feet high. Together they decide to go off on a ramble through the fields of space. The Saturnian has been recently married, and his bride is very unwilling to let him go after their all-too-brief honeymoon of only two hundred years. But the Saturnian consoles her with the assurance that he will soon return, and the two friends jump upon the tail of a comet and go sailing away among the stars.

They finally land — of all places! — upon the insignificant dust speck known as the earth.

Walking through the Mediterranean, which to them is nothing more than a puddle, they chance upon a vessel that is returning, with a group of philosophers on board, from a polar expedition. This vessel is (to the Sirian) so small that he cannot see it without a microscope. He scoops it up from the ocean and places it upon his fingernail for closer examination. He is very much astonished, after observing the vessel for some time, to discover living atoms upon it. His astonishment turns to amusement when these atoms tell him that they are human creatures with an immortal soul, that they are made in the image of God and that they consider themselves to the centre of the universe!

Inquiring to learn something about their life, the Sirian

is told that these funny little mites devote most of their time upon earth to the killing of one another. "At this very moment," one of the philosophers informs him, "there are one million creatures of our own species, covered with hats, slaying an equal number of their fellow creatures, who wear turbans... The object of this dispute," continues the human spokesman, "is an insignificant little molehill (called Palestine)... Not that any one of those million who cut one another's throats pretends to have the slightest claim to the smallest particle of the clod. The question is not whether it shall belong to any of the men who are fighting for it but whether it shall go to a certain person who is known by the name of Sultan or to another person whom (for what reason I know not) they dignify with the appellation of King... And this (senseless slaughter)" concludes the philosopher, "has been going on all over the earth from time immemorial."

Such, then, are the crazy atoms that inhabit this funny little earth, muse the two celestial travellers. They then hold further converse with the tiny philosopher (a disciple of Locke) and they find his rather likeable little creature. But unluckily there is a scholar upon the ship, a squirt of a fellow in a square cap and gown, who cuts short the conversation of the philosophers. He looks the celestial visitors up and down and declare that they and their world, their planets and their suns and their stars, have all been created solely for the sake of man. "At this speech our travellers gave way to that hilarious, inextinguishable laughter which is, according to Homer, peculiar to the gods.

Their shoulders and their stomachs rocked back and forth, and in these convulsions the vessel that the Sirian held on his fingernail fell into the pocket of the Saturnian's breeches."

The Saturnian took the ship out of his pocket, placed it back upon the sea and started with his companion upon their return journey to their celestial home. The earth, they concluded, is a lunatic asylum for the inhabitants of the other planets who have gone mad.

III

MICROMEGAS was not the only book which resulted from Voltaire's visit to England. His *Letters on the English* was a far more important, if somewhat less diverting, work than his *Micromegas*. In these letters he tried to contrast the freedom of the English as against the slavery of the French. But he did it indirectly, sandwiching his truth between layers of laughter. Without actually referring to the autocratic system of the French monarchy he pointed out the wisdom of the British system of government "which leaves the king all-powerful to do good but ties his hands if he tries to do evil." He praised the house of Commons, "which, though it is only the second in rank, is the first in influence." He commended the British system of taxation. "Everyone in England pays," he said. "Each gives, not according to his rank but according to his income." He called attention to the happy lot of the British peasant as compared with that of his Freneh brother. "The (British) peasant's feet are not bruised by sabots: he eats white bread; he is well clad; he does not hesitate....to cover his roof with tiles, from fear lest his taxes be raised the next year.... He does not disdain to till the soil that has enriched him. On it he lives a free man. Above all, Voltaire applauded the comparative freedom of speech that prevailed in England. "Anyone has the right to speak in public.... or to have his thoughts on public affairs printed."

Yet in spite of his admiration for the English he was happy when his exile was revoked and he was allowed to return to Paris. For the London fog had penetrated his bones. He was anxious to stretch his "withered limbs" once more in the warmth of the Parisian suns. "I love England," he said, "but after all I want to live in Paris."

And so he came back to Paris after his enforced exile of three years — and promptly found himself in deep water again. His *Letters on the English*, which he had written not for publication but for private distribution, had been issued without his knowledge by a dishonest publisher. A copy fell into the hands of one of the government officials, who took it for what it was actually meant to be — a cargo of explosives concealed in a pleasure yacht. This sort of dynamite was too dangerous for the safety of French absolutism. The book was burned in public and a warrant was issued for Voltaire's arrest.

But Voltaire had no desire to pay another visit to the Bastile. He fled from the clutches of the police — straight into the arms of his mistress.

This young lady, the Marquise du Chatelet, was married. But she had already borne the marquis three children; and having performed her marital duties, she was now ready to attend to her extra-marital pleasures. This was quite in keeping with the fashion of the times. The marquis was away with his regiment, and Voltaire took advantage of the old gentleman's absence by making himself master of his wife and his castle. The Marquise du Chatelet was perhaps the most extraordinary woman of her age. Tall, commanding, stately, she was a very Venus of enticement when dressed in her fashionable clothes. But for the most part she went about with ink — stained fingers and wrapped in an old black apron, delving into the mysteries of chemistry, physics, philosophy and mathematics. Not infrequently she would sit up all night gazing at the stars through her telescope. In her "spare" moments she translated Newton's Principia and Virgil's *Aeneid.* She was one of those rare creatures with a superb mind in a superb body. Her chateau at Cirey with Voltaire as the presiding genius, became the temple of Dionysian revelry and philosophical disputation. Here Voltaire and the marquise entertained the most brilliant wits of the day. From the letters of some of his visitors to their friends we get an intimate glimpse into the colourful life of Cirey. The philosopher and his mistress rose early in the morning and worked in their own studies until luncheon, which they generally ate at ten-thirty. After lunch Voltaire invited his guests for an informal chat in the lobby of his study. This chat lasted exactly half an hour, at the end of which period Voltaire bowed and the company withdrew. The hosts then returned to their studies and worked till nine o' clock in the evening, when supper was announced. During the day, while the hosts were at work, the guests were expected to amuse themselves in their own way. If any of them were rash enough to visit Voltaire in his study, they found no easy chair to sit on. For this was a workroom and not a play–room. At supper, however, Voltaire expanded into his exuberant and playful self. And never since the symposium of Plato had the world seen anything so brilliant as the suppers at Cirey. Voltaire entertained his guests with his best wine, produced for them his most amusing plays and sent them into gales of laughter with his satirical romances. For it was at Cirey that he began to write those exquisite fairy tales for cynics — *Candide, The World As It Goes, Zadig, The Pupil of Nature* and *The Princess of Babylon.*

The leading characters in these stories were not creatures of flesh and blood but mere figureheads which Voltaire dressed up in his favourite ideas. But what sumptuous ideas! And what a fantastic dress he gave them! His *Candide,* the most ineresting of these romances, was written in three days. His pen literally "laughed as it ran." He proved, in this book, that the world we live in is the worst of all possible worlds. He could hardly have chosen a gloomier subject for a story. Yet even Despair, under the magic touch of Voltaire's genius, can become an adorable jester. *Candide,* the Gospel of Pessimism, is one of the most joyous books in the history of literature.

His other romances, too, are a summons to laughter.

He calls upon men to laugh at the spectacle of their own suffering and their own stupidity. In *The Pupil of Nature (L' Ingenu)* he contrasts the wholesome simplicity of the savage mind with the complexities and the corruptions of the civilized mind. A Huron Indian is brought from America to France and the missionaries, out of a sincere desire to save his soul, try to convert him to Christianity. The Huron makes a study of the New Testament and then offers himself for circumcision as well as for baptism. "For", he observes "every character in the New Testament is circumcised. It is therefore obvious that one must become a Jew before he can become a Christian."

The matter is explained to him, and he is ready for the next step. He plunges into the river up to his neck for baptism. When his teachers inform him that it is no longer customary for Christians to be baptized in this manner he shrugs his shoulders, puts on his clothes and goes to the priest for confession. As soon as he is through with the recital of his own sins he drags the priest from the confessional chair, places himself in the seat and orders the good father to confess in turn. For the Bible, insists the Indian, expressly states that "we must confess our sins to one another."

Again explanations are in order, whereupon the bewildered Indian remarks: "I perceive that an infinite number of things are done in your country which are not in your Bible and that hardly anything is done which is commanded in it. I must acknowledge to you that this greatly astonishes and distresses me."

Then the story races along with the adventures and the misfortunes that the savage undergoes as a result of his contact with civilization, until he is finally driven to the conclusion that the devil alone must have misguided him to become a civilized member of society. "My Indian countrymen in America," he complains, "would never have treated me with the barbarity that I have here experienced, Indians may be crude savages, but the men of this country are refined scoundrels."

And so on, throughout the romances of Voltaire. There is nothing in literature that can quite compare with these stories. They are plotless — or rather each of them is a series of disconnected plots strung upon the thread of Voltaire's philosophy. His heroes marry peasant women and heiresses and queens; they lose their eyesight and feel happy because they can philosophize about it; they are disappointed in love and feel unhappy because they *cannot* philosophize about it; they help people in distress and are kicked for their trouble; they commit crimes and are repaid with honours and riches, in short, they dance through the whole puppet show of human existence with Voltaire holding the strings in his agile fingers. His wit is like a perpetual well, but it is a well that bubbles with wine instead, of water. Intoxicated with the humour of life, he made the whole world dizzy with the merry-go-round of his thought.

Yet within the shell of his humour there was always the kernel of serious philosophy. This was especially true of the histories he wrote at Cirey — *The Century of Louis XIV* and the *Essay on Customs* (a history of civilization). Voltaire was one of the first "debunkers" in the modern world. His purpose in writing history, he said, was to disenthrone the mere pretenders to greatness and to put the real great men in their place. He despised the tyrants, the dictators, the conquerors, the aggressors and the oppressors of the world. He deplored the foolishness of historians who held up these men as objects of admiration for their fellow men. "Such is the wretched stupidity of mankind that they revere those who have done evil brilliantly." On the other hand, Voltaire regarded Pope Alexander III as the greatest man of the Middle Ages because "this Prince of the Church, unlike the princes in the palaces, has tried to free the slaves instead of enslaving the free." Indeed, the aim of all history is the physical, mental and moral emancipation of the human race, and the weapon by which this emancipation is to be achieved is the human reason. "God gave us reason as He gave feathers to birds and fur to animals..... In the end it always gets the better of tyrants." Voltaire believed in the fundamental principle of democracy. *Vox populi vox dei,* the voice of the people is the voice of God. "In the long run the people can be trusted to judge what is best for them."

In his business of "debunking" the great he could transfix a personality on an epigram like a butterfly on a pin. Of Mazarin, the intriguing minister of Louis XIV, he wrote; "This man was guilty of all the good he did not do." Voltaire paints in a single brief sentence the unfogettable picture of a starving nation whilst their king is celebrating his military victories. "The people perished of hunger to the music of Te Deums." And time and again he warns the tyrants that their ambition is destined to end in revolution. "You lose everything when you drive the people like a herd of bulls. Sooner or later they are bound to gore you to death.

IV

THUS far Voltaire's outlook upon the world had been whimsical rather than deep. He was too prosperous to be bittter and too popular to be sad. He had not as yet lived sufficiently to have a proper understanding of life. He was the Puck of the eighteenth century, the playboy of intellectual Europe, but his mind was still immature. He had not grown to the stature of a great man because he had, thus far, experienced no great sorrow. He needed suffering for a teacher before he could be numbered among the true leaders of men.

In 1749 Madame du Chatelet died, and for the first time Voltaire forgot to laugh at sorrow. His own health began to fail, and on top of that he was once more exiled from France.

Then came, in 1755, the news of the earthquake at Lisbon. Thirty thousand people had lost their lives in this catastrophe. Many of the victims had been crushed to death while at their prayers, for the earthquake had come on All Saints' Day, when the churches were filled with worshippers.

Voltaire began to see the world in a new light. His work took on a more sombre tone. His superb mind had become mature at last. He realized that life was much more than a subject for pretty epigrams and careless laughter. He composed an epic poem in which he depicted the devolution of his thought from frivolity to philosophy.

With heedless gaiety bygone times
I sang of pleasure in seductive rhymes.
The times are changed and fate has schooled my mind
To share the common sorrows of mankind.

He bought an estate at Freney, in Switzerland, just beyond the borders of France, and enlisted in a vigorous crusade against human suffering. He attacked every sort of injustice. He issued a veritable flood of books and pamphlets, all of them written at white heat. These works, brilliant with the sincerity of a noble faith, were directed against the evils of social oppression and religious intolerance. He adopted as his motto the words *Ecrasez l'infame*, crush the infamy of man's inhumanity to man. He directed his fight not against the religious beliefs of men but against their superstitious hatreds. His quarrel was not with the *pillars* but with the *caterpillars* of the Church. "Let us detest these creatures who are eating away the heart of their Mother, and let us honour those who are fighting against them." He was not, as is commonly believed, an atheist. He was a deist. He believed in the existence of God. Indeed, "if God did not exist," he said, "it would be necessary to invent him." But Voltaire's God is not an exclusive king of a single ecclesiastical order. He is the world's,

"Supreme Intelligence, a Workman infinitely able" — and infinitely impartial. He has no favourite people, no favourite country, no favourite church. For the true worshipper there is but a single faith, equal justice and equal tolerance to all mankind.

Voltaire did much to lessen the sum of religious intolerance in the world. He established, once for all, the principle of non–interference in religious worship. He drove militancy out of the Church and resorted morality in its place. "To laugh and to let laugh" had been the motto of his earlier career. He now changed it to the more enlightened motto — to think and to let think.

V

WHILE this revolution was going on in the mind of Voltaire his life externally remained as restless as ever. Invited to the court of King Frederick the Great, he came there officially as his literary secretary and unofficially as his intellectual fencing master. Voltaire enjoyed the suppleness of Frederick's mentality but he disliked and feared the exuberance of his ambition. One of the courtiers reported to Voltaire a witticism of the King's. "I shall have need of Voltaire for a year at the most," said Frederick. "One squeezes the orange and throws away the skin." Voltaire laughed at the jest but gave Frederick no opportunity to put it into effect. "I had better save the skin before the orange is sqeezed dry." He left the king to his ambitions and returned to his philosophy. Joining the circle of Diderot, D' Alembert, Condorcet, and the other inconoclasts who paved the way for the French Revolution, he helped them in the preparation of the great *Encyclopedia of Free Thought*. The Encyclopedists accused him of being a Christian and the Christians accused him of being an infidel, and between the two parties he had his hands full.

Yet busy as he was with his controversies and with the writing of his tragedies and his romances and his histories and his *Philosophic Dictionary* and his numerous other works — there were about a hundred in all — he was never too busy to throw himself into every fight on the side of the oppressed. He spent his time and his money and his strength in his continual efforts to rescue the victims of social injustice and ecclesiastical bigotry. He built model homes for the poor people of Ferney. He set up a silk mill and a watch factory for the unemployed; he personally directed the sale of their finished goods — for he was a shrewd businessman — and he turned over the entire profits to the workers. He built a church for them and he inscribed it with the words — *Deo erexit Voltaire* (Voltaire erected this to God). For he believed in giving others the freedom to worship, just as he expected others to give him the freedom *not* to worship. He had become, in short, not only the prophet of common sense but the champion of the common man. "Everyone, far and near," writes Sainte-Beuve, "claimed his good offices;

people consulted him, related the wrongs of which they were the victims and solicited his help." And none of these appealed to him in vain.

He was accessible to everybody — expect the "irritating rabble of celebrity hunters." For them he reserved the keenest shafts of his wit. One day an Englishman came to see him. "Tell him," said Voltaire to his servant, "that I'm dying." But the Englishman persisted. "Tell him I'm dead," said Voltaire. The visitor insisted upon paying his last respects to his dead body. "Tell him I'm already buried and consigned to the devil. If he still wants to see me, tell him to go to hell."

VI

HE was eighty-three years old now and as restless as ever. Realizing that his end was near, he paid a last visit to Paris. The greeting that he received there was "one of the historic events of the century." But it was too much for his strength. He went, against his doctor's advice, to see the production of one of his plays. This was his last public appearance. He took to his bed, never to rise from it again.

Shortly before his death he met Benjamin Franklin, who was at that time the American ambassador to France. Voltaire complained that he was no longer as nimble as he would like to be. "I feel," he said, "like a statue with feet of clay." "Yes," replied Franklin, "but with the heart of gold."

The American philosopher had brought his grandson along with him. He begged the French philosopher to give his blessing to the boy. Voltaire placed his hand on the boy's head and said. "God and Liberty."

These two words are the sum and substance of Voltaire's philosophy.

****

Important Works By Voltaire

Henriade.
Oedipe.
Artemire.
Brutus.
Zaire.
Merope.
Mahomet.
Irene.
Pucelle.
Littlebig.
Letters on the English.
Candide.
The World As It Goes.
Zadig.
The Pupil of Nature
The Princess of Babylon.
The Century of Louis XIV.
Charles XII
Essay on Customs.
Philosophic Dictionary.
Diatribe on Doctor Akakia

12

IMMANUEL KANT

1724 – 1804

THE goodly Burghers of Konigsberg had an infallible way of setting their clocks. Every afternoon, precisely at three-thirty, Immanuel Kant left his house for his daily stroll. He was a quaint little elfin of a man — scarcely five feet tall, flat chest, protruding abdomen, right shoulder twisted back, left shoulder depressed, head perched to one side, gray hat, gray coat and gray cane daintily tapping the ground as he directed his steps towards the avenue of lindens which his townsmen had nicknamed The Philosopher's Walk. Trudging faithfully behind him, with an umbrella in his hand as a protection for his master in the event of an unexpected rainstorm, came his old servant Lampe, who adored Kant and for whom, as we shall see, Kant was to create a religion and a God.

The crippled little sage of Konigsberg was as punctual in his habits as the sun. He rose, dressed, drank his coffee, wrote, lectured, dined, walked — each at the selfsame hour everyday. "Kant's life," observes one of his biographers, "was like the most regular of regular verbs." But it was not a *conjugated* verb. For Kant never married. He was hardly the man to fill a woman's head with romantic thoughts.

Yet when he lectured he filled his audiences with something akin to veneration. For, standing behind a desk which concealed his inadequate body, he appeared to his students to be nothing but a head. A strong, broad -- browed high-cheekboned head, with large, piercing blue eyes, a ruddy complexion and an eloquent mouth out of which flowed "the profoundest language" — to quote Herder — "that ever came from the lips of man."

II

"FIRE" says an old Eastern proverb, "destroys wood but strengthens iron." The iron in Kant's soul was strengthened by a childhood of privation. He was born (1724) into a poor, conflict-stricken and plague-stricken Europe. More than sixty per cent of the people had lost their lives in an almost endless succession of wars, and many of those who had managed to survive were on the verge of starvation. The Kant family were numbered among the slarvelings of fortune. Immanuel's father was a cutter of leather straps who, as he humorously remarked, "could never make the ends meet." But he had the Scotch tenacity of purpose — the Kants, or Cants, had emigrated from Scotland in the seventeenth century — and he knew how to "raise good men on sma' means." Though he was unable to supply his eleven children with sufficient physical fare, he brought them up on a rich diet of mental food and moral inspiration. To the Kant children white bread was a dream but honest thought and simple affection was a daily reality. They were brought up in a practical religion based upon the teaching of the Bible.

For the Kants were Pietists — a sect of German Puritans who called themselves Soldiers of Peace.

It was in this religious atmosphere that Immanuel received his home education and his early schooling. The school curriculum especially was calculated to develop the moral rather than the mental faculties of the children. "I would rather," said one of his Pietist teachers, "save one soul than produce a hundred scholars." Little did he dream that here in his school he was producing one scholar who would enlighten a million souls.

Indeed, Kant resented the overemphasis of the religious as against the intellectual side of his education. He disliked the endless catechisms, the ceremonious formalities, the long hours of religious instruction and the continual round of prayers from breakfast time until bedtime. As a result of his early acquired distaste for formal religion Kant refused throughout his mature life to attend public worship.

Yet Kant was not blind to the ethical values of Pietism. "Say what you will of this doctrine, no one can deny the sterling worth of the characters which it formed." And doubtless it played no small part in the formation of Kant's character, for his Pietist teachers had given him "the highest thing that man can possess — that peace, that cheerful spirit, that inner harmony with self which can be disturbed by no passion."

He remained in this "character-building" school for eight years, and then he entered the Konigsberg University. Throughout his college career he remained "a familiar of poverty," tutoring his backward classmates for his tuition and his bread and frequently — especially on the days when his tuition fell due — going without his bread. His clothes during this period were on the ragged edge. But he kept his trousers, like his thoughts, always neatly pressed, and he held them up with an ingenious invention of his own — he attached them to bands which he passed up into his trousers' pockets and which he kept taut by means of springs contained in little boxes. Not for nothing had he been born into a family of strap makers!

Yet with all his hardships he managed to preserve his health. For he took care of himself with German meticulousness and with Scotch perseverance. When he walked outdoors, especially in the winter, he breathed only through his nose and refused to enter into conversation with anyone. He was determined not to allow those "pneumonia winds" to come in through his open mouth!

Kant had enrolled in the university with his parents' blessing and with their hope that he might someday "wag his head in a poo'pit." For the ministry was the height of the professional ambition of the Scotch artisans of the day. But Kant preferred philosophy to theology — especially so since the philosophical department at Konigsberg just then enjoyed the services of two of the most brilliant German intellects — Professors Knutzen and Teske. These men were, in the parlance of the day, regarded as *polymaths* — scholars in many fields. Their interests were not only philosophic but scientific. And under their broadening influence Kant was able to dip not only into the abstractions of metaphysics but into the realities of physics, geometry, algebra, psychology, astronomy and logic. In short, he took a brief but comprehensive survey of the entire world as it was known at that period.

And the general picture that he received of the world was that of an infinite estate with an absentee landlord — God. Kant decided to devote his life to the examination of the estate and to the search for the landlord. "Nothing," he said, "shall swerve me from that course."

But first of all he must earn a living. And so he hired himself out as a servant-tutor in the country. This was a degrading position for a young philosopher but not quite so degrading as the position of his sisters, who had been obliged to hire themselves out as maidservants. Indeed, so superior did Kant regard himself to his sisters that — and this is the one serious blemish upon his character — he never went to visit them after his graduation from the university.

He continued his tutoring among the Prussian gentry for nine years — a period in which he was able to acquaint himself with the "ways of the world." And strangely enough for a philosopher, he found these ways not to his distaste. Among the employers who admired his knowledge though they despised his station were the Count and the Countess von Keyserling. Under their benevolent patronage he was introduced to the "higher social circles" where, to everybody's surpise, he found himself at home "like a fish in the water." He dressed his twisted little body in trim if inexpensive clothes; he enlivened the soirees in the salons of the great ladies; he became the "harmless director" of the local gossip; he played a skillful hand at the card or billiard table; and he developed into an elegant *causeur* and *bon vivant*. In short, the son of the leather cutter had learned to cut a figure in the society of the day.

But only for a short time. Temperamentally he enjoyed the inner rather than the outer life. After his brief physical and social excursion into the world of his fellows he withdrew into the shell of his own mind. Appointed as instructor (*Docent*) at the University of Konigsberg (in 1755), he settled down to a life of study and never travelled more than forty miles beyond the limits of that town. His adventures from now on were to be over the mountains of human imagination and into the labyrinths of human thought.

III

KANT began his academic career not as a philosopher but as a scientist. He wrote treatises on *Fire, Winds, Natural History, Anthropology, The Theory of the Heavens* and *The Ageing of the Earth.* He foreshadowed the nebular hypothesis of Laplace and the Darwinian theory of evolution. But his chief interests were speculative rather than analytical. Gradually he turned his mind away from physics in the direction of metaphysics.

The stream of his metaphysical speculations was fed

by many tributary influences, of which four may be mentioned in particular — the idealism of Berkeley, the materialism of Hume, the rationlism of Voltaire and the emotionalism of Rousseau. Berkeley had destroyed matter. Hume had demolished mind. Voltaire had said: "A plague on both your houses! Let's forget abstractions and stick to reason." And Rousseau had countered: "Let's forget reason and rely upon feeling." Kant, with German thoroughness, decided to examine each of these four conflicting theories in turn and to discover, if possible, some common denominator which would combine all these fractional theories into an integral unit of truth.

He published the results of his investigations in three monumental works: *The Critique of Pure Reason, The Critique of Practical Reason* and *The Critique of Judgment*. These three books may be roughly compared to a three-storied temple — a dark basement which serves as a crypt for dead idols, an auditorium which allows a mystical light to stream in through the stained — glass windows, and a dome which towers into the blue beauty of heaven. Let us briefly glance at these three books.

IV

IN his introduction to *The Critique of Pure Reason* Kant warns the reader of the book's difficulties. "We are here" he writes, "oppressed with problems which cannot be ignored... and which cannot be solved." To add to the necessary obscurity of the subject, Kant exasperates the reader with an unnecessary obscurity of style. The German philosophers have a habit, figuratively speaking, of scratching the left ear with the right hand. Why be simple when you can be complex? Why please your reader when you can plague him? Kant invented a whole dictionary of abstruse terms, and he was so long-winded that in his effort to *explain* a passage he often explained it *away.* When he finished the manuscript of his *Critique* he sent it to Marcus Herz, his fellow metaphysician, for his opinion. Herz returned the manuscript when he was only half through with it. "If I finish it," he explained, "I am afraid I shall go mad."

Yet it is possible even for the lay reader to find here and there a beam of light in the dark mazes of its speculation. First of all let us translate the title of the book into everyday language. The *critique* of pure reason doesn't mean the criticism but the *examination* of pure reason. And *pure* reason doesn't mean *ethical* but *independent* reason — that is reason or knowledge which does not depend upon our senses but which resides in our intellect.

Bearing in mind the above interpretation of the title, let us now go on. Our knowledge, maintains Kant, does not all come through our senses. For our senses are but imperfect measures of reality. They can conceive neither a finite world nor an infinite world. They can envision neither a beginning and end of time on the one hand nor a beginningless and endless time on the other. The real world, accordingly, is beyond our sensory comprehension. But it is not beyond our intellectual comprehension. We can "see" the world with our "inner" eye. We can understand it without the help of experience. "My question (therefore) is," writes Kant, "what can we hope to achieve with the intellect when all the material and assistance of experience are taken away?" And he answers this question by asserting that we can hope to employ our intellect — that is, our reason — not merely as a receiver of impressions but as a creator of ideas. We can, and we do, subordinate our *senses* to the service of our *sense*. "The eye without the mind is important and blind."

We must try to understand the real world, then, "not through our perceptions but through our conceptions," not through our impressions but through our intellect. For our intellect is not only a scientist that observes but a philosopher that classifies. Science *and* philosophy are necessary if we wish to acquaint ourselves with the truth.

And where does this truth lead us? To the conviction that the world as it is, or the *thing-in-itselfi*, is quite different from the world as it appears, or the *phenomenon.* "Kant's greatest contribution to philosophy," said Schopenhauer, "was the distinction he made between the real world and the phenomenal world." Our notions about man and nature, life and death — these are merely perceptions of our senses but not conceptions of our mind. "It remains completely unknown to us what (these) objects may be by themselves and apart from the receptivity of our senses." The same is true of our notions about free will, the soul and God. We cannot, owing to the limitation of our senses, prove their existence. We therefore have no right to be positive about anything. We must dispose of all dogma.

It is interesting to note how positive this philosopher can be in his denunciation of the positive point of view. Kant is a profound believer in the rational testament of unbelief. He slays dogma with a dogmatic sword.

V

HAVING destroyed God in his mind, Kant then proceeded to create Him in his heart. *In The Critique of Practical Reason* the gentle philosopher performed this act of creation, as Heine half jestingly and half seriously points out, for the sake of his old servant Lampe. "Hitherto," writes Heine, "Immanuel Kant has appeared as the grim, inexorable iconoclast. He has stormed heaven, put the whole garrison to the sword; the ruler of the world swims senseless in his blood; there is no more any mercy or fatherly goodness or future reward for present privations; the immortality of the soul is in its last agonies — death rattles and groans! And old Lampe stands by with his umbrella under his arm as a sorrowing spectator, and the sweat of anguish and tears run down his cheeks. Then Immanuel Kant is moved to pity and shows himself not only a great philosopher but a good man. "Old Lampe," he observes, "must have a God, or else the poor man cannot be happy; and people really ought to be happy in this world. Practical common sense *requires* it. Very well then, let practical reason *guarantee it."*

"And in consequence of this argument Kant distinguishes between theoretical reason and practical reason and with the latter as with a magic wand, revives the corpse of deism, which theoretical has slain."

The Critique of Practical Reason is therefore a refutation of *The Critique of Pure Reason.* In his latter book Kant declares that if you cannot base religion upon science you can base it upon morals. *Accept* a belief in God because you need such a belief. Your practical needs are more important than your theoretical speculations. After all, if there is one absolute reality in this world it is the reality for our moral sense, our *ethical obligation.* This ethical obligation — Kant calls it "the categorical imperative" — guides our conscience to a definite distinction between right and wrong. And our conscience is not a matter of science but of intuition; not a matter of *pure* reson but of *practical* reason. And practical reason in the philosophy of Kant is closely akin to, if not actually identical with, feeling.

Our feeling reveals to us first the existence of God as the guide of our conscience, the prompter of our duty, the organizer of our individual and our social life. Second, our feeling proves to us the existence of free will. For if we had no free will we should have no conception of any moral obligation. We cannot feel *obliged* to do what we are not able to do. Third, our feeling demonstrates to us the existence of a life after death. For we follow the dictates of our conscience even when we realize that we shall receive no reward for such conduct in this world. We act upon the instinctive principle that goodness is its own excuse for being. Why? Because we feel, and therefore we *know,* that the drama of our present life is but an uncompleted act in a larger drama and that the plot, however incongruous it may appear in *this* world, will come to a logical and satisfactory denouement in the *next* world. Tennyson has well expressed this idea in his philosophical poem, *In Memoriam.* Relying, like Kant, upon his "practical" rather than upon his "pure" reason, he assures us.

That nothing walks with aimless feet;
That not one life shall be destroyed,
Or cast as rubbish to the void,
When God hath made the pile complete

God, the free will and the immortal soul — these are the facts of the real world of the heart as opposed to the fancies of the imaginary world of the mind.

VI

IN the first book of his philosophical trilogy Kant has *denied* God. In the second book he has *affirmed* God. In the third book, *The Critique of Judgment,* he *finds* God. And where does he find Him? In the beautiful design of Nature — a design based upon the "pattern laid up in the heavens." Behind beauty there is always purpose. The work of art presupposes the artist. When man experiences the beautiful he feels within himself an infinite power which corresponds to an infinite power outside of himself. Like calls unto like. God has spoken to Man, and Man replies, "I understand." The genius — the painter, the sculptor, the musician, the poet — lives for the greater part of his life in the presence of this vision. But the layman, too, has his moments of sublime insight. And in such moments he recognizes the presence of God in the two great mysteries of the world — "the starry heavens above, and the moral law within."

And yet — here Kant himself falls away from his "sublime insight" and allows the scientist once more to override the seer — and yet there is ugliness in the world as well as beauty, destruction as well as creation, wrong as well as right. Nature is such a reckless spendthrift in the elaboration of her design. So many wasted seeds to produce a single flower, so much needless suffering to round out a single life. The beauty to the world, then, though it points definitely in the direction of a benign Providence, is not to be regarded as an absolute proof of the benignity, or even of the existence, of Providence. And so Kant ends exactly where he started: Man must try to solve the riddle of God, but God is a riddle that cannot be solved. Once more Tennyson gives poetial expression to his Kantian thought:

Behold we know not anything;
I can but trust that good shall fall
At last– far off — at last, to all,
And every winter change to spring.

So runs my dream; but what am I?
An infant crying in the night;
An infant crying for the light:
And with no language but a cry.

VII

SUCH, in very brief outline, is the substance of the Kantian system of philosophy — a system which stirred up a veritable revolution in the philosophical and theological circles of the day. The sceptics regarded Kant as a foolish little idealist, and the idealists looked upon him as a cantankerous old sceptic. As for the clergymen, some of them called Immanuel Kant a dog and others called their dogs Immanuel Kant. But Kant — he was now past seventy — serenely drank his coffee and took his daily walk and looked undismayed into the face of the storm. The minister of education, a fanatical Pietist by the name of Wollner, forbade the further publication of Kant's work in Prussia. Whereupon the unperturbed philosopher dispatched his latest book, an essay on religion, to be published in Jena, a city which lay outside the jurisdiction of the Prussian king.

The king was outraged at the temerity of the humpbacked little professor. "Our highest person," he wrote to Kant, "has been greatly displeased to observe how you misuse your philosophy to undermine many of the most important doctrines of the Holy Scriptures.... If you continue to do this, you may expect unpleasant consequences." Kant, who had already spoken his last word on theology, quietly replied to the king that he would express no further religious views in public.

But he continued to express *political* views in public. He hailed the French Revolution with tears of joy. "Now at last," he exclaimed, "I can say with Simon — *Lord, let The servant depart in peace, for mine eyes have seen Thy salvation.*

He believed — how blind even a philosopher can be to the future! — that the French Revolution would bring about an era of peace. He failed to see the red sunrise of Napoleonism just beyond the dawning of the new day. But perhaps he saw beyond that sunrise to still another day, "when the constitution of every state shall be democratic and war shall not be declared except by a plebiscite of all the citizens." We can hope for universal peace only when monarchs and dictators, "who regard themselves as the sole owners of the state," are a thing of the past, when every man in every country "is respected as an absolute end in himself," and when the nations learn that "it is a crime against the human dignity of any man to use him as a mere tool for another man's gain."

Kant had come at last to the end of his philosophical quest. He had sought for God and he had discovered Man. "Man," we are told in an Eastern legend, "lifted the veil from the goddess of Sais and beheld — himself."

****

Important Works By Kant

The Critique of Pure Reason.
The Critique of Practical Reason.
The Critique of Judgement.
Metaphysic of Nature.
Metaphysic of Ethics.
Religion within the Limits of Pure Reason

Among the best English translators of Kant's works are J.P. Mahaffy, Belfort Bax, T. K. Abbot, Meikeljohn and Max Muller.

13

GEORG WILHELM FRIENDRICH HEGEL

1770 – 1831

GEORG Wilhelm Friendrich Hegel came from a line of civil servants. In Germany the civil servant was a servile civilian, whose sense of initiative and instinct for freedom had been paralyzed by the virus of bureaucracy. Hegel's father kept the records of the Wurtemburg finances. He was a humdrum, white-collar toiler of the till. His family emblem was red tape.

Born on August 27, 1770, Georg Wilhelm was sent to the Latin School and then to the theological seminary at Tubingen. But he turned out to be a mediocre student of "the verities of the heavens." He was far more interested in the vicissitudes of the earth.

And, indeed, there were many things happening on earth during the student days of Hegel. France had declared the "Reign of Reason." The wine of the Revolution had reached the lips of all the liberals throughout Europe. They lifted their hats and clicked their heels to Liberty, Equality, Fraternity.

Hegel, in a burst of exuberance, planted a "liberty tree" in the public square at Tubingen as a salute to the new Republic of France. Then he turned to salute the greater Republic of Philosophy — a commonwealth in which every free intellect was given the opportunity to cast his sovereign vote of thought. Hegel dreamed of joining that splendid commonwealth and of contributing his decisive vote.

II

BUT even a philosopher must eat. In accordance with the Biblical maxim, "seek ye first food and clothing, and the kingdom of heaven shall be added unto you," he decided upon teaching for a livelihood. For some years he barely managed to make his way as a struggling tutor. His chief asset was a love for Greek literature and for the philosophy of Kant; his chief liability was the lack of worldly goods. And then his father died and left him fifteen hundred dollars. Hegel now considered himself financially independent, even rich! He wrote to his friend Schelling, announcing that he was about to retire to the life of a gentleman of leisure. He asked Schelling to advise him where he ought to settle down in order to enjoy his inheritance. It must be a place with good books and good beer. Schelling answered, "Come to Jena."

Jena was a university town in Prussia where some of the leading young intellectuals of Germany had gathered to teach philosophy and history and Greek. It was the centre of a cultural Renaissance, one of the glowing points of the perisphere to which the rays of liberal thought had penetrated from Paris.

He came to Jena. He was appointed a teacher at the university. By this time his early enthusiasm for the wayward Goddess of Liberty had been quenched. Indeed, many of the sensitive spectators of the Revolution had turned away in disgust when the Reign of Reason had degenerated into the Reign of Terror. A revolution that had begun in common sense had ended in murder. A movement to liberate mankind had led to the dictatorship of Napoleon Bonaparte. Men had dreamed of a better, freer world. And with a stunning suddenness their dreams had turned to ashes.

III

WHILE Hegel pursued his quite life of research in the little university village of Jena, Napoleon invaded it with his drummers and his grenadiers. In a pitched battle he had demolished the Prussian army. Now he put the shackles of slavery upon the Prussian state. He had successively and successfully conquered the Austrians and the Italian and the Dutch. He had reduced the princes of south and central Germany to a state of Vassalage. He had sent an army into Spain. Freedom on the Continent was a memory. The present was engraved in blood. The future was written in clouds.

Hegel escaped from Jena and sought a new lease of life in Bavaria — a German province which had appeased Napoleon from the first and which was now a “friendly” country in good standing and abject slavery. The young philosopher accepted the position of headmaster at the Nuremberg Academy. And here he was able to pursue his studies in peace for many years, quietly dreaming his philosophic dreams until long after the nightmare of Napoleon had become a myth and the ambitious dictator had been chained to his destiny on an obscure little island in the middle of the sea.

...And men were free again. Hegel had married a lady of intelligence and refinement. Gradually philosophy had become systematized. And his life too. Indeed, so absorbed was he in his thoughts that he had become legendary for his absent-mindedness. Though he was still in the prime of his life he was prematurely bent, with a studious brow and emaciated cheeks. There was nothing about his external conduct or appearance to distinguish him. His essential personality was his inner life.

Never for a moment had he abandoned the mental attitude of the family from which he was descended. As he thought about the unknown quantities in the equation of existence he did not conclude his search with the shrug of a sceptic. For he was not like the Englishman Locke nor like the Scotchman Hume. The German character within him constructed a philosophy of faith. And his inherited punctiliousness spun out as complicated a fabric of metaphysical speculation as the world has ever seen. He was a civil servant hard at work in the vast administrative offices of red tape under the jurisdiction of a bureaucratic God.

The world is intelligible, said Hegel. Reason lies at the heart of things, under their apparent disunity on the surface. Sceptics like Hume had thrown doubt into men's minds and had created an atmosphere of cynicism that had produced unscrupulous adventurers like Napoleon. When man loses faith in the values of human life, civilization is on the retrograde. For life is a great and systematic scheme of truth. Man can understand this truth through his faculties of reason even if he cannot apprehend it through his faculties of sense. In other words, Hegel directly throws out a challenge to Hume. After all, it is posible for man to know things beyond his experience. Through his reason. There are two types of reason: the *practical reason,* which deals with everyday affairs and with sensible objects that have a tangible existence, and the *abstract reason,* which deals with ideas beyond our sensory existence.

And here we come to the crux of the matter — the principal issue between the sceptics and the metaphysicians. The sceptics maintain that those things alone exist which we can apprehend through the senses. The metaphysicians, on the other hand, insist that there are things beyond the senses which have an equally real existence.

All our conceptions which are not material — declares Hegel — exist just as surely as a material table or chair. Consider, for example, our conception of *quantity.* We have seen two pencils but we have never seen the abstract *quantity,* two. And yet the abstract conception of *two* exists in the reason just as surely as the conerete *two pencils* exist in space. For without the existence of an abstract measure of quantity we would never be able to distinguish between the concrete quantities of things in experience.

There is therefore pure reason as opposed to practical reason — or, to put it in another way, there is a *formal* existence as opposed to a material existence. The proposition that two and two equal four has a formal existence. It does not exist in space; it does not exist in time. It does not exist even in our minds, for regardless of what happens to our minds the proposition remains true. Yet it exists in the abstract with as much reality as the house of my next — door neighbour exists in the concrete.

This is the fundamental assumption of Hegel. And upon this assumption he rears his structure of philosophy. Hume has maintained that we can never discover a first cause for the world, or indeed a cause for anything. And Hegel agrees. But he insists, if we cannot find a *cause* we can at least find a *reason* for things. This may sound like a quibble, but it is not. A cause is an active force that produces an effect in time. A reason is a logical necessity which has nothing to do with time. The *cause* of the world's existence, Hegel would agree with Hume, is an expression which makes no sense. But the *reason* for the world's existence is an expression which makes very good sense indeed. The reason for the world has a logical non—temporal priority to the world, just as a mathematical problem has a logical non—temporal priority to its solution. The logical exists just as truly as the physical. The *real* is the *rational* — this is Hegel's battlecry.

Reason, continues Hegel, is self-explanatory. The world is reason. For reason is identical with existence. To the question as to what is the reason for everything we must answer — *everything.* But since existence is all-inclusive, maintains Hegel, it comprises within it the state of not–being as well as of being. Everything contains within itself *its own opposite.* It is impossible to conceive of anything without conceiving at the same of its opposite. You cannot think of finiteness without thinking of infinity or of time without thinking of timelessness. A cow is a cow and is at the same time not a cat. A thing is itself only because at the same time it is not something else. Every thesis for an argument has its antithesis. Life has death and love has hate. Day has night, and youth has age. Hegel goes a step beyond this perfectly obvious conclusion and comes forward with a startling pronouncement. Not only has everything an opposite but everything *is its own opposite!* The truth lies on both sides of every question. The truth is either side. After all, life is a struggle of opposing forces attempting to combine with one another into a higher unity. And this unity, the quest of the philosophers and the dream of the poets, is achieved only at the cost of much blood. It is a unity born out of strife and agony and despair. It is the concord of love that rises out of the discord of hatred, the precept of denial that is translated into the principle of affirmation, the spirit that dies in order to live!

All nature, then, is a reconciliation of opposites. And, like everything else, man too finds his opposite. He wrestles with nature. He is finally overcome by nature. But only to achieve his immortality. For when he yields himself in death he is merely yielding his one self to his other self. For life is death. And nature is man. Here, too, underneath the surface diversity as apprehended by our fragile senses, there is a profound and moving unity. Nothing external to man is really different from man.

The world around us is our other self. We see a tree. The tree is known to us. It exists for us only as it is known to us. Therefore its existence is included in our faculty for knowledge which exists in us. Its existence is part of us. Our existence is part of it. Nature is the *objective* self as opposed to the *conscious* self. If we wish to obtain the truth, we must not only view the world from the standpoint of our inner selves but we must view our inner selves from the standpoint of the world. This is the supreme test we must pass if we are to follow the highest laws of reason. We must regard ourselves with complete objectivity as our own opposite, or *antithesis*. And then we are ready for the highest union, or *synthesis* known to human experience. Liberated from the petty prejudices of our sensuous perceptions, we may now breathe the clear cool air of freedom. By withdrawing from our imperfect and fragile consciousness we have achieved a far greater consciousness, the sublime and perfect consciousness of Self. And this Self, as we then realize, is completely aware of its own organic unity and all-inclusive power. Nature rises to self-consciousness in Man. And Man rises to self-consciousness in Freedom.

IV

HUMAN freedom emerges as the product of the grandest struggle between the two supreme forces

— nature and man, body and mind, energy and soul, savage and saint. And now Hegel transfers this principle of synthesis through antithesis, of unity through struggle, from the individual to the mass, from the contemplation of man to the philosophy of mankind. Hegel climaxes his life's work with a new outlook upon history.

The subject of human history is the development of human freedom. History began when a spiritual consciousness dawned upon man.

Hegel divides his historical survey into three stages. Each stage manifests a period of development in the struggle for freedom. The first stage presents the drama of the original world — China, India and the Near East — the countries in which our civilization began. The second stage represents the world of the Greek states. The third comprises the epoch of the Roman Empire. There is a fourth stage still to come — and here the Teuton in Hegel rises to the surface — the Germanic world in which "the idea of freedom will reach its highest expression."

The oriental world is the home of the childhood of man. In China society was based upon the family and the state. The prevailing mode of religion was ancestor worship. The government was paternal. The emperor was the great yellow father who ruled over his children with an iron hand. All punishment was corporeal. Every inhabitant of China was a minor before the law.

While the spirit of China, declares our philosopher, was the spirit of an *alert* child, the spirit of India was that of a *dreaming* child. The religion of India was shadowy, pantheistic, abstract. Its God was a dozing ghost of Nirvana — nothingness. The Hundu led a static, vegetative life. He was physically and politically and socially unprogressive.

In Persia it was different. The Persians had a religion of *light.* Their supreme deity was a solar energy. The sun puts into motion all the processes of organic growth. It is the power of good struggling against the forces of evil. And this struggle, remarks Hegel, is the very essence of life. Until man awakens from his slumbers and becomes aware of the opposition between good and evil he can never be conscious of his mission to achieve a spiritual freedom.

In Egypt — continues Hegel — man became even more aware of the dynamic struggle between good and evil. The Egyptians symbolized this awareness in the supreme riddle of their national art — the Sphinx. Man is struggling to emerge from the beast. But he is not as yet successful. In fact, the Sphinx is both man and beast, and no one in wise enough to guess as to which of the two natures is predominant.

Next to the Egyptians came the Hebrews, who marked a great transition in man's ethical and religious history. It was a transition from a naturalistic to a spiritual conception of morality. Hitherto men had worshipped animals and stars. The Jews worshipped the spirit of Jehovah, the one and absolute God.

And then arose the second stage in human development — the civilization of the Greek states. "Greece is the fresh morning of human history." Humanity has emerged from childhood into youth. Greek art and religion and philosophy and politics manifest the eager innocence of the youthful spirit. The gods of the Greeks are eternally beautiful and immortally young. They are human in their wisdom and in their folly. They are perfect guides for struggling humanity. Says Schiller, the German poet, "When gods were more human, men were more divine." And the Greeks were a divine race, with all the splendour and with all the weakness of their own Olympian deities.

In Athens the citizens governed themselves. They were the members of a democratic community. But mankind was not altogether free in the Athenian world. For the majority of men were slaves. As yet there was no idea of freedom as the common property of all men.

And then the world advanced to the third stage of history. The Greek world gave way before the Roman world. "Rome was the practical spirit of early manhood which had forgotten, or had learned to despise, the happy dreams of youth." The first community of Rome was a community of robbers. And "a state founded on force had to be held together by force." The evolution of Roman history is the development of the Roman robber into the Roman soldier. Yet with the growth of the Roman Empire certain essential forces began to emerge for the good of mankind. A universal code of law was established, the first of its kind in history. *Duty* as well as *booty* became the maxim of the Romans. The individual for the first time had arrived at a self–consciousness of his rights in the eyes of the law — at least *formally*. Actually the case was far different. For the majority of the people were still enslaved and for them the law was an empty form.

But then a new power arose — Christianity. This religion, mighty in its humility, took the lowly masses and gave them a father in God, a brother in Christ and a knowledge of love. And thus, side by side with the legal equality as expounded by the Romans, Christianity introduced an *intrinsic* equality — the inherent and infinite worth of all men.

Thanks to the adoption of Christianity, justice gradually triumphed over injustice in man's historic struggle for freedom. Men began to see, faintly at first but more and more distinctly as time went on, the intimate relationship that exists between justice and mercy, between law and love. The legal code of the Romans, which had been devised to protect the strong against the weak, was step by step transformed into a new code, designed to protect the weak against the strong. Absolute monarchy gave way to constitutional monarchy, the legal rights of the people were amplified into political rights, and freedom and democracy became almost synonymous terms.

And finally, as Hegel brings history down to his own day, he sees before him a new synthesis of freedom emerging out of the welter and confusion of diplomatic and military rivalry. This new freedom, he declares, will come in Prussia. For Prussia "is fast developing a formidable power. Soon it will dominate the entire continent." The freedom of Prussia at the expense of the rest of the world!

V

HEGEL had left Jena, had taught for a spell at Heidelberg and had spent the remainder of his life at the University of Berlin. He was now on excellent terms with the reactionary and absolutist Prussian government. The Prussian state transcended all the rights of the individual. Yet Hegel fancied that he saw in this state the highest type of "community" life. The individual self, he declared, must sacrifice everthing for his "better" self, the state. As Hegel grew older he became an arch conservative. His earlier days as a liberal were far behind him. He lent his moral support to every oppressive measure of the Prussian king. He was just as shocked at the second revolution of France, which overthrew the Bourbon Charles, as he had been jubilant at the first revolution, when he had planted a liberty tree at the fall of Louis XVI. He wrote an article criticizing the British constitution, which he termed an "ungodly jungle." He would substitute the "rational institutions" of Prussia for the popular government of England. A government, he said, is not obliged to express the will of the people. The people never know what it wills.

Such was the anticlimax of the man. Such was the irony at the apex of his grandiose political thought. He succumbed to an attack of the cholera before he realized how his philosophy would fare in the hands of his disciples. Its fate has been remarkable. On the one hand, the backward-looking statesmen from the Austrian Metternich to the Russian czars adopted it as a justification for their tyranny. For, according to Hegel's dialectic, every state must accept the divine right of oppression that belongs to it as a necessary stage in the evolution of government. Here, said the tyrants, is a classic philosophy *against* all revolutions. But, on the other hand, the liberal disciples of Hegel have seen in his philosophy a justification for *all* revolutions. Does not this philosophy proclaim the right of every force on earth to contend against its opposing force? Does it not assert the doctrine of the violent change through violent strife? Out of this Hegelian doctrine sprang the class struggle theory of Karl Marx the father of modern Socialism.

Such was Hegel's contribution to the history of thought. Thanks to a Frenchman who had asked the German philosopher to state his theory, Hegel replied in ten books. But when an ancient prophet was asked to define his philosophy he replied in one sentence: "Thou shalt love thy neighbour as thyself." And long after the logic of the ten books had become merely a dead curiosity, the logic of the one sentence will remain a living faith.

****

Important Works By Hegel

Science of Logic.	*Philosophy of Right.*
Phenomenology of Spirit.	*Philosophy of History.*
Aesthetics.	*History of Philosophy.*
Philosophy of Religion.	*Encyclopedia of philosophical Science.*
Philosophy of Art.	
Philosophy of Mind.	*Life of Jesus.*

14

ARTHUR SCHOPENHAUER

1788 – 1860

THE news reached the clerks in the counting-house of Herr Schopenhauer that their employer had become the father of a son. "If the boy is like Master Heinrich," whispered one of the clerks to his neighbours at the high desk, "he will look like a baboon."

"Hush, here comes the master."

"It's safe to talk. The old man is stone deaf."

"For a man that keeps our noses to the grindstone fifteen hours a day, Heinrich Schopenhauer has a strange device on his family coat of arms — No *happiness without liberty,* Liberty indeed!"

The Schopenhauers were a strange and ingenious people. Everybody still repeated that story about Old Andreas, Heinrich's great-grandfather, who had entertained Peter the Great and his empress on the occasion of their visit to the imperial city of Danzig. The royal family had chosen to sleep in a room that had neither a stove nor a fireplace. It was a bitter cold night. But Andreas was unperturbed. He brought up a load of barrels filled with brandy, emptied them over the tiled fioor and set the room ablaze. Then precautions were taken to keep the fire from spreading. The room was shut, and the host and his guests retired to another section of the house until the air had been completely warmed. When Czar Peter and his wife entered the room again it was delightfully hot and steamy. They spent a comfortable night.

The grandson, Heinrich, was a wealthy and independent merchant. Frederick the Great had designs on the free city of Danzing and in order to ingratiate himself with her leading citizens he invited them into his royal cabinet. He had met Heinrich and taken a fancy to him. He offered him a lucrative post. But Heinrich refused the offer. He would not accept patronage from the man who threatened the freedom of his city.

Later on Heinrch's worst fears were realized. The prussinas invaded Danzing, and the merchant was compelled to fleet to Hamburg together with his young and pretty wife Johanna. Their son Arthur was five years old at the time.

Arthur was the only male child of heinrich who, like Dombey, hoped someday to turn his son into a merchant like himself. But he never lived to see his hopes realized. One day he leaned too far over a window in the attic and slipped into the canal. He was instantly drowned. The boy was left fatherless at seventeen. His mother, pretty, young, light- hearted, had never been faithful to her husband. Indeed , it was generally believed that Heinrich had taken his own life.

After his father's death Arthur tried his best to prepare himself for a mercantile career. He wanted to be true to his father's memory. But he loathed his work.

He was a melancholy lad. Never could he get the horrible story of his father's death out of his mind. His father had been his one and only friend. He did not like the giddy little social butterfly who was his mother. His father hadn't liked her either. And she had driven him to his death.

The young widow who had gained popularity as a novelist and notoriety as a practitioner of free love, moved to the congenial atmosphere of Weimar, the literary and artistic center of Germany. Here she organized a salon and entertained all the celebrities with her scintillating mind and her flashing smile. Even Goethe found it not unpleasant to be counted among her visitors. But her son's contempt toward her increased with his years. He settled down in Danzig, attended to his father's business and, Hamletlike. Brooded over "his father's business and, his mother's shame."

Frau Schopenhauer, on her part sent him taunting letters. She disliked him as heartily as he disliked her. It gave her great pleasure to plague him. "You are unbearable and burdensome," She told him in one of her letters, "And impossible to get along with." And in another letter, when Napoleon entered Weimar with his army, she wrote: "I could tell you many things that would make your hair stand on end. But I refrain from giving you the hair stand on end. But I refrain from giving you the satisfaction. For I know how you love to dwell upon human misery."

This son of hers was a monster, she said. He puzzled her. He frightened her. Once, when he was planning to visit her at Weimar she wrote hastily: "I like to hear of your happiness. But I don't wish to be a witness to it.

I will not hide the truth from you.... I would rather sacrifice anything than have you come here.... I have always told you it is difficult to live with you.... Your illhumour, your complaints of things inevitable, your sullen looks, the extraordinary opinions you utter, like oracles none may dare to contradict- all this depresses and troubles me... Your eternal quibbles and your laments over the stupidities of the world and the sufferings of humanity give me bad nights and unpleasant dreams."

Little by little hostility between mother and son grew into a passion of hatred. And from hating his mother Schopenhauer came to hate everybody else. "From the first dawn of my thought," he wrote, "I have felt myself in discord with the world."

II

UNHAPPY in his choice of a commercial career, he finally gave it up and plunged into the study of the classics at the Gymnasium of Gotha. But he got into a quarrel with one of his teachers and resigned from the gymnasium.

He then entered the University of Gottingen, where he continued his education with a voracious appetite. Everything was grist to the mill of his receptive mind. He read books on history, natural history, mineralogy, physics, botany, philosophy, astronomy, physiology, ethnography and jurisprudence. And he came to the conclusion that "the dead world of a brilliant writer is worth incomparably more than the living voice of a blockhead lecturer." From Gottingen he went to the University for Berlin. Fortunately his father had left him a competent income so that he was able to indulge himself in his mental hobbies. These hobbies now embraced, in addition to his other studies, the subjects of experimental chemistry, magnetism, electricity, ornithology, ichthyology and Norse poetry. And he attempted an original investigation into the causes of insanity.

His fellow students were awed into silence by this frowning scholar with his high forehead and his massive mop of hair. He let it be known that he was sensitive to sound and that he preferred to walk alone. "Noises torture me. When I am interrupted in my work, by the cry of an animal especially, I feel as if my head were severed from my body under the executioner's axe."

On rare occasions, however, he emerged from his shell and associated with other people. At times he even visited his mother — arriving and leaving, however, not with the intimacy of a son but with the formality of a guest. On one of these visits he withdrew immediately after dinner to a window and was gazing abstractedly into the night. Some of the girls at the table giggled, "Children," said an old genteman who was sitting next to them, "leave that young man alone. In due time he will outgrow all of us."

The speaker was Goethe. The old poet had a great admiration for the young philosopher. But Schopenhauer's mother did not share Goethe's admiration for her son. Upon the publication of his thesis for the doctorate, *On the Four Roots of Reason,* she was insanely jealous. For she too, was a writer of books and she hated any rivalry from her son. "The fourfold root," she said sarcastically. "It sounds like a book of prescriptions for druggists."

The young man looked at her. "It will be read, Mother," he said quietly, "when even the rubbish heap ceases to contain a copy of your books."

III

SCHOPENHAUER never saw his mother again. He settled down in Dresden and lived the life of a grumbling gentleman of leisure. He enjoyed his solitude. "Men of intellectual worth more especially if they have genius," he told himself, "can have but few *friends.*" He justified the idleness of his physical life on the ground that he was thereby left free to lead a vigorous mental life. A man of genius need not occupy himself with a job. "By merely existing...he labours for all mankind; therefore he is exempt from all other obligations." He sacrifices himself through his sensitiveness, his suffering. "Suffering is a condition of genius." Did anyone believe that Shakespeare and Goethe could have created their dreamworld if they had found contentment in the actual world of their everyday life?

And he, too, was a genius. Was not a great system of philosophy coming to birth in his mind? "It was revealing itself to me by degrees, like a beautiful landscape out of a morning mist." Modesty was not one of Schopenhauer's virtues.

And so he idled and dreamed and allowed his philosophy to mature slowly in his mind. For hours he sat in the Dresden Art Gallery and gazed at the Raphael Madonas. They were the very spirit of peace, beatitude, transfiguration. He walked up and down the banks of the Elbe with the fixed expression of a maniac. Often he visited the municipal greenhouse and the orangery. Once he talked in whispers to the shrubs and bent his ear to the orange blossoms that had fallen on his shoulder. An attendant, fearing for the wits of this young man who acted so strangely asked him who he was. Schopenhauer looked up at him with a puzzled air, "If you could tell me who I am," he said to the attendant, "I should be greatly indebted." Then he walked hurriedly off as the poor fellow looked on in amazement.

But to Schopenhauer the question was perfectly natural. He had been speculating on the philosophical problems of the world. "The world is my idea." he had jotted down in his notes. "The sun exists only as I see it; the earth exists only as I feel it. Man himself is a dream." His existence at Dresden was part of the dream of Life. Living and dreaming, man and the earth and the sky, all these are chapters out of the selfsame mysterious book. And what is this dream called *Schopenhauer*? "I shall be greatly indebted if you give me the andwer."

Schopenhauer's dream life at Dresden had for a while taken on a rosy hue. For in spite of his misanthropic declarations Schopenhauer really enjoyed the society of other men. And he found this society in the city which, next to Weimer, was the magnet of European art and culture. Here Schopenhauer was "an equal among equals." He accepted invitations and frequented the theatre and dined in the cafes. He dressed in immaculate and expensive clothes. Yet he couldn't get over his old habit of brooding. "My condition is miserable," he said. And as if to underline this statement he slept with a loaded revolver under his pillow. He went about perpetually angry, suspicious, irritable. He suffered from an abnormal sense of fear for his own life. He had no faith in people, no faith in God. "Better trust fear than faith," was his grim motto. He never allowed himself to be shaved by a barber's razor. At the mere mention of a contagious disease he would run away from all company. He carried a leather drinking cup with him whenever he went out to dine, that his lips might not be forced to touch another's glass. And he kept his pipes and his cigar butts under heavy lock and key lest they be "contaminated" by his friends. He was obsessed with the notion that he might lose all his money. Indeed, the concrete value of money played a large part in the life of this man who so emphatically stressed the abstract value of thought. He was convinced that the world wanted to cheat him of his fortune. He hid his coins under the inkstand and he put his bonds among old letters. As for the accounts of his property, he never recorded them in the German language but in ancient Greek and Latin — forgetting that these "secret" accounts could be read by any thief who was a classical philologist. To deceive his own friends he labelled his valuables with misleading names.

And, truth to tell, he despised himself for these habits. But he was comforted by the thought that persons of genius, according to no less an authority than Plato, "are often morally weak, despicable, aye, even bad." One half of him could afford to be a savage if only the other half was developing into a sage.

And so he brooded and dreamed and distrusted his fellows and planned his great system of pessimistic philosophy. How can man differentiate himself from the large dream of the cosmos? How does he know himself? Through his will. The action of the body is nothing but the will. To will is to act. But more — the manifestations of the will are not only the voluntary actions of the body but are also the so-called involuntary reflexes of the mind. The will is the instinct. It is the very drive of life.

The emotionally abnormal young philosopher was fascinated by this conception. Did not his own personality demonstrate the truth? It is the will that is fundamental in man. And he of the high forehead and the strong eyes and the determined mouth knew the power of the will. It is the will that rules. The mind is merely its servant. We do not want a thing because we reason. We find reasons for a thing because we want it. The mind is always inventing logic for the whims of the will.

The mind and the body, then, are the instrument of the will. It is the will that forms the grooves in the human embryo and builds the vessels for the circulation of the blood. It is the will that fashions the brain. It is the will to eat that shapes the mouth, the teeth and the throat; the will to reproduce that shapes the sexual organs; the will to grow that attracts the plant to the sun. Can the agitated struggle of men for food and mate and children be the work of reason? Not at all. It is the will. Life is the instinctive will to live. Rivalry and struggle and destruction are therefore the essentials of life. For the wills of all individuals wage a ceaseless war upon one another. The will itself has no motive, no aim, no purpose and no limit. It is a blind and endless and futile striving. Victory alternates with defeat and life with death. The will to live drives everything ultimately to self-destruction. And finally each man succumbs to the will of the worms.

With such a declaration Schopenhauer commenced the book which contains the systematic conclusion of his speculations — *The World as Will and Idea.* Upon sending this book to his publisher he wrote; "Whoever has accomplished a great immortal work will be as little hurt by its reception from the public, or swayed by the opinions of the critics, as a sane man in a madhouse is affected by the upbraiding and the aggressions of the insane."

Sixteen years later Schopenhauer was told by his publisher that he had been forced to sell the greater part of the edition as waste–paper.

IV

BUT in the meantime Schopenhauer, for all pessimism, desired to live. After the completion of his book he had travelled to Italy, the land of Petarch's verses and, Rosinis' music. Wherever he walked men and women stopped to stare at the "surly stranger" whose eyes flashed fire under a massive forehead. "I like to sit opposite you," a young Englishman remarked shyly to him at table. "You have the face of Beethoven."

As usual, he wore his clothes with spotless extravagance. But the words he flung at people were not always spotless. He frequented Cafe Greco, which enjoyed an international clientele. "You know," he said to his companions on one occasion, "I think that Germany is the most stupid nation in history. But it is so far superior to all the other nations that it has already attained to the point of dispensing with religion."

He was thrown into the street by his enraged listeners. "Such philosophers," declared a fellow German, "ought to be jailed for the good of our country!"

But Schopenhauer was unperturbed. "I am a tender spirit in an iron age," he sighed and settled down to hear the public reaction to the book he had just sent to the printers. No reaction of any sort was forthcoming. The work fell stillborn from the press.

He shrugged his shoulders. "The more I see of men

the less I like them," he remarked. Then he turned to more mundane affairs. With an acute sense of business he managed to foresee a crash in the stock market. He took out every cent of his investments in the nick of time. He decided that he had better obtain a teaching position to guard against the possibility of financial losses in the future. Full of confidence in his scholastic ability he hastened to Berlin, the university centre of Germany. It mattered little to him that "the most formidable intellect of the day" was lecturing on philosophy to crowded halls in the same city. Hegel was the man of the hour. But Schopenhauer showed his contempt for his colleague by announcing a lecture on the same night on which Hegel had scheduled one of his own lectures.

His opening remarks to the audience were anything but tactful. "Soon after Kant had gone," he said, "sophists arose who wore out the thinking power of their time with a great deal of noise and barbarous speech." Then, as if he hadn't made his point clear enough, he continued: "People like Hegel (with their rationalistic metaphysics) should be shut out from the ranks of philosophers, as of yore the money-changers were cast out of the Temple.... A fitting motto for Hegel's writings is Shakespeare's 'Such stuff as madmen tongue, and brain not.'"

He was left standing in an empty room. Did it occur to him that his audience had been offended at his lack of professional courtesy towards the revered professor? Not at all. The public had refused to understand his genius, he was convinced. "How highly was Socrates esteemed by his contemporaries?" he remarked sarcastically.

Another unpleasant incident occurred during his stay in Berlin. Peeved at the unresponsiveness of his audiences he had begun to quarrel with his landlady. During one of the altercations he lost his temper and pushed her violently out of the room. She fell on her arm, injured it severely and sued Schopenhauer for substantial damages on the ground that her injury prevented her from further earning her livelihood. Though the philosopher vigorously contested the case, he lost the verdict and was compelled to support the woman for the rest of her life. Unfortunately for Schopenhauer she turned out to be a hardy soul and lived a great many years. When Schopenhauer finally received the certificate of her death he celebrated the occasion with a wry pun: "Orbit anus, abit onus." The dame's deported, the doom's departed.

After the trial Schopenhauer took a second trip to Italy and then returned to live in Berlin.

Always he was driven by the will to live. "We note now a dry seed preserves the dormant forces of life through thirty centuries and how at last, when favorurable circumstances arise, it grows up into a plant." For countless generations galvanism slumbers in copper and zinc.... for aeons toads lie imbedded in limestone in a state of suspended animation — all biding their day — all greedy to live. The world was born in a compulsion of selfishness and lust. And the eternal enemy is death...

The living present is constantly receding into the dead past. For what is the past but dead time? Life is a postponed death, just as walking is a postponed falling. Every breath we draw, every step we take, every meal we eat is an attempt to fight off death. But to no avail.

Death Claims us at own birth. No wonder the wise oriental monarchs go around with a vial of poison which they can take at any moment. For they and we live on borrowed time.....

Schopenhauer was very tenacious of his own borrowed time. An epidemic of cholera broke out in Berlin and he who had preached the futility of life was filled with such a moral dread of losing it that he fled from the city in panic. He took refuge in Naples, only to run away when a smallpox epidemic broke out in that city. He fled on to Verona — and here he became obsessed with the idea that he had swallowed poisoned snuff.

He was dreadfully unhappy. People began to avoid him, for "wherever he gazed a gloom pervaded space." His friends begged him not to paint the devil so black. "A good gray will suffice. "

But the devil couldn't be black enough to suit his dark moods. His obscurity as a philosopher had produced an almost pathological effect upon him. He was starved for the adulation of the public who had failed to recognize him as Arthur Schopenhauer, the Supreme. "I have been born to impress the mark of my intellect upon the whole human race," he had once confided to a friend. "Yet I am compelled to hear the trumpet of fame proclaiming the base and worthless — I who have lifted the veil of truth higher than any mortal." Well, the imbecility of those who had attained success would console him for the loneliness of his failure. He was proud and defiant and he would never succumb. There had been no philosophy between Kant and Schopenhauer that deserved the name, he believed. All those who had pretended to be philosophers were only university charlatans. "One giant calls to another through the weary space of the centuries, and the myriads of pygmies who are crawling below can hear nothing but a faint sound overhead... These pygmies ape one another in an orgy of buffoonery, adorn themselves with what the gaints have dropped and acclaim as their greatest heroes those who are pygmies like themselves...."

With these thoughts he came to the drab little city of Frankfort, where he determined to settle down, away from the eyes of the world. "It enters my mind as little to mix in the philosophic disputes of the day as to go down and take part when I see the mob having a scuffle in the street." He was forty-five and in the adventurous prime of life. Yet he never left Frankfort again. He lived the life of a lonely recluse to the end.

V

SUCH was the German Achilles, sulking in his tent away from the scholastic and literary battles of the world. His daily routine for the next twenty-seven years never changed an iota. Cold baths at dawn, strong coffee for breakfast, scowling and cursing at his landlady, three hours of study and writing in the forenoon when his brain was most fresh, half an hour's practice on the flute before his noonday meal, dinner at the Hotel d' Angleterre, home again, another cup of strong coffee and an afternoon devoted to reading. Towards evening a long brisk walk, accompanied by his white poodle, another meal at the hotel and a bout with the wine cups. Then usually a concert or the theatre, a brief perusal of the Hindu mystics and so to bed — "to sleep the sleep of the righteous."

He was actively interested in all phases of art, and when his friend Goethe died he lent his wholehearted support to a campaign which had been organized to collect funds for a monument. Even in this work, however, he was not without his strange suggestions and theories. He declared that scholars, philosophers and poets, who work for humanity with their heads, should be represented by busts; but that statesmen, rulers and generals who serve humanity with their whole being, should be commemorated by their entire figure.

His eccentric theories ranged from the place of women in society to dietary laws. It was one of his favourite thesis that originally man had been completely black and that he had dwelt in the south where a vegetable diet was practicable, but that later, when he had migrated north and his skin had become blanched, the change in the climate had necessitated more warmth in his blood and he had therefore adopted a diet of meat. He was disconcertingly frank in his conversation and eager to disemburden himself of his ideas whenever people were willing to listen. In the knowledge that Kant and Goethe had been prodigious eaters before him, he was not the least bit ashamed of his huge appetite. Once, when a stranger across the table from him looked on with amazement at his voracious eating, Schopenhauer remarked quietly: "Sir, you seem to be astonished at my appetite. True, I eat three times as much as you, but then I have three times as much brains as you."

Day after day he placed a gold piece beside his plate at the commencement of his meal and, to the waiter's chagrin, put it carefully back in his pocket at the conclusion. When asked about this peculiar habit he replied: "This piece of gold is to go to the poor whenever I hear the officers at the table discuss anything more serious than women, dogs and horses."

Though stingy with his money, he loved his comforts.

He sat for hours in his study smoking a five-foot pipe that twisted from the chin to the floor like a tuba. The smoke, he said, had thus an opportunity to cool properly before it reached his throat. And as he puffed away at this monstrosity he kept gazing at a gilt bust of Buddha that stood silently on his bureau next to a head of Immanuel Kant. The Hindu mystics were the deities of his philosophic system. It was they who had preached the glory of resignation, who had retired from the strife of the world to sit in meditation upon the futility of life and who had longed for the approach of death, not because they believed in an afterlife of blessedness but rather because they saw in death a return of the individual to a state of nothingness. Such was the peace of the soul that the Hindu mystics had dreamed about. It was the complete obliteration of man.

This philosophy was thoroughly congenial to Schopenhauer. "I get more out of one page of these ancient Hindu books," he declared, "than I do out of ten volumes of European philosophers after Kant." He was exasperated with "false optimism" of the modern philosophers. Man is essentially a creature of pain. His will is constantly driving him on to desire one object after another in life. But the moment he obtains his desire what follows? A terrible boredom, an empty void. Existence becomes again an unbearable burden. So he strives anew. What is life but a pendulum swinging between pain and emptiness, desire and boredom? For all, satisfaction in this life is a negative quality. When we fulfil a desire we have merely freed ourselves from this desire in order to succumb immediately to the slavery of further desires. Paradoxically enough, it is only the absence of bliss that can make us understand bliss. We are unable to recognize its value until after it is gone. Happiness is a negative state. The only positive state is pain. In such a scheme of things is there any place for hope? Decidedly no. Nothing but satiety and tedium alternating endlessly in the human will. The very presence of the will implies in us a deficiency, a want, a lustful craving for something that can never be fulfilled.

And what is the end? Can death stop the mad process and free man from his misery? Why, no. Even if the individual commits suicide he has not put an end to the general craving for life. For though the part dies, the whole moves persistently onward. The universal will to live conquers its eternal enemy, death through the reproductive organs of the species. Nature doesn't care at all about the individual; she is concerned only with the type. As soon as the individual reproduces his kind he has lost all value for Nature. After he has completed his task man is ripe for the grave. Nature has deceived the individual into perpetuating the misery of his race. She has endowed woman for a few years with a wealth of charm... at the expense of the rest of her life, so that during those years of youth she may capture the fancy of some man to such a degree that he is hurried away into undertaking the honoarable care of her..... Then, just as the female ant, after fecundation, loses her wings, which are now superfluous.... so, after giving birth to one or two children, a woman loses her beauty. Her mission has been accomplished. Time to make way for younger, healthier bodies to carry on the work of reproduction. What an irony, this perpetuation of the race. And how foolish we are to *love?*

Thus spake the prophet Schopenhauer. And who was

his constant companion, his "most persistent disciple"? His little white poodle whom he had named *Atma*, the soul of the world. This little poodle had become as legendary a figure in the streets of Frankfort as his famous master. The children of the neighbourhood called him "Young Schopenhauer." He slept on an elaborate bearskin rug under the picture of William Shakespeare. No matter how busily he was engaged Schopenhauer was always ready like a slave to attend to the needs of Atma. At precisely four-thirty in the afternoon the master and his dog took an airing in the streets of Frankfort. Though he was nearsighted, Schopenhauer avoided wearing glasses. He struck his cane impatiently on the ground as he walked and made meaningless grunts, looking neither to the one side nor to the other. The philosopher had an aversion to people who couldn't keep to the right when passing him on the sidewalk. Whenever a pedestrian failed to observe this rule he made an issue of it, shaking his cane and muttering, "The idiots, can they never learn how to walk properly?" He was fond of mimicking the carriage and the gait of the people he passed. Indeed, he turned the action of the people on the street into a "cosmic" subject for philosophical observation. "It is physiologically remarkable," he wrote, "that when conversation begins to interest most people they are immediately obliged to stand still, because as soon as their brain has to connect a few ideas they no longer possess the strength to keep their legs in motion by the motor nerves. So scantily is everything meted out to them by nature."

He tried to find a weighty philosophical reason for everything including his own conduct. Having lost the taste for travel, he deplored the love of travel in modern youth as a "revival of the nomadic instinct prevalent in the lowest stages of civilization."

At various stages in his own life he had contemplated marriage. And in spite of his unromantic philosophy he had been guilty of one or two romantic indiscretions. Indeed, he was the father of an illegitimate child whom he stubbornly refused to acknowledge. But as a general thing, when his thoughts turned to female companionship, he reiterated his motto with grim lips: "Were I a king, my prime command would be — *Leave me alone."* And then he would follow up the attack with a second motto: "Matrimony means War and Want." The institution of marriage was a trap set for man by Nature for the perpetration of the greatest evil in the world–life. No wonder that so much shame is attached to sexual love! It is the most miserable affirmation of the will to live. "We see the glances of two lovers meet longingly; yet why so secretly, fearfully and stealthily? Because these lovers are the traitors who seek to perpetuate the whole want and drudgery of the human race which would otherwise speedily come to an end." No man with intelligence could possibly be a partner to the farce called love for the "fair" sex. How any man "could possibly give the name of fair sex to that undersized, narrow–shouldered, broad–hipped and short–legged race called *woman"* is, to Schopenhauer, one of the inexplicable mysteries of the world.

If Spinoza's philosophy, as has been remarked, was the God-intoxicated spirit of affirmation, Schopenhauer's philosophy was the devil–intoxicated spirit of denial. As he grew older, though he became quite deaf, his mind lost not a whit of its keenness. His teeth fell out, his lips hung loosely against his gums and his untrimmed moustache drooped down in disorder over his mouth. But he still retained the mockery upon his face and the fire in his eyes.

VI

AND then recognition came to him at last. It had been his custom to go at times for weeks without talking. And for seventeen years he had desisted from publishing any of his work. In 1835 he broke his silence and "patronized" mankind to the extent of publishing an essay *On the Will in Nature.* In this essay he continued his lifelong discussion on the essential evil of all existence. Then the wrote a sequel to *The World as Will and Idea.* And the public began to read his books. He who had said that "a friend in need is not a friend indeed but merely a borrower" now discovered that he had hosts of friends all over the world — young and old students of philosophy who had been attracted by the brilliant lucidity and incisive analysis of his work and who proclaimed him as the prophet of a new age. This outburst of adulation did not surprise the incorrigible pessimist–optimist. He had never lost faith in himself. He had been expecting acclamation all along. But it was rather late. He was in the Indian summer of his life. "Now that I have spent a long, lonely life of insignificance and disregard," he said with his customary sneer, "they escort me to the end with trumpets and with drums." The world had finally discovered Schopenhauer. It had found in his pessimistic utterance the stimulant to a new kind of courage — the courage of despair. Misanthropy became a fad. Everybody devoured *The World as Will and Idea* and found in the acid originality of its thought the height of "sophistication." Young disciples everywhere mouthed with delight the old master's assertion that the "only honest wish man can have is that of absolute annihilation."

And Schopenhauer basked like an old tom-cat in his glory. He caused every review on his books that appeared in the papers to be sent to him at his own *personal expense* — which for a pinchfist like Schopenhauer was no less than a revolution. When visitors came to his house they stood and gazed at him for hours, as if he had already been petrified into a monument. One ardent disciple begged him to establish a literary society for the purpose of keeping a constant watch that not a syllable of his writings should ever be altered by adapters or translators. And Schopenhauer in the meantime had looked into his mystic Hindu literature and had seized with satisfaction upon the Vedic belief that the healthy man could look forward to a life span of a hundred years. "My opponents declare that my fame has come too late. They think I'm old and ready to die. Well, I shall outlive them all." For the older he got the more he loved life — this German Koheleth who taught the vanity of existence and the wisdom of self-annihilation. He firmly believed he would reach the century mark. "I shall still have more than thirty years of fame before I die."

There was a fair in the city of Frankfort. Schopenhauer had reached his sixty-ninth year. Every afternoon he went to the fair and stared impressively at an orangoutang who stared back at him, unimpressed, from his cage. Schopenhauer was fascinated by "the probable ancestor of our race." He urged his friends not to miss the opportunity of seeing this orangoutang. "Mon ami," he said to him on one of his visits. "I regret exceedingly that I have not been able to make your acquaintance at an earlier date... Yes, yes the frontal bone of your head is decidedly better formed than that of most humans..... I am thrilled at the manner in which you stare through the bars. You have the strange and melancholy mien of a prophet gazing into the Promised Land."

And then he added bitterly. "But for myself, unhappy creature that I am, there is no such place as the Promised Land."

VII

ONE day as he was hurrying home for dinner — he always walked rapidly even at his advanced age — he was seized with palpitation of the heart and a shortness of breath. This wouldn't do. He must have at least thirty more years in which to taste the sweets of success. He couldn't afford as yet to be slowed up in his gait, to be weakened by an unsteady heart and a shortness of breath. From time to time the palpitations recurred. But rather than slow up his step Schopenhauer shortened the compass of his walks. His doctor advised him to take medicine, but he growled back that he had never taken a pill in his life and that he wouldn't start now. Those who hoped to purchase health at the druggist's were fools and scoundrels!

And what was the reason behind man's endless struggle to live? What was the grand result of all the skill and trouble of life's creatures to continue their existence? What, but death? How ingenious the preparation, how mighty the cost, how eager the hope, how hopeless the end! Surely no one could reasonably wish to prolong such an unfair contest? Yet Schopenhauer struggled on.

The old philosopher's illness was diagnosed as an inflammation of the lungs. He struggled violently against the suggestion that he take to his bed. He sat on his sofa. Above him hung an oil portrait of Wolfgang von Goethe. On the bureau stood the bust of Immanuel Kant. Nearby on the table, lay on open volume of Descartes. How wise these philosophers! How well they understood the futility of man — the stupendous irony of his will to strive for a little greater share of greed! Does anyone believe he can enjoy his pleasure while his neighbour suffers pain? On the contrary, he who seeks for himself a happy life in a world which is a tempestuous sea of evil is like a beggar dreaming he is king. This is the law of Eternal justice. There is no gulf between mine and thine, my happiness and your happiness, my will and the general will of mankind. Let the wise men proclaim this transcendent truth — that each and every one of us must bear all the suffering of the world as his own. And we who have sipped a drop from the fountain of eternal wisdom, we who have dedicated ourselves as humanitarians and saviours of men, let us pay out our hearts to all those who suffer, that in so doing we may relieve our own suffering. We who have stripped our power of its blind and futile desire to struggle against our fellows, we who have merged our individual will into the general will, we shall become saints — *hopeful* saints, will-less, wise and free.

Dr. Gwinner came very often to see old Schopenhauer. They had long conversations on philosophy and on the political events of the day. 1860...The Italians had risen like a tidal wave to sweep away their Austrian oppressors. Louis Napoleon had brought France into the war on the side of Italy. In America the North and the South were arming themselves for the titanic struggle of the house divided. The Southern senators were leaving the halls of Congress in tears. Momentous days, these, days that provided much food for philosophic thought.

VIII

"LET us dispense with the emptiness of existence. The great man is not the conqueror, but he who denies the will to live." Histories in the future will not be written about the warriors but about the peacemakers — the men of resignation who in the morning of their reason are ready to cast away the masquerade dress which they have worn in the foolish carnival night of their life. No regrets no will, no world — and peace.

His voice was still strong, remarked the philosopher's friends. His eyes showed scarcely a trace of old age. His health, he insisted, was really nothing to complain about, except that now and then he was seized with violent coughing spasms.

.....Seated quietly at his breakfast table, correcting the proofs of his latest book and waiting for the landlady to serve coffee. He had found hope, a real escape from the needless flux of desire.... Had not Kant discovered the secret, this wise old philosopher looking down from the bureau in a peaceful marble repose? In his early days Schopenhauer had gone to the Dresden art galleries to study for hours the Madonnas of Raphael. What was written in the many different faces of the Virgin as painted by the master? Life, labour, death — and transfiguration. Art alone was the escape from the endless flux. Art, the pure idea that lies outside the whirlpool of space and time — "like the rainbow quietly resting on the raging torrent."

"Doctor Schopenhauer, have you taken your cold bath?" His landlady entered to let the morning air into the room.

But Schopenhauer's mind was far away from his room. Art — what does it mean? It means the renunciation if one's individual personality, the divorce from all practical desires, the reverent contemplation of the selfless Idea as a sacrament. The average man turns his attention to things insofar only they have some relation to his individual will. But the artist steps outside of his will to comprehend each thing as it really is. And then he realizes that the "thing" is no longer a purpose. It is only an idea. He has learned to interpret the world in terms other than those of his own petty desires. He has subjected his will to the pure, untrammelled wisdom of is mind. He has risen above himself and looked over the landscape of wisdom beyond the mountain peaks of desire to the vast horizon of peace. Life, labour, death — transfiguration...

"Doctor Schopenhauer!" called the landlady as she put the coffe down beside him. He did not answer. He was dead.

****

IMPORTANT WORKS BY SCHOPENHAUER

- *The World as Will and Idea.*
- *On the Fourfold Root of Sufficient Reason.*
- *Of the Will of Nature.*
- *The Two Fundamental Problems of Ethics.*
- *The Art of Controversy*
- *Essays.*

15

RALPH WALDO EMERSON

1803 – 1882

ON July 15, 1838, Ralph Waldo Emerson delivered an address before the senior class of the Harvard Divinity School. In this address he pointed out "the simplicity and energy of the Highest Law — the oneness of mankind." He proclaimed the doctrine of individual liberty and universal tolerance — the New World principle of mutual collaboration between free men as against the Old World formula of mutual distrust between enslaved individuals and nations. He placed the ethical code of humanity upon a practical American basis — *to live, let live and help live.*

This address marked the moral Declaration of Independence for the United States. "From now on," observed a member of the audience, our young men will have a Fifth Gospel in their Testaments — the *American* Gospel."

What sort of man was this New England Isaiah who paraphrased the Bible into the Yankee dialect?

II

He came of a pioneer stock — poor but self-reliant

unconquerable, free. "My American forebears" — Thomas Emerson had come to Concord in 1635 — "had hard labour and spare diet, and off wooden trenchers, but they had peace and freedom... The light struggled in through windows of oiled paper, but they read the word of God by it." One of his ancestors had prayed every evening that none of his descendants might ever be rich. His prayer was answered. The Emersons were born "not to be rich but to be educated." William Emerson, Waldo's father, was a clergyman — "the most liberal preacher who had yet appeared in Boston. But those who supply the bread of life are often repaid with stones." He died, like most of the Emerson tribe, a poor man. He left five children, all boys, of whom Waldo was the second. At the time of his father's death (1811) Waldo was eight years old.

His mother opened a boarding house in order to support the family. From the very beginning, therefore, Waldo learned to know and to like people. And he also learned to be cheerful in the face of poverty. In the winter he and his older brother William had but a single overcoat between them, so that one of them was always compelled to stay indoors when other was out.

Waldo missed his play, but he made the best of his winter evenings — listening to the conversation of the boarders and feasting voraciously upon the books in his mother's library. In bed, covered to the chin with his woollen blankets, he followed Plato in the breathless adventures of his *Dialogues;* and during the Sunday sermon at church be dipped into the *Thoughts* of Pascal, a copy of which he always carried in his pocket.

And thus his growing mind was nurtured upon Yankee common sense and metaphysical philosophy — not a bad combination, thought his mother, for a future minister of the Gospel. For that was the career — the Emerson career — to which she was trying to dedicate him. In 1817 she sent him to Harvard, where he added Shakespeare and Spinoza and Montaigne to the intimate circle of his "beloved masters." Scholastically, however, his college career was undistinguished. He was appointed class poet only, after seven others had declined the honour. But he was barely eighteen at the time of graduation — tall and thin as a lamp-post and with a lamp-like glow in his large and gentle eyes. He had fallen a prey to "the Emerson plague" — consumption — which had destroyed his father and was soon to carry off two of his brothers. For twelve years he lived "in the House of Pain," fought desperately against death and strove to find a financial as well as a physical foothold on life. He tried teaching among the hills in Roxbury, "where man in the bush with God may meet." He wrote poetry that was a poor substitute for prose and prose that was the very essence of poetry — and failed to sell enough of either to make a living. He was invited to "preach on trial" at various churches, where he was unable to reap the harvest of a job but succeeded in planting many a seed of job. "O Sally!" wrote a woman in Northampton to her sister after she had heard one of Emerson's "trial" sermons. "We thought to entertain 'a pious indigent,' but lo! An angel unawares!"

Finally, however, a few of the New Englanders became aware of the "angel in their midst." On March 11, 1829,

Emerson was ordained minister of the Second (Unitarian) Church in Boston. He had a most remarkable voice, a soft and golden instrument that melted away the frosts of New England Calvinism like an April sun.

But he preached a doctrine which was unpalatable to the reactionary mind. He advocated a practical application of the Sermon on the Mount rather than a conventional adherence to the ceremonials of the church. Indeed, he definitely objected to some of these ceremonials — especially the one dealing with the sacrament of the Lord's Supper. "The kingdom of God," he said "is not meat and drink but righteousness and peace." The deacons of the church, while expressing their "undiminished regard for our pastor," nevertheless insisted upon the continuance of "the customary administration of the Supper. Whereupon Emerson resigned from his pastorate. His interpretation of religion, he explained, was too unorthodox for the rigid formulas of the established church. "Christianity, as I see it, has for its object simply to make men good and wise. Its institutions, then, should be as flexible as the wants of men."

In severing himself from his church Emerson attacked no institution and no man. He merely observed that since he was unable to see eye to eye with his congregation it would be best for them to get another pastor. Thus by a single simple act, he banished from his soul the idols of an ancient — and to him outmoded — tradition. But, as Oliver Wendell Holmes remarked, "here was an iconoclast without a hammer, who took down his idols from their pedestals so tenderly that it seemed like an act of worship."

Yet to many of the reactionaries his iconoclasm was anything but tender. Indeed, they maintained that he had enthroned the devil in the place of God. He would be punished for his sins. "We are sorry for Mr. Emerson, but it certainly looks as if he is going to hell." "It does indeed look so, "replied one of his friends. "But I am sure of one thing — if Emerson goes to hell, he will so change its climate that it will become a popular resort for all the good souls of heaven."

III

WHEN Emerson left his pulpit he went out to search for the meaning of life. He took long walks in the country. He tried to attune his ear and his heart to the music of Nature. And before long he made a strange discovery. He learned that the heart of Nature was beating in unison with his own heart. He was an intimate part of a living world. His mind was an important cell in the world mind — or, as he called it, the World Soul or Oversoul. And this abstract discovery led him to a practical observation. He noticed, when he reflected upon the intimate relationship between himself and the rest of world, that his whole being was electrified with a surge of power, an overmastering confidence in himself and in his fellow men. This power was infinite. He could draw upon it at will. *And he could teach others to draw upon this same power within themselves.* Each of us, he concluded, possesses the spiritual capital for developing an enormous business — the business of acquiring and exchanging beauty and joyousness and freedom and friendship and peace.

It was a doctrine admirably suited to the temperament and genius of America. We are forever, he said, "on the verge of all that is great." Trust in yourself. Claim your share of the greatness of life. Assert your relationship to the divine. Surrender yourself to the power within you — not the power to enslave but power to liberate, to help. Dare to become the master of your own fate and teach all and sundry to dare likewise.

And thus Emerson became a teacher of man, the immortal pupil — "a professor," to use his own expression, "of the Science of Joy."

His own life, however, was not a life of unmixed joy. He had fallen in love and married and lost his wife — all within eighteen months. For two years after her death he paid a daily visit to her grave. He himself expected to follow her shortly, for his painful cough was "like a sexton singing a funeral dirge" in his chest.

But Emerson was the philosopher of life. He refused to die. He took a trip to Europe in order to sit at the feet of the masters of the Old World. One evening he came to see Carlyle. The "hermit of Craigenputtock" gave his young American visitor a pipe and took one himself. In perfect silence — so the story goes — the two puffed away at their pipes until bedtime, when they shook hands and congratulated each other on the fruitful evening they had spent together. On his subsequent visits, however, when he had become more familiar with philosophy of Carlyle, Emerson found him somewhat disappointing.

Carlyle's eyes were fixed too intently upon dead glory of the Old World and were insufficiently open to the living beauty of the celestial region." He was so eager to praise the *great* men, thought Emerson, that he failed to appraise the greatness of the *common* man.

Emerson found the same fault with many of the other celebrities of Europe. For these men were still encumbered with political beliefs and ethical dogmas which Emerson had long outgrown. "For a thousand years these poor men (of Europe) have sat before the gates of Paradise to catch a glimpse of the beauty within. And now that the gates have been opened, these men have fallen asleep."

Disappointed with his European trip, Emerson returned home. Europe had little to say to him, but he had much to say to America. He found a new kind of schoolroom, the village lyceum. Here, liberated from the shackles of conventional creeds, he expressed his independent thoughts on mice and men and angles and gods. The intellectual Brahmins of Boston and Cambridge didn't like his ideas. For he was too irreverent toward the old traditions and professions. Once they hooted him off the platform at Harvard College. But the common people, the men and the women with the homespun thoughts, understood his simple teaching even though they couldn't always follow his elegant phrases. For the lesson that he brought home to them was but an echo of the ambitions and the hopes that were stirring vaguely within their own minds. "We are simple folk here," said a Lexington woman after one of his lectures, "and we understand Mr. Emerson because he speaks directly to our hearts."

His lectures were, for those days, fairly remunerative. They brought him about eight hundred dollars a year. To this he was able to add an annual income of twelve hundred dollars, a legacy which he had inherited from his wife. He felt himself a rich man. He bought a "mansion" in Concord for thirty-five hundred dollars, married a second time and settled down to cultivate the flowers in his garden and the friendship of his neighbours.

And his friends were among the richest personalities in the world. For some mysterious reason which the scientists have not as yet been able to explain the gods occasionally select a single spot on earth and people it with the citizens of heaven. This happened in the Athens of the fifth century (B.C.), with its Aeschylus and Euripides and Phidias and Socrates and Plato; in the London of the Elizabethan period, with its Beaumont and Drayton and Fletcher and Johnson and Shakespeare; in the Germany of the early nineteenth century, with its Goethe and Schiller and Heine and Mozart and Schubert and Beethoven; and in the Russia of the latter part of the nineteenth century, with its Turgenev and Tchaikovsky and Checkhov and Dostoyevsky and Tolstoy. In a lesser sense the Concord of Emerson was the scene of another of those periodic flowerings of the divine mind on human soil. Among the intimates of Emerson were Nathaniel Hawthorne, the man who immortalized the struggle between the Puritan love of religion and the pagan religion of love; Margaret Fuller, a female

Merlin whose eyes were "visible at night" and who could play with ideas as a juggler plays with coloured balls; Bronson Alcott, the peddler-prophet whose personality was a combination of the wisdom of Plato and the wholesome-ness of Saint Francis; Henry Thoreau, the saintly vagabond whose capital was about twenty-five dollars a year and an infinity of love; Sarah Riply, a Greek goddess in a Yankee wrapper, who washed the family clothes and scrubbed the floors and translated Klopstock and taught Homer and Virgil and Aristotle in her husband's school; and "Aunt Mary" Emerson, a living flame of four feet and three inches who galloped over the fields of Concord dressed in her shroud and a scarlet shawl and whose wit could tear into shreds the conventions and pretentions of the day.

With these friends and many others, in Boston and in Cambridge as well as in Concord, Emerson exchanged ideas; and then he went into his study and transformed these ideas into the minted gold of his essays and his lectures. He travelled over New England, into the South and across the continent to California. He delivered talks to all sorts of people — sailors and blacksmiths and poets and teachers and farmers and shoemakers and politicians and pioneers. He took another trip to England — this time to bring the idea of Democracy, the message of the New World, to the inhabitants of the Old. Everywhere they listened in amazement to this New England apostle, "straight and thin as a birch tree in winter," whose keen strong face was like a block of granite chiselled out of Mount Monadnock and whose optimism was grounded upon a firm foundation of

American faith. Faith in the Justice of the American idea and in the heroism of the average American man.

IV

EMERSON had no cut–and–dried system of philosophy. There was no dogmatic consistency to his thought. And purposely so. "A foolish consistency," he observed "is the hobgoblin of little minds." He did not pretend to know the truth. The truth, he said, is as hard to capture and bottle up as light. All that he tried to do was to pick out, here and there, a stray thread which to him seemed to be part of an intricately woven yet definite design of benevolent Providence. These threads may be briefly pieced together into the following pattern:

All men are vital parts of one organism—mankind. This philosophy, to distinguish it from Pantheism, may be called Panhumanism. In *The American Scholar* Emerson repeats "one of those fables which out of an unknown antiquity convey an unlooked — for wisdom — that the gods, in the beginning, divided Man into men that he might be more helpful to himself; just as the hand was divided into fingers, the better to answer its end." But unfortunately, continues Emerson, the individual units which compose this united human organism have allowed themselves to be "peddled out," to be "spilled into drops," so that our present–day society is one in which "the members have suffered amputation from the trunk and strut about so many walking monsters — a good finger, a neck, a stomach, an elbow, but never a man."

It is our business therefore to reaffirm the "oneness of mankind." Indeed, we must not only reaffirm this fact but we must actively dedicate ourselves to it. American philosophy is a philosophy of action. "Good thoughts are not better than good dreams, unless they are executed." The prophets of the East had preached the passive doctrine that God is One. But now came the prophet of the West with the added active doctrine that Man, too, is One. Man is one, declares Emerson, because his soul is part and parcel of God.... Let us stun and astonish the intruding rabble of men and books and institutions by a simple declaration of (this) fact. Bid the invaders take the shoes from off their feet"; for every man, every human part of that divine entity known as mankind, is a god in the making.

Emerson applied the term *transcendentalism* to this idea of the oneness of man through his relationship with God. It is an unfortunate term, for it obscures a simple idea with a difficult name. Many of Emerson's contemporaries sneered at this exotic name and failed to understand that it encompassed a vital American thought. One of Emerson's critics, Dr. Burnap of Baltimore, characterized transcendentalism as "the new philosophy which maintains that nothing is everything in general and everything is nothing in particular" — a definition which is as false as it is facetious. For, properly understood, the philosophy of Emerson is but the ethical foundation for the political doctrine of American Democracy.

And this brings us to the second point in Emerson's philosophy — his insistence upon the dignity of the common man. "In all my lectures I have taught one doctrine namely, the infinitude of the private man." With the annunciation of this principle Emerson turned his back completely upon the European institutions with their superficial nobilities and their artificial class distinctions. Come out of the cemeteries of the past! Look forward into the woodlands of the future! "The eyes of man are set in his forehead, not in his hindhead." We have outlived the despotic traditions of the old. "There are new lands, new men, new thoughts. Let us stop imitating our brothers of the Old World. For "what is imitation but the (backward) travelling of the mind? Our houses are built with foreign taste; our shelves are garnished with foreign ornaments: our opinions, our tastes, our faculties lean and follow the Past and the Distant." Stop being followers and leaners; become founders and leaders. "Build your own world." Build your own life. "The private life of one man" can be made "more illustrious than any kingdom in history."

And it is the business of the American thinkers, the American scholars, to teach their fellow citizens how to build. "Let each one of us begin at home." Here in Concord, observed Emerson, there are no manufacturing industries. "Well, then, let us manufacture school teachers and make them the best in the world." *American* Teachers — teachers of the American Way.

But what is the American Way? The recognition of the importance of each in the summation of the whole. Size doesn't matter; neither does pomposity or blatancy or fame matter. The gods descend upon the earth in lowly disguises. In the folklore of may nations the most powerful creatures are the smallest. Let each man attend to his own work, and let every man respect the work of his fellows. What, the blacksmith is unable to write a poem? Well, but the poet is unable to hammer out a horse-shoe. "If I cannot carry forests in my back," declares the squirrel to the mountain, "neither can you crack a nut."

Emerson's philosophy pointed out the nobility of the commonplace. "Know, whoever you are, that the world exists for you." In each and every man "there is an angel in disguise who plays the fool." It was to these "angels in disguise" that Emerson spoke when he addressed his audiences, exhorting them to cast off their foolish outer garments of servitude and sycophancy and humiliation and prejudice and hate and to stand forth in all their divine splendour as free men. He told them to liberate themselves from the European philosophy of resignation and to accept the American Gospel of aspiration. He urged every man to assert himself — not his isolated self but his *inclusive* self. Strengthen your heart with the knowledge of this inclusive self, this social individualism which is yours by right of birth and you have mastered the secret of all power. "All that Adam had, all that Caesar could, you have and can do." Unshackle your mind from its chains and learn to know yourself for the man that you are destined to become. "There are no bounds to the possibilities of man."

Emerson's was the voice which, as he remarked in a letter to a friend, he had sought in vain among other philosophers — "that profound voice which might speak to the American heart, cheering timid good men, animating the youth, consoling the defeated and intelligently announcing duties which clothe life with a joy and endear the land and sea to men." America, he said, needs a new kind of virtue — virtue "with guts in it." Pride in our work and justice for our workers. For the workers are the channels through which aspiration flows into creation. This is to be a country of great deeds and of great ideas. Free, dynamic and daring ideas. America "shall be the asylum and patron of every new thought, every unproven opinion, every untried project which proceeds out of good will and honest seeking."

America is to be the Great Experiment. It is to be dominated by the strong courageous will of pioneers and guided by the wise and gentle counsel of the scholars. And the goal of the Experiment? Complete Democracy, social, political, economic. A future hope, founded upon past mistakes. Keep on trying and blundering and failing- and trying again. Do not despair. In spite of your failures in spite of your sufferings, in spite of your discouragements, keep "antagonizing on." The race is not to the swift but to the resolute. Have you been pushed aside? Have you stumbled? Never mind the ridicule, never mind the defeat. Up again, old heart! "Be of good cheer.... Patience and patience, we shall win at last."

Be of good cheer! "This world belongs to the cheerful, the energetic, the daring." Dare to assert yourself as an accredited citizen in the great Republic of Mankind. Your birth into this world has been no mistake. You are an invited guest to the banquet of life. And He who has sent you the invitation is no niggardly host. Divine generosity is hidden somewhere behind the mystery of creation. "There is intelligence and goodwill at the heart of things."

And — here Emerson stresses again the idea which dominates his entire thought — this divine intelligence has created individual men as the vital component parts of a united mankind. One for all, all for one. "The heart is the is the heart of all. Not a valve, not a wall, not an inter section is there anywhere in nature, but one blood rolls uninterruptedly and endless circulation through all men, as the water of the globe is all one sea, and, truly seen, its tide is one."

Again and again Emerson appeals to this one tide of humanity which flows in the hearts of all living men. Indeed, Emerson may be said to have written the final clause to the American Declaration of Independence. For his brave and gentle philosophy represents the Universal Declaration of *Interdependence*.

This philosophy of interdependence receives perhaps its highest utterance in Emerson's essay on *Friendship*. The beauty of friendship lies in the recognition of the ultimate relationship that exists between man and man. "The essence of friendship is entireness," the intuitive knowledge that you and I are an undivided unit. When we are in the presence of our friends "let us be silent-so that we may hear the whisper of the gods." And in the music of that whisper we can feel "the flowing of two souls into one". Wherever two friends engage in conversation there is a third party present — God. "Shall I not call God the Beautiful, who daily showeth Himself to me in His gift of friendship?" When I encounter my friends "it is not I but the Deity in me and in them" which "derides and cancels the thick walls of individual character and now makes many one."

The life of man is a quest for friendship, a striving for the class reunion of the human soul. But true friendship is not merely a passion but it is also an action of the soul. It is a divine game of give and take. "The only way to have a friend is to be one." We must learn to "grasp heroic hands in heroic hands." The active and heroic conception of friendship is to Emerson the one solid thing in a world of shadows. It is a substance of such reality and duration that compared to it "the Alps and the Andes come and go as rainbows."

Cultivate that art of friendship and you come close to the heart of reality. You stop looking at the rainbows and you begin to see the true source of light. "If man could be inspired with a tender kindness to the souls of man and should come to feel that every man was another self... this feeling would cause the most striking changes of external things; the tents would be struck; the cannon would become street posts; the pikes, a fisher's harpoon; the aggressors would be disenthroned, and the marching regiment would be a caravan of emigrants, peaceful pioneers."

Peaceful pioneers. This was the philosophical dream of Emerson — a warless world of courageous independent, joyous, loving and adventuring friends.

V

HAWTHORNE gives us a gracious picture of the serene and friendly sage of Concord as he met him on his daily walks. "It was good to encounter him in the wood paths, or some times in our avenue, with that pure intellectual gleam diffused about his presence like the garment of a shining one; and he, so quiet, so simple, so without pretensions encountering each man alive as if expecting to receive more than he could impart. But it was impossible to dwell in his vicinity without inhaling the mountain atmosphere of his lofty thoughts."

There was in his make-up no hatred, no rancour, no disdain, only infinite forgiveness and love. When he lost his son Waldo a Unitarian preacher attributed the loss to Emerson's "lack of faith." Emerson merely replied: "Neither my friend nor I can understand the ways of life and faith and death." Once, when he had concluded a lecture at Middlebury College, the presiding minister offered up a prayer as an antidote. "We beseech Thee, O Lord, to deliver us from ever hearing any more such transcendental nonsense as we have just listened to from this sacred desk." Asked to comment on this public insult, Emerson remarked: "The minister seems a very conscientious, plainspoken gentleman."

He failed to get excited at the foolishness of men. One day a "Millerite" came to him with alarming news. "Mr. Emerson," he cried, "do you know that tonight the world is coming to an end?" "I am glad to hear it," smiled Emerson. "Many will get along better without it."

Yet on occasion his voice could grow sharp — especially when he cried out against injustice. On November 7, 1837, when opposition to slavery was still regarded as a crime in the intellectual circles of Boston, he dared at a public lecture to express his admiration for the abolitionist martyr, Elijah P. Lovejoy. "The brave Lovejoy gave his breast to the bullets of a mob for the the right of free speech and opinion and died when it was better not to live." One of Emerson's friends who was present at the lecture, remarked that "a sort of cold shudder ran through the audience at this calm braving of the public opinion."

Emerson was fearless not only in braving the opinions of others but in changing his own opinion whenever he found himself to be in the wrong. The one great hero of his early youth had been Daniel Webster. "There is the Bunker Hill Monument, and there is Webster," he once wrote, referring to the "two wonders of the New England world." Yet when his hero surrendered to slavery Emerson was one of the first to stigmatize his conduct in public. At a political rally in Cambridge one of the few in which Emerson ever took an active part — he pictured "the car of slavery and its abominations," with Webster as the leading horse. His words were greeted with a storm of hisses. Emerson waited patiently until the noise subsided and then he went on; "Every drop of Webster's blood has eyes that look downward. He knows the heroes of 1776, but he cannot see the heroes of 1851 when he meets them on the street."

When Webster died he received perhaps his most fitting epitaph in the paradoxical tribute of Emerson: "He had honour enough to feel degraded."

In the tragic days preceding the Civil War, and throughout the war, Emerson always spoke "the best and bravest word." Several of his close friends were killed in the war, and his only living son was wounded. In spite of his advanced age and his always precarious health he was tireless in his advocacy of the black man's cause. He had the highest admiration for Lincoln, "the Protector of American Freedom," and Lincoln, returned this admiration for Emerson, "the Prophet of American Faith." At the conclusion of the war Emerson proclaimed this faith in one of his most inspired lectures, "America means opportunity, freedom, power. The genius of this country has marked out her true policy: opportunity — doors wide open every port open. If I could, I would have free trade with all the world, without toll or custom-house. Let us invite every nation, every race, every skin; white man, black man, red man, yellow man. Let us offer hospitality, a fair field and equal justice to all."

VI

"LIFE," said Emerson in one of his lectures, "is unnecessarily long." He had always hoped that he might not outlive the decay of his mental faculties. This hope was not completely fulfilled. In 1872 his house burned down. "The morning after the fire," he said, "I felt something snap in my brain." From that day onward his "naughty memory" gave him "but fitful service." One evening his daughter read to him a passage from his lecture on *Nature.* "I don't know who wrote this," said Emerson "but he must have been a great man."

Yet there were moments when his former greatness broke through like a flash of lightning in the gathering dusk. One day, as he was walking through his garden with his friend Moncure Conway, he handed the young man a plum. "Take this," he said. "At its best it is the fruit of Paradise."

These words were symbolical of Emerson's attitude not only toward the humblest of fruits but also toward the humblest of men. "At his best he is the child of Paradise."

****

Important Works By Emerson

The American Scholar.
English Traits.
Nature.
Essays.
Representative Men.
The Conduct of Life.
Society and Solicitude.
Letters and Social Aims.
Self–Reliance.
The Oversoal.
The Natural History of the Intellect.
Duty.
Truth.
Beauty and Manners.
Literary Ethics.
Journals.
Poems.
May Day and Other Pieces.

✦✧✦

16

HERBERT SPENCER

1820 – 1903

IN his old age Spencer wrote his autobiography. Referring to his Quaker ancestors he observed "I have never showm the unfailing diligence that was common to them, yet there has not been displayed by me as great an amount of altruistic feeling." In this book he also recorded his "youthful indifference to a sense of duty" and his early "divorce from religion." All this, he said, seemed to demonstrate "that in my brain the blood supply, when not increased by excitement, has been below par." Here speaks the apologist for the "spiritually anaemic" age of scientific scepticism.

His hands, Spencer tells us, were unusually small and well built. And — always the evolutionist he points out proudly that he has inherited these hands from his father and his grandfather who did "nothing more arduous, day by day, than wield the pen or pencil." The theory of hereditary characteristics had swept Europe in Spencer's time.

He speaks proudly of his early "freedom from moral fear." And with malicious relish he quotes the criticism of his uncle: "The grand deficiency in Herbert's natural characters is in the principle of Fear. By Fear, I mean that 'Fear of the Lord' which is the beginning of wisdom." This "grand deficiency" was a matter of pride to the philosopher who was the spokesman of the age of agnosticism.

And here speaks the original thinker: "I inherited an unusual capacity for the intuition of cause. Without instruction.... I had reached (as a child) a true insight into ultimate dynamic relations than (was the case with) those who were much older and far better cultured.... At the age of thirteen I called in question the doctrine of inertia set forth in Dr. Arnott's *Physics* and defended by my uncle, and persisted in my dissent in spite of this combined authority against me."

And finally, here speaks the man of tragedy, with a body maimed by overwork at the age of five and thirty, a pitiable wreck reduced at middle age to wearing "stoppings" in his ears to quiet his nerves and to taking nightly doses of opium to induce sleep; "Of literary distinction, as of so many things which men pursue, it may be truly said that the game is not worth the candle."

II

HE was the oldest of seven children and the only one to survive his infancy. He obtained under his father and his uncle, both of them teachers and social reformers, a smattering of natural science, physics, chemistry and anatomy. But he studied no Latin or Greek to speak of, and he received no regular instruction in his native language. Indeed, he boasted that he had practically no knowledge of English grammar. Up to the age of forty he gulped down his knowledge piecemeal. Nothing formal — a hasty lunch — counter sort of education. Yet he became an assistant schoolmaster in his native Derby at seventeen. Shortly thereafter he found an outlet for his mathematical talents as a civil engineer with the London and Lirmingham Railway. He was discharged from his job, however, when politics held up the further construction of branch line. "Got the sack — very glad," he remarked.

He was free to devote his time to himself. He collected fossils, studied modelling and phrenology, produced a number of inventions including a "binding pin" for fixing together the loose sheets of a blankbook, and then decided to come down to London for a literary career. He secured a position as sub editor of the *Economist,* hobnobbing with such members of the London intelligentsia as George Henry Lewis, Thomas Huxley and Marian Evans (later to become famous as George Eliot). But he was so poorly off that he thought of migrating to another country where he might find perhaps "better luck under fairer skies." New Zealand was his choice. With scientific meticulousness he jotted down on paper a list of the relative advantages of the life in the two countries. Each item was valued at a definite number. England presented "greater domestic comforts," valued at ten points; "excitement in literature," twenty points; excitement in science," six points. New Zealand, on the other hand, offered the chance of a more profitable living wage and the prospective "excitement of marriage," valued at one hundred points.

When he made the final computation New Zealand outnumbered England almost three to one. But Spencer grew critical of his plans and gave up the idea of migrating — with its living wage, its chances of marriage and all its other advantages. Later in life he remarked, "It seems probable that this abnormal tendency to criticize has been a chief factor in the continuance of my celibate life."

However, his financial luck turned. His uncle died and left him a small inheritance. He gave up his job on the *Economist* and wrote a book on Psychology. He had already prepared a number of essays on sociological and scientific subjects. He had inherited from his father the "synthetic tendency" of theorizing scientific figures into sociological facts. And he was anxious to offer his findings to the world.

While he was busy editing his various essays into a collection for publication it occurred to him that these essays might serve as the basis for a "new scientific philosophy" that would revolutionize the world.

III

HIS scientific philosophy grew into a work of eighteen volumes. He was recognized as the leader in all the important controversies on evolution. He wrote one of the most important texts on psychology in the nineteenth century without any study of the works of his predecessors in the field. He prepared a book on biology and performed only one laboratory experiment to test his theories. And he became one of the most talked of men in England!

During these productive years of his life his interests ranged from a metaphysical doctrine to a binding pin; from, a classification of all the sciences to an improved fishing — rod joint; from the general law of evolution to a better way of dressing artificial flies." But widely as they roamed within the limits of science, his interests extended no further. He was one of the most dogmatic intellects of his century. He had become so obsessed with the business of devising synthetic formulas for life that "he stopped living."

At thirty–eight he had drawn up the tremendous outline of his *Synthetic Philosophy,* and the remaining forty–three years of his life he spent in completing the task.

Spencer's Synthetic Philosophy is the universe in miniature. It deals with the birth of the stars, the evolution of the earth, the life of man, the growth of his intellect and the progress of his spirit. It is impossible in the space of a few pages to come anywhere near to an adequate summary of this comprehensive work. Let us, however, try to dip up, as it were, a thimbleful of knowledge out of this vast ocean of speculation.

Spencer based his entire system of thought upon the theory of evolution. He had expressed the idea of evolution in an essay some years before the publication of Darwin's *Origin of Species.* And now he extended the principles of evolution from the earth to the heavens. All nature, he said, is progressively and regressively rhythmical. All life is an integration of matter and a concomitant dissipation of forces. Matter passes from an "indefinite incoherent homogenety" to a "definite coherent heterogeneity" and then back again to an 'indefinite incoherent homogenerity." Translated into everyday language, this means that the destiny of the universe is from chaos to creation to chaos. The epic of life and death — the rise and fall of planets and nations and men. All things — culture and morals and art and science and religion — are born from the embryo, pass through youth, prime and old age and finally end in decay. What is biology but "life, the continuous adjustment of internal relations to external relations." What is psychology but a continuous evolution "from nebula to mind" — a developent of the consciousness through the stages of simple and complex responses, instinct, memory, imagination, to intellect and reason. Society, too, is an evolving structure, having organs of nutrition, circulation, co-ordination and reproduction. Families grow into clans; clans into states; and some day, let us hope, state will grow into the federated superstate of the world. But in the end everything will dissolve into the nothingness out of which it came. The life of man, the life of the world, is a fitful dream between a sleep and a sleep.

No man of the century had undertaken such a monumental task. Spencer's world was laid out in the pattern of a geometrical diagram. His mind, remarked William James, "had not the lights and shades of an ordinary style; it was a remorseless glare throughout." His friends and critics, as they watched this iconoclast dictating his thoughts to a number of secretaries day after day for nearly half a century, shook their heads and murmured "All brains and no heart."

IV

HIS writing was an immense monument of egotism. His mind was utterly unreceptive to any idea that was not his own. For a philosopher he was singularly unappreciative of Plato. He attempted time and time again to read the *Dialogues* and with each succeeding attempt put them down with greater exasperation. "There is more dramatic propriety in the conversations of our third-rate novelists," he said. He felt contempt for the fine arts. He ascribed this feeling to his analytical habit which rendered him prone to dwell "upon defects" and which diminished his "appreciation for the beauties....So is it also with my (lack of) appreciation for literature more especially poetry."

He seemed to have as much spirit as an adding machine. "The passionless thin lips told of a total lack of sensuality, and the light eyes betrayed a lack of emotional depth," observed one of his secretaries. Once as a young man, Spencer tells in his diary, he met a young lady of exceptional beauty in face and figure. After the meeting his friends asked him what he thought of her. "Any other young fellow," he writes, "would have launched out into unmeasured praise. But my reply was, 'I do not like the shape of her head' — referring, of course, to my phrenological diagnosis." He was fond of making mental measurements of people's skull when he was introduced to them and of using these measurements as a basis for his judgment of their character. As a young man he had been very friendly with Marian Evans. Spencer and Miss Evans were seen constantly together. People waxed romatic about them.

They even expected an engagement. But the only thing that ever came of their "romance" was the following observation about Marian Evans in Spencer's atuobiography: "Usually heads have, here and there, either flat places or slight hollows, but her head was everywhere convex."

He was continually correcting himself in his speech, to attain more accuracy even in his most casual observations. And his speech, like his mind, was utterly devoid of aestheticism. When he took his first trip to America all that he could say about the majesty of a ship sailing over the Atlantic was this entry in his diary: "Terrific disturbance from fog whistle. Getting bored." He couldn't look at a sunset without thinking of the speed of the earth's progress through space. Asked upon his return to England from his American visit to tell what he thought of the people in the New World, he replied that they had left no impression upon him. "I am a bad observer of humanity in the concrete, being too much given to wandering into the abstract." His diary contains constant references to the size and the population of the Americam cities and to the latest improvements in their hotels. He turns every casual observation into a subject for a scienetific essay. Referring, for example, to the American habit of drinking ice water in restaurants, he remarks: "There can be no doubt that the habit is an injurious one....The cold liquid may, by reaction, stimulate the gastric circulation, but by perpetually exciting the blood vessels it inevitably produces.... an abnormal state, resulting in a chronically deficient circulation."

When he reached Niagara Falls – the honeymooners' paradise he felt himself inspired to write the following description of its grandeur:

"The fall is 160 feet high; and it is calculated that it delivers 100,000,000 tons of water per hour, or more than 27,000 tons per second...... This mass of water, as it curls over, is probably some 20 feet thick... At the bottom it is subject to a lateral pressure of, say fifteen pounds to the square inch... hence the rocks on which it falls have to bear the brunt of say, 20,000 tons per second, moving with a velocity of more than 100 feet per second." And so on!

He possessed, he said, but a single emotion — a pride in his unemotionalism. He boasted that until the age of thirty six only one oath had passed his lips — on an occasion when he had caught his fishing hook in his arm.

"He would be a much better fellow," remarked his friend Tyndall, "if he had a good swear now and then."

V

ONE day while Spencer was travelling in a carriage he sat opposite a poor labourer who was busy with his lunch. "His mode of eating was so brutish as to attract my attention and fill me with disgust which verged into anger." But after a time the labourer finished his meal and became quiescent. "Then I was struck by the woebegone expression of his face. Years of suffering were registered on it... And while I gazed on the sad eyes and the deeply marked lines I began to realize the life of misery through which he had passed."

So wrote the old philosopher in his *Autobiography.* At last he had recognized the truth about himself — the truth of the really deep emotions that lay within him. Spencer's friends had been wrong in estimating him. Each one of us is a compound of two personalities — the outer and the inner man. The outer man in Spencer was the compassionate, tender hearted, impartial humanitarian. If his life was not an epic poem, it was at least a thoughtful essay.

And a *tragic* essay. For no man was ever less equipped physically for the mental job at hand. At thirty-five he had begun to experience peculiar sensations in the head and to suffer from chronic insomnia. These symptoms were the prelude to a general nervous breakdown from which he never recovered. A year later his condition had become so pathetic that his physician advised him not to live alone but to take up his residence with other people who might be able to look after him. It was under such handicaps that he prepared the first draft of his *Synthetic Philosophy.* As soon as the outline was finished his friends got busy securing advance subscriptions. Spencer planned to issue the work in quarterly instalments. Six hundred people agreed to underwrite the venture, and the philosopher seemed assured that he would draw a sufficient income to keep his mind at peace.

But when the first issues appeared, with their strong anti-religious doctrines, many of the subscribers withdrew their support. Time after time Spencer was compelled to dip into his small inheritance in order to keep on with his work. At last his funds were exhausted and he was brought to the verge of despair. But somehow his friends managed to get enough subscriptions to keep him going.

And Spencer, his body racked with pain and his mind distracted with worry, kept travelling with his manuscripts from one boarding house to another, a restless nomad. So weakened was he physically that he was able to dictate only a few hours at a time. He resorted to all sorts of methods in order to ward off cerebral congestion. He wrote the opening chapters of *First Principles* in a rowboat at St. Regent's Park. He would row for five minutes and then dictate for fifteen. Thus he relieved the severe pain in his head.

Under these conditions his work advanced at a snail's crawl. And then, as if his other difficulties were not enough, his printers suffered a financial collapse. His friends offered him donations so that he might be able to continue, but he obstinately refused to accept them. He issued an announcement that, owing to unforeseen difficulties, he would be unable to finish his manuscript. Whereupon several of the leading philosophers and scientists — among them John Stuart Mill, his great professional rival – generously and anonymously invested seven thousand dollars in the further publication of his work. His friends pretended that a new batch of subscriptions had come in.

Spencer continued doggedly. He still took constant doses of morphia. His walks were restricted to two or three hundred yards a day when he was at his best. A drive of fifteen minutes in a carriage with India-rubber tyres was his only exercise in the afternoon. Toward the end of his life he was unable to dictate for more than ten minutes at a time. And the sum total of his dictation period for the entire day was fifty minutes. For the rest of the day mental as well as physical excitement was taboo. Reading, even of the lightest kind, was injurious to his eyes. So, too, was the use of his microscope. Social intercourse was strictly prohibited during the last ten years of his life. He was allowed to dine out only twice in that decade. Public amusements were rigorously excluded. His waking hours had become a torture. He did not permit himself to think of any serious subject after his morning's dictation. He lay on the sofa or sat in the open air watching the drifting clouds and waiting for the night. And when the night came it brought him anything but relief. During a "good" night with a strong dose of opium he managed to get three or four hours of broken slumber. And on all nights, good and bad alike, there were long stretches of tossing and waiting for the dawn.

This was the state to which he had brought himself "by forty years of brainwork — a brainwork which would have been by no means too much had I not at the outset overstrained myself." And it was under these circumstances that he wrote some of the most interesting sections of his monumental work. *The Principles of Sociology,* which was the product of this period, is a comprehensive plan for universal peace through the development of industry and international trade.

For the justice in men's heart grows out of the needs of society. The social structure of the human race is the highest expression of life. "Hitherto," writes Spencer, "history has been little more than the Newgate (Prison) calendar of nations." The record of man's story on earth has been a catalogue is inflexible. There has been throughout the ages an evolution from "the belief that individuals exist for the benefit of the state to the belief that the state exists for the benefit of the individuals." There has been an evolution from a Society of the Status Quo to a Society of the Social Contract.

Spencer was distrustful of the state. It should "be limited merely to preventing breaches of equal freedom among its members." He had witnessed the rise of the military state in Prussia and he wanted none of it in his society. The growth of state power, he said, means militarism and imperialism. "Beyond maintaining justice, the state cannot do anything else without transgressing justice." Such views were the liberal expressions of nineteenth century free-trade economy. The "anarchist" thinkers of that day refused to concede that the state can exist for good as well as for evil. In his declaration of individual independence as against state regulation Spencer reminds one of Thoreau. The Englishman had such little faith in government institutions that he carried his manuscripts to the printer himself instead of trusting them to the post office!

He was an uncompromising individualist. It was

impossible to argue with him on any subject at all. As he grew older he developed what may be termed as a hardening of the intellectual arteries. And this was due in no small degree to his shattered nerves. One day he called on a scientist friend at the Athenaeum to obtain information on biological matters. Spencer stated his own theories with regard to the case. But as soon as his friend offered an objection Spencer hastily withdrew his ear pads from his pocket and fastened them over his ears. "My medical advisers will not allow me to enter into discussions with anyone," he snapped. And then he added by way of explanation, "It is on account of my physical collapse."

But a worse fate than mere physical collapse was in store for him. He lived to see the decline of his fame.

VI

HE had formulated his philosophy and achieved renown comparatively early in life. And then he spent long, dreary years defending his doctrines against a tidal wave of hostile attack. The scientific specialists exploded on inaccuracy after another in his voluminous work; the religious leaders assailed his irreligious attitude; the socialists took exception to his doctrines on limiting the power of the state; and the British imperialists launched out against his anti–war stand. Slowly his followers deserted him. And he was left late in life, as he had been early in life, pathetically alone. He was an old curiosity, the butt of the younger generation — a man without a country, without a faith, without a God, an old and bewildered and friendless invalid. Once he had made the vain assertion, "I am never puzzled." But with the sunset coming on he was forced to admit to himself that throughout his career he had merely *formulated* rather than *informed.* Life could not be conceived in physico-chemical terms. It presented a riddle he had failed to grasp.

As he wrote the final pages of his *Autobiography* just before his death, he asked himself: "Had all my subsequent disappointment and the prospect of shattered health been known to me when I embarked upon my career, would it have discouraged me from continuing?" And with a brave hand he answered, "I cannot say yes."

****

Important Works By Spencer

Social statics.
The Development Hypothesis.
Progress, Its Law and Cause.
Synthetic Philosophy, ten Volumes.
First Principles.
Principles of Biology.
Man Verses the State.
Principles of Psychology.
Principles of Sociology.
Principles of Ethics.
The Theory of Population
The Universal Postulate.
Education: Intellectual, Moral, Physical.
Autobiography.

17

FRIEDRICH WILHELM NIETZSCHE

1844 – 1900

HE was named Friedrich Wilhelm, after the Prussian King. Yet he looked upon himself not as a Prussian but as a Pole. For he was a descendant of the Nietsky family — a hardy race of aristocrats, fighters and "supermen" who had come to Germany from the kingdom of John Sobiesky. A family of "Olympian demigods."

But Nietzsche himself was a puny branch of this mighty tree. He had inherited a feeble constitution from his father — neuralgia, weak eyes, dizzy headaches. These dizzy spells had led to the death of his father. One night, as Pastor Nietzsche was walking up the steps to his house, he had suddenly staggered and fallen backwards, striking his head against the stones.

Pastor Nietzsche suffered a paralysis of the brain. Within a year he passed on. Little Friedrich, who had just turned seven, followed the entire tragedy with a terrified fascination. He looked on as they brought the stricken form of his father into the house and laid it on the bed. He saw the slow suffering through the months, the gradual disintegration of the brain, the death, the burial and the grave. All this he observed and remembered.

At the death of their father Friedrich and his little sister Elizabeth were subjected to the sombre influence of four women — their mother, their grandmother and their two aunts. Friedrich grew up with a "sissified" psychology — all the more so because he was unable to take part in sports. Those irritating headaches and those weak eyes! They sapped him of his strength. He was the laughing–stock of his schoolmates, this squint–eyed "little minister" with the diminutive body and the enormous head. Fit to associate only with his sister.

And indeed, outside of his sister's company Nietzsche was almost completely alone. He was afraid of boys. Didn't know how to talk to them. Couldn't use their slang or their "cuss" words. It was either playing with his sister or digging his tousled head into books.

He was always reading some book or other "just like his father before him," as his mother proudly remarked. She wanted him to follow his father's footsteps into the pulpit. He was such an eloquent little fellow and so solemnly impressive with his owlish blue eyes and his bushy brown hair. He would make religion an edifying experience for all the old ladies in his congregation. His face was the very image of the eternal *Weltschmerz — the* World's Sorrow. Why the moment he was born, the bystanders had remarked, his eyes seemed to be filled with the suffering of Christ. He had a great destiny, insisted his mother. Perhaps a *prophet's* destiny.

She sent him to the Pforta Preparatory School. Here he studied poetry and science and Greek and Latin — everything, if fact, but life. His eyes bothered him as usual. He went throughout hours of torture after a session with his books. He threw himself on his bed and lost his will to live. He couldn't bear to keep his eyes open in a bright light. The sun turned him dizzy, made him feel like screaming with pain. Only the night, with its cool shadows, gave him relief. And so he would look forward to the dark, the dormitory without lights, the silence of his bed. The night was his best friend — the night and loneliness.

But he had discovered a hobby to comfort him in his lonely hours. He had developed a passion for music. Whenever he played or heard others play he lost himself in dreams. Indeed, his dream of life had little by little become his real life. He found in his fancies the energy that had been denied him in fact. He relieved the adventures, the ambitions and the battles of his fighting ancestors. In his dreams he knew violence without pain.

But in his waking moments he knew pain without violence. His suffering had become chronic, exhausting, almost unendurable. He composed a piece of music and dedicated it to sorrow.

Yet he was young and he wanted to live. He possessed the curiosity of youth to experience the world — the intellectual and, so far as possible, even the physical curiosity. He left the Pforta School and entered the University of Bonn. He began to drink; he told off-colour jokes; he wrote obscene poetry; occasionally he visited the brothel. He read Byron's *Childe Harold,* the battle cry of selfish individualism, "the Bible of Youth." He even fought a duel. Would he become another Goethe, another Faust? Not he — with that sickly body of his. His breath came short and sharp. His pains increased. His strength had given out. After a few months he left his debauchery, renounced life, wandered into a corner and resumed his solitary seat on the sidelines of the world. And he despised himself.

He transferred from Bonn to the University of Leipzig and plunged into the study of language. He wanted to devote his life to teaching rather than to preaching. For he had begun to doubt the tenets of religion. He had lost faith in a life of faith. He wondered whether one could get along with a strong soul in a weak body. Above everything else he craved for physical strength, for the vigour of youth. He resented the fact that he had been born an old man. He wanted to take a plunge into the invigorating ocean of life and to feel the surf beat against his breast. But his feet refused to move off the shore. He must lie on the beach and allow the sun to pump a little warmth into his sluggish blood. Sexually he had little desire, and this appalled him. Why were the fruits of life denied him? Why was he compelled to renounce the pleasures of the senses? He resented his religion because it encouraged this renunciation. It was a perfect defense mechanism for his weakness. To be sure, the saints had preached that our passions were to be despised.

But wasn't it possible, thought Nietzsche, that these saints had made a virtue out of necessity? Why should anyone be ashamed of his body when it is completely healthy and completely able to perform its functions? Wasn't it true perhaps, that few neurotics had first conceived the doctrine of original sin to justify their own neuroses and that all the subsequent generations of normal men had been following these abnormal thinkers like stupid sheep? Wasn't our so-called morality fraud? Wasn't the aim of life happiness? Wasn't the very act of living meant to be an acceptance of life? What part, then, did religion play in life? As he pursued this idea further his blood ran cold. For he found himself faced with the following deduction: Religion, far from being an *acceptance* of life, is a *denial* of life.

What, then, insures life? *The will* to *live*. If Nietzsche could will strongly enough, he would overcome his headaches, his dizziness, his pain. The will alone can make man free.

Such were the thoughts that came out of the sick man's chamber. Many miles away similar thoughts were being born out of sickness. In America there had arisen sects of people who believed that man can overcome sickness through the will. You merely have to will yourself into health. These were the proponents of mental healing. And at the other end of the world, in India, a group of mystics had transformed the human will into an uncanny magic. They stopped breathing and willed themselves into death. They lay buried for many hours and then they willed themselves back into life. They walked barefoot over hot coals and willed away their pain. This idea of the power of the mind over the ills of the body was not new. The old Christian ascetics in the deserts had endured hunger, flagellations, almost superhuman torture, in their will to become one with God. Had not Christ willed himself to the Cross for the salvation of man? In Germany Arthur Schopenhauer had seized upon this doctrine of the power of the will and had proclaimed it as the dominant principle of life. Plants, animals and men — asserted Schopenhauer — increase their species merely through a blind and irrational will to live. And being a pessimist who saw no good in life, he argued that if man turned this will to life into a will to death — that is, if he *willfully* stopped marrying and reproducing and breathing — there would be an end to all suffering in this world. Man would then be enthroned as a victorious prince in the heavenly kingdom of nothingness.

Nietzsche accepted Schopenhauer's idea of the will, but he transformed it from a negative into a positive philosophy. Man must use his will not to die but to live. It is cowardly to will death as a release from suffering. On the other hand, it is noble to will life in *spite of suffering.* Such a positive assertion of the will raises us above ourselves. Indeed, it transforms man into God.

II

NIETZSCHE had now found a meaning in his own life. He was to live the life triumphant. Yet the spells of renunciation and terror still seized him at intervals. He had not as yet become the God of his own religion. When an epidemic of cholera broke out at Leipzig he ran away and died a thousand deaths. He was obsessed with the premonition of an untimely grave. His father had passed on at an early age. Died of softening of the brain. Nietzsche shuddered. He was a miserable specimen, trying to will. The Prussian government drafted him for military service. He begged for exemption on the ground that he was the son of a widow and her sole means of support. This did him no good; he was inducted into the cavalry. After a few months of training he fell from his horse and wrenched a muscle in his breast. He breathed a sigh of relief. Again he was able to avoid the danger of an active life in the passive shelter of a disabled body. He lay on his bed and rested from his injury and thought about the relentlessness of the human will.

Discharged from the army, he returned to his academic life. His brilliance as a linguist had reached the ears of the faculty at the University of Basle. They offered him the chair of classical philosophy though he was scarcely twenty-five. He accepted the position and found contentment for a while in the quiet atmosphere of the university. But then his perennial self-inquisition began once more to trouble him. What about that will power which he was so eager to assert? And where could he find a field in which to assert it? Surely not in the province of Latin prepositions and Greek verbs!

And so he began once more to fashion his adventurous dreams as he sat quietly in the classroom lecturing to his students. But suddenly he awoke out of his academic dream life. Titanic events were stirring in his country. Germany and France had gone to war.

He saw a troop of Prussian cavalry marching to the front. At that moment, he tells us, his entire philosophy took shape. "I felt for the first time that the strongest and highest Will to Life does not find expression in a miserable struggle for existence but in a Will to War, a Will to Power, a Will to Overpower!"

But Nietzsche was a poet as well as a philosopher. Owing to his poor eyesight he was excused from active service in the war. His duties were confined to the nursing of the wounded soldiers. His harsh philosophy of the will to overpower *man* was now transformed into the gentle poetry of the will to overpower *misery*. For months he lived, like Walt Whitman, among dying men. He saw the blood, he smelt the perspiration, he sat in water–soaked cattle vans packed with soldiers who were suffering from gangrene. And his heart was filled with disgust — disgust and pity. What was the meaning of all these scenes? Where was the "eternal glory" of existence as preached by the prophets and the persons? Was it not rather eternal suffering?

When the war was over and he had been through a siege of diphtheria he went to the mountains and in the cool clear air gave further thought to these problems. He came to the conclusion that somehow all this suffering of the world must be justified. Man, in spite of everything, is an invincible optimist. And why? Because misery perchance is a worthy and even holy experience.

Yes, man through his own strength of will overcomes his baser inclination to renounce life; he rises to affirm it. The greatest poets humns of joy to their existence.

So thought Nietzsche. All about him there was tragedy. And yet from tragedy we draw not spiritual suffering but spiritual rejoicing. Who were the greatest writers of tragedy in history? Why, the Greeks. The recurrent theme of the tragedies of Sophocles and of Aeschylus is the punishment meted out to mortals by the immortal gods. Man is the play thing of the gods. He is the victim of their cruel sport. Yet the hero of the Greek tragedies, in spite of all his buffetings, refuses to bow his head. In the face of the unhappy lot of mankind he wills with all his power to be man and to remain man. He will not change places with the gods, not he! He will not surrender his mortal misery for the immortal bliss of the Olympians. He is far too proud of his ability to defy the gods. Prometheus steals the secret of fire from heaven and brings it down to his fellow men. This is the first attempt of the human will to assert itself.

For fire, observes Nietzsche, is the light of freedom. The myth of Prometheus is a parable that symbolizes the birth of civilization. When man ceased to look upon the forces of nature with superstitious awe and commenced to take his destiny out of the "lap" of the gods into his own mortal hands, when he started systematically to subdue the forces of his environment to his own advantage instead of praying blindly for a miracle, when he asserted his own will to live instead of relying upon the will of the gods to let him live then began the greatest rebellion in the history of the world.

The pages of Greek tragedy and mythology are filled with examples of the nobility of the human will. Man suffers because he wills to be free. He is struck down because he dares to proclaim his rights against the interests of the gods who would keep him enslaved. Such was the fate of Prometheus who was chained to a rock and tormented by the elements. And such, too, was the fate of Adam and Eve who were driven from the Garden of Eden. The Lord, observes Nietzsche, cannot tolerate the rebel.

Yet the greatest rebels have been the supreme liberators of men. And Nietzsche prefers the pagan to the Christian attitude towards rebellion. For while the Christians renounced the transgression of Adam, the pagans have *justified* the transgression of Prometheus. The Christians are weak, the Greeks strong. The Bible, maintains Nietzsche, is a document of enslavement; the Greek mythology a hymn to independence. Only by asserting his will against the alien domination of heaven can man in his own right be free.

And only by suffering the tragic consequences of such an assention can man grow in the strength and worthiness of his freedom. For tragedy forges the will into a mighty instrument of power. Stupid and short-sighted ate those who desire anything but the test of tragedy and suffering and sorrow. Away with the "appeasers" who would sell their humanity for a life complacent, will–less resignation!

So reasoned Nietzsche, the pagan son of the Christian priest.

III

HE grew a heavy drooping mustache to conceal the sensitive corners of his mouth. For he wanted to present himself to the world with a sneer. His eyes were sunken and half blind. The sublimely disregarded persons and objects at close range and looked only into the vast spaces on the infinite. He spoke gruffly to hide the real warmth of his voice. He hid himself away from most people because he was afraid of them. But one man fascinated him. That man was Richard Wagner. He too was a Prometheus who had dared to steal the fire of God and to transform it into the music of Man.

But with the exception of Wagner, Nietzsche had practically no other friends. He lived alone with his strange philosophy about the splendour of darkness and the happiness of pain. A doctor alarmed at his frequent headaches, was tactless enough to warn him against a gradual paralysis of the brain. Nietzsche was terrified. He adopted a vegetarian diet in the hope of regaining his health. He succeeded merely in losing his strength. He became convinced that he was dying of cancer. He fled from one sanatorium to another and finally returned home in despair. He had not been able to flee from himself. And then, as he entered upon his thirty-fifth year he prepared to die. Had not *his* father died in his thirty-fifth year? Had he not died of paralysis of the brain accompanied by frequent frightful headaches? Nietzsche recalled the tragedy with superstitious horror. The tides of fate were regular in their ebb and flow. They recurred eternally. They had swept his father away. And they would sweep him away also. He shivered. He wrote grimly in his notes, "My hour may come upon me at any moment..."

His thirty-fifth year passed and still he lived. During that terrible year he had suffered more than a hundred attacks of pain. He resigned his professorship and went to Marienbad for the climate. But the southern sun sent the fever to his head. He could stand it no longer. He shut himself up in an attic. Still did not die.

And with coming of the next year the pains in his head had stopped. He was once more able to think of life. He tramped through the mountains and looked long at the Mediterranean waters. They were blue, defiantly blue. And all around was the dignity of massive cliffs aspiring upwards. And the heavens were silent. They were empty, infinite heavens. They were waiting for Man to ascend them, to take his place as Lord and Master over his rightful domain. There was nothing to bar his way but his own stupidity, his own fear. In an evil moment Man had invented a myth called God. And ever thereafter he had been chained to the story of his own creation. There was only one real divinity — Man. If only Man would have the courage to be himself and then — to surpass himself. That was it — Man must strive to become Superman!

Nietzsche came down from the mountains and went to Rome. Here his contemplative life was interrupted by a stormy incident. He was introduced to a young girl from Finland, Lou von Salome, and fell in love with her. She was handsome, ardent, desirable. She seemed an ideal companion. Nietzsche asked for her hand. But the young lady refused. She respected him for his mind, but she was afraid of being cut by its keen edge. Moreover, he was practically an invalid — no fit mate for a healthy -bodied woman of the North.

Nietzsche was undaunted. He had completely misunderstood her refusal. He believed that she had objected to her marriage because it would interfere with her plans for a career. But surely, he pleaded, she would not refuse an offer to free love. After all, was she not a disciple of his? And had not their mutual friend, Richard Wagner, entered into a free-love arrangement with Cosima?

But again she rebuffed him. Hurt and humiliated, Nietzshe returned to his books. And then the news reached him that the young lady had accepted a similar proposal from another man — not a philosopher.

For once in his life Nietzsche turned cynical. (Cynicism, someone has observed, is the weapon of the wounded). "After all," he said "I didn't create either the world or Lou von Salome. If I had done so, both would have been more perfect."

His unfortunate love affair directed him into another channel of speculation — the question of morality, of good and evil. All our ideas about good and evil, he concluded, come not from God, for there is no God, nor from a higher moral law, since there is no such higher law. These ideas have developed through the evolution of the human mind. The term "good" was originally not an ethical qualification but social and political distinction. The "good" men were the ruling classes. They were the warriors, the aristocrats in every society. *Good* meant *brave, athletic, strong.* The prestige of the aristocracy was founded on its strength. The strong men imposed their own values upon society and drew up their own moral code which happened to fit their own characteristics. The "bad" men in this society were the people who occupied the inferior positions owing to their physical inferiority. A good man was a fighter and a master; a bad man was an underling and a slave.

But as time went on, argued Nietzsche, a very unfortunate development took place in the history of morality. The concepts "good" and "bad" slowly lost their original meaning. For a new class of men had slowly risen to the top. The leaders of the class were not the fighters, or the "strong" men, they were the priests or the "weak" men. These men relied upon their mental rather than upon their physical vigour. In their struggle against their former warrior masters they imposed a new code of conduct upon the society they wished to dominate. Lacking the powers of the body, they invented the so-called virtues of the "soul." They created a system of ethics to cover their own infirmities. Unable to conquer, by the sword, they ruled by "piety and prayer." They proclaimed the "rights" of underdog, the dignity of the timid and the glory of the weak — all this to shackle the natural instincts of the strong and to perpetuate their own impotent rule. And they founded a religious propaganda that exalted their own impotency. "The wretched," they said, "are alone the good, the poor, the weak, the lowly are alone the good; the suffering, the needy, the sick, the loathsome are alone the pious and the blessed; for them alone is salvation. But you, on the other hand, you aristocrats, you men of power, you are to all eternity the evil, the horrible, the covetous, the insatiate, the godless; eternally also shall you be unblessed, the cursed, the damned!"

In such a way "did the fox replace the eagle," in such a manner was the code of morality "subverted." It was an act of clever revenge on the part of the cowardly against the courageous. The masters were banished from the kingdom of heaven. The morality of the vulgar man had triumphed. And what is the emergency of this slave morality called *The rise of Christianity.* "It is the most pious fraud in history," alleges Nietzsche. Strength is made a devil, weakness a god. The old doctrine of virility is transformed into the new doctrine of debility. "Christianity is the subterfuge of the slave."

Such is the teaching of Nietzsche, the suffering philosopher. All the talk about "good and bad conscience" that has crept into "civilized" society is sheer balderdash. Actually no one who is strong and free feels a sense of shame for any of his deeds. Do the great birds of prey feel ashamed because they seize upon the helpless sheep? Should we demand of strength not to express itself as strength? The strong has no more the option of being weak than the weak has the option of being strong.

In the happy days, said Nietzsche, when the "blond beast" that lies at the core of all aristocrats had not as yet been chloroformed by "civilization," the strong had exercised their rightful power over the weak. The warriors had roamed at will, venting their natural instincts upon their helpless fellows. They had felt no compunction over their cruelty. They had ruled by terror. They had inflicted punishment without regard for any so-called "higher law."

But as man lost his nomadic habits and settled down in villages, as he formed communities for self–protection, as he developed a social consciousness and a feeling of interdependence, he found himself in a peculiar pligt. Adapted though he was by nature to the savage life of war and prowling, his instincts were suddenly "switched off" and rendered worthless. "I do not believe there was ever in the world such a feeling of misery, such a laden discomfort. Man's ancient instincts had not ceased their demands. Only now it was difficult and rarely possible to gratify them. He was compelled to satisfy himself by new and, as it were, hole-in-the-corner methods. All instincts which do not find an outlet, *turn inwards.* Hatred, cruelty, the delight in persecution — all these emotions had now become instruments which man, that creature of perversion, had turned *upon himself.* And this, asserts Nietzsche, is the origin of what we call a "bad conscience." Imprisoned as he had now become in the oppressive narrowness and monotony of custom, and impatient at his monotonous restraint, man "lacerated, persecuted, gnawed, frightened and ill-treated himself.... He beat himself against the bars of his cage... He created out of his own self a torture chamber.... from which the world has not as yet recovered." What a spectacle, man suffering from the disease called man! A will for self–torture, an ingrowing cruelty! After the natural outlet for the will to hurt others had become blocked up he resorted to hurting himself. He turned martyr. He used as a supreme instrument of torture the conception that he "owed" something to a higher deity. He placed himself between the horns of the dilemma — *God and devil.* He invented a heaven and a hell. And finally this tormented creature found "his supreme expression of self-abasement in that made stroke of genius called Christianity." What a paradox — "God personally destroying himself for the debt of man, God paying himself personally out of a pound of his own flesh — the creditor playing the scapegoat out of a sense of love (would you believe it?) out of a sense of love toward his debtor!"

Too long has the world been a madhouse, said Friedrich Nietzsche.

IV

THESE doctrines of Nietzsche came like staggering blow to the few friends that he had. They looked with horror at the shy, drooping little man who had poured such volcanic fire from his lips. From that day on they left him severely alone. He had committed the unpardonable sin, not of being antisocial in practice — that could be tolerated — but of being antisocial in theory. Too tender in his actual life to tread upon an insect, he was ready to annihilate heaven itself — in his books. Everybody was frightened at this dual personality. Wagner went so far as to call him insane. Nietzsche repaid the compliment. The two men had been taking one of their walks. Wagner had talked about his new religious opera, Parsifal, and he had remarked that he was becoming interested in the church services, that his formerly "atheistic" thoughts were now tending more and more toward God and Christianity. Nietzsche looked at him without a word and never visited him again.

The trouble with world, thought Nietzsche, was that it

contained too many Christians and not enough savages. And since nobody agreed with him in this thought he was "content to dwell in majestic solitude like that other great lonely hero, Achilles." From time to time he went into the mountains. He fancied himself as an ancient Nordic god destined to live among the thunderclouds and to overwhelm the world with the lightning flashes of his philosophy.

But he was a *pitiable* god. His health was as bad as ever. Many a night he took an overdose of chloral in the hope that he would not awake again. But when morning arrived he was still alive — a fatality doomed to self-torture, the very exemplification of the masochist he so lustily despised in his writings. And as he looked down upon the earth from the Alpine heights he made a vow: "Ye lonely ones of today, ye who stand apart, ye shall one day be a people; from you who have chosen yourselves a chosen people shall arise; and from it, the superman." Slowly, the vision arose in mighty dimensions before his weak and dazzled eyes. The superman! Yes, he was the prophet of a new religion. He had chosen himself to "sing a new song."

V

NIETZSCHE sang this song through the lips of the Persian prophet, Zarathustra — a prose poem of inspiration, splendour and confusion. It was a stately and terrible testament of hate.

Behold, Zarathustra descends from the mountains and advances to the gates of the city. He comes with a mighty and portentous message on his lips. In the forest he has met a hermit mumbling his prayers. He has seen the priests offering their sacrifices. And now as he enters the city he sees the business folk and the mother and the sons bending their knee and soliciting the protection of the Lord. "Can it be possible that they have not as yet heard of it, that God is dead? He, the prophet Zarathustra, has buried the ancient myth. The new Era had dawned. "Dead are all the gods; now do we desire the Superman to live." All created things have hitherto surpassed themselves. The tide of life rises ever higher and higher. Are you, then, content to be the ebb of that great tide? Would you rather go back to the beast than go forward to surpass man? For man is to be surpassed. "I say unto you, what is the ape to man? A laughing stock, a thing of shame. And so too shall man be to Superman: a laughing stock, thing of shame."

Only take heart, my fellow men. Cast off the rusty virtues that have enchained the human race. Say "Ego" over and over again. And be proud of it! I command you not only to *say "Ego"* but to do "Ego". For behind your thoughts and your feelings, my brothers, there is an almighty god – and his name is *self.* He dwells within your body. He *is* your body. He cries unto you continually, "Seek for pleasure!" He cries unto you continually. "Since humanity came into being, man has enjoyed too little: this alone, my brethren, is our original sin." I say unto you, "Too modest even is the thief in the presence of sheep: he always stealeth softly through the night. Immodest, however, is the night watchman; immodestly he carrieth his horn." I say unto you, "Blood is the spirit of man. Of all that is written, I love only what a man hath written with his blood." I say unto you, "Be not ashamed of the hatred and the envy within your hearts. It is glorious to hate and to be envious." You ask me, "Is it the good cause which halloweth even war?" and answer unto you, "It is the good war which halloweth every cause."

Remember, my brothers, men are not equal. So speaketh eternal justice. Be strong. Be unafraid. I command you to laugh at what little men call sin. You who proclaim the Ego as something holy and divine shall openly avow that selfishness, voluptuousness and passion for power are the true virtues of manhood.

Lo, I walk among men as the fragments of the future. I see beyond the great noontide of our life. I hear the voice of a new and greater and more individualistic race of men — *the voice of their will to power!*

Thus spake Zarathustra. Nietzsche offered this book to the world, and the world refused it. He printed forty copies at his own expense and was compelled to give them away. He had hurled a thunderbolt across the landscape of humanity, and he himself recoiled at the force. The old headaches gripped him. Pain blinded the eyes that had dared to look too far.

VI

"THERE is no one among the living or the dead with whom I feel the slightest affinity," he often told himself. And this became literally so when his old sister, a woman who had nursed him and comforted him throughout his life left to get married. Her husband was anti-Semitic, and Nietzsche, the philosopher with the malevolent pen and the gentle heart would have nothing to do with him. For Nietzsche's hates were never personal. He felt bitter neither against Jew nor Gentile. He was at war not with persons but with an impersonal force. He had entered upon a crusade, he said, against civilization itself, and he was determined to overthrow it single-handed.

And so he travelled from Switzerland to Venice, from Genoa to Nice, from Turin to Marienbad, always restless, always seeking peace through war. His eyesight had become so impaired that he could write nothing but short aphorisms. But this, he thought was divine omen. Had not the ancient oracles spoken their wisdom briefly? It was well that he was finished with writing books. After all, his works were not philosophy; they were revelation. Was he not the prophet of a new religion, the religion of the Antichrist? He had set in motion, he declared, the greatest revolution in history. Someday after his death history would no longer be divided into B.C. and A.D. — the era before Christ and the era after Christ; men would speak of B.N. and A.N.– the dark centuries before Nietzsche and the enlightened centuries after Nietzsche. Jesus would be entirely forgotten now that the German philosopher had supplanted him. The blond beast would rise again in the future as he had risen in the past. All things return in precisely the same manner in the tides of time. Eternal recurrence. Let the nations of the world beware! Let the democracies of Europe tremble! "Within fifty years these Babel governments will clash in a gigantic war for the markets of the world..." Then the world shall see a more terrible, more systematic flaring up of the old conflagration. "The beasts of prey, the race of conquerors and masters, shall rise again from the ashes of men — they shall rise in a mightier, more deadly form." "Those who cannot bear my philosophy are doomed, and those who regard it as the greatest blessing are destined to be the masters of the world."

And he, Friedrich Nietzsche the satyr, would he not be worshipped as a saint?

VII

As Nietzsche approached the high noon of his life he longed for the evening. The sun within him, that blazing eye of his analytical reason, was burning itself out in an excess of its own brilliance. "I am not a man," he whispered; "I am dynamite."

Slowly his mind gave way. The light was yielding to the shadows. On January 3, 1889, at the age of forty-five, he suffered a mental stroke. He sat at the piano and ploughed through the keyboard in a mad ecstasy of music. His cheeks were flushed.

"Tis night; now do all the gushing fountains speak louder...." 'Tis night, now only do all the songs of the lovers awake."

His senses for the first time were atingle. "I am Dionysus," he shouted: "I am the God of Joy!" At last he had reached the supreme moment of physical affirmation — now that his mind was dead.

It was the only possible ending to this great Greek tragedy. The man had dared to rise up against the gods, and for his wilfulness the gods has struck him mad. For ten years he lingered in an asylum before his body joined his mind in death. Among his papers they found a note in his handwriting. It was signed — "The Crucified."

****

Important Works By Nietzsche

The Birth of Tragedy.	*The Joyful Wisdom.*
Human All, Too Human.	*Thus Spake Zarathustra.*
The Dawn of Day	*Beyond Good and Evil.*
The Genealogy of Morals.	*The Will to Power (un-finished.)*
The Twilight of the Idols.	
Schopenhauer as Educator.	*Antichrist.*
Richard Wagner in Bayreuth	*Ecce Homo (Autobiography.)*

✦✧✦

18

WILLIAM JAMES

1842 – 1910

HIS Grandfather, an Irish immigrant, was a practical man of the world. His father, an intimate of Emerson, was a free-thinking mystic. Take the practicality of the grandfather and the mysticism of the father, add to them a pinch of Irish humour and generous dose of American forthrightness, and you have the combination that was the personality of William James.

He was born (January 9, 1842) at the Astor House in New York City, and he lived in or near big cities for the greater part of his life. His attitude towards the world, therefore was coloured by his conception of the earth as a "parcel of nature crowded with company."

He loved company from his earliest childhood. And in spite of the easy circumstance of his family he was not snobbish in his attitude toward his companions. To a youngster who boasted about the exclusiveness of his playmates, he declared, "I play with boys who curse and swear!"

He was an active youngster — in sharp contrast with his brother Henry, who was a quiet and contemplative little fellow. Since both of them showed an early aptitude for literature the friends of the family predicted that William would take up fiction as his field and that Henry would choose philosophy. It turned out just the other way around. To some extent, however, the prophets were correct. William James developed into a philosopher who wrote like a novelist, and Henry James developed into a novelist who wrote like a philosopher.

As to their early preparation for their respective careers, both William and Henry regarded it as a waste of time. In their effort to provide their children with best education available their parents took them to Europe and enrolled them in one school after another-in London, Paris, Boulogne-sur-Mer, Geneva, Bonn. Always they sought for "the one perfect channel of truth" in which to bathe the precocious minds of the two youngsters. The result of this eclectic education was that the boys learned "a little of everything and not much of anything."

They did, however, acquire a facility in language which enabled them to devour all sorts of books on every conceivable subject. Thus their minds were trained to resemble long-distance swimmers rather than skilful divers. They were able to cover wide horizons of experience though they were incapable of plunging into the depths of the world's mysteries.

The mind of William James especially was ever restless, ever eager for adventure, ever curious for the new landscape before it had become thoroughly familiar with the old. His interests were so manifold that he found it difficult to make a final choice among them. And so he sampled every intellectual and artistic dish that was offered to his healthy appetite, dabbling in biology, anatomy, philosophy, chemistry, physics, natural history and even painting. And in spite of his intellectual pursuits — or rather because of his intellectual curiosity —he managed always to find plenty of time for his social activities. In 1860 he joined the Swiss student's club, Societe de Zoffingue, where he showed an active interest in his debates and a somewhat more passive though no less fascinated interest in its debaucheries. In the social parlance of the day, William James was "a hail-fellow-well-met" young specimen of the dynamic nineteenth century.

His dynamic versatility, however, must somehow be co-ordinated into a unified profession. It wasn't in his nature to drift aimlessly through life. He must now choose definitely between art and science. He chose science, entering the Lawrence Scientific School. (Harvard University) in 1861.

But he had given up his brush only to become a painter with the pen. For few writers in the history of philosophy have been blessed with a more colourful style.

II

THOUGH he had decided upon a scientific career, William James was still uncertain as to the particular branch of science that he wanted to adopt as his life's work. For a time he thought of chemistry. But then his interest shifted to medicine. He entered the Harvard

Medical School, took his degree and then quit medicine for natural history. He joined the Brazilian expedition of Professor Louis Agassiz, a man whom he admired more than any other of his teachers. "Since Benjamin Franklin," he wrote many years later, "we had never had among us a person of more popularly impressive type."

Together with Agassiz he studied the fishes of the Amazon. And under the influence of Agassiz he learned to regard the objects of natural history as the "translation into human language of the thoughts of the Creator." The philosophic scientist of Harvard had transformed the young naturalist into a scientific philosopher.

When he returned to the United States William James had a pretty clear idea as to the future course of his life. He would write and, if possible, teach philosophy. He attended a philosophical lecture by Charles S. Peirce, a man who was trying to introduce a new system of thought called *pragmatism*. "I couldn't understand a word of the lecture," said James, "but I left that it had a definite message for me." He was to spend the rest of his life in the effort to understand and to interpret this "definite message" of Pragmatism.

Before he entered upon this work, however, he underwent a physical breakdown and a siege of mental depression. For a time he thought of committing suicide. "No man," he said in later life, 'is psychologically complete unless he has at least once in his life meditated on self — destruction.' He took a trip to Europe for his physical and his mental health and within a few months was so completely recovered that he was able to "flirt in Bohemian" with his landlady's daughter. He had brought along with him his American democracy– or was it his Irish sense of humour? – for he accepted a "social" invitation to dine with an innkeeper's family. The talk, he said, was salty enough but the soup tasted like the "perspiration of pigs."

On his return to America he was appointed instructor of physiology at Harvard College. From physiology he moved to psychology and from psychology to philosophy. These successive steps from one academic department to another were quite in keeping with the steps of his own mental development. For his intellectual progress was not "from the sky down, but from the ground up." Like Socrates, he was more interested in the problems of men than he was in the Providence of God. Not that he was sceptical about God. On the contrary, he found himself "less and less able," as he wrote to his friend Thomas Davidson, "to get along without Him." His main preoccupation, however, was with the Here rather than with the Hereafter. His philosophy grew out of his own needs. He had suffered a serious illness and he had "pulled himself back" into health. Man's salvation depended upon his own will. In the course of his reading during his sickness he had come upon the Essais of Renouvier, and he had been struck with the French thinker's definition of free Will – "the sustaining of a thought because one *actively chooses* to sustain it when he might have other thoughts." William James had chosen to sustain the thought of becoming well. He had willed himself out of sickness. "From now on I will abstain from speculation and depend upon action." For action is the human will transformed into life.

This was but a continuation of Emerson's philosophy of optimism. But James added something to it. Or rather he modified it. He transformed the somewhat impractical idea of optimism, the theory that all's well with the world, into the more practical idea of *meliorism,* the theory that all's *not* well with the world but that we can make things better if we will. It was an excellent philosophy for America at that period (1872), for the country had just entered upon its Golden Era of Expansion. It was the industrial age of Rockefeller, Carnegie Gould, Harriman, Drew, Cook J.P. Morgan. William James was one of those fortunate children of destiny — the right man born into the right time. He came as the prophet of the Free Will to a free nation.

Thus far, however, his philosophy was still in its seedling stage. He had no opportunity to develop it further at this time because he was asked to write a text-book on psychology for Henry Holt's American Science Series. He expected to produce the book within two years. It was twelve years before the manuscript was finished.

In the meantime he met, wooed and married Miss Alice Gibbens. Legend has it that his father, Henry James the elder, had first seen her at the Radical Club in Boston and had exclaimed upon his return home, "William, I have just met the woman you're going to marry!" Whereupon the young philosopher, resenting his father's interference in his private affairs, replied "I shall refuse to see that woman." "I don't care whether or not you *see* her," retorted his father. "All I want you to do is to *marry* her."

In spite of his rebellious rejoinder to his father's suggestion James did manage to see Miss Gibbens. And he fell a willing prey to "the great dark luminous eyes, soft brown hair, wildrose complexion... and especially the smile which lit up her face and seemed to light up the world."

His marriage worked a miracle in his health – and in his habits. "She saved me from my *Zerrissenheit* (torn-to-pieces-ness) and gave me back to myself all in one piece." He had now found his mate and his métier. He settled down in Cambridge and devoted himself for the rest of his life to the cultivation of his philosophy.

III

His first book, *The Principles of Psychology,* marks the formal transition from William James the scientist to William James the philosopher. For this book is more valuable as a masterpiece of literary abstractions than as a repository of concrete facts. James cared very little for the objective phenomena of the mind, but he cared very much for the subjective personality to whom the mind belonged. His psychology, therefore, is a study of persons and not a data. Human thought, to William James, was not a mechanically connected series of separate ideas – a doctrine of the European psychologists – but a continuously flowing stream of consciousness analogous to the blood stream that flows continuously through the body.

Furthermore, said James, the study of human

consciousness must be subordinated to the study of human conduct. Psychology is a preface to Morality. "The physiological study of mental condition is... the most powerful ally of hortatory ethics."

The mind, in brief, is not a material but a spiritual instrument. It is not a recorder but a prompter of our ideas. it is our teacher and guide toward a freer, juster and better world.

And this brings James back to his philosophy of *betterment or meliorism.* Let us at the outset, he said, admit the fact that the world is full of evil. But precisely because of this fact we find our life worthwhile. For the presence of evil has given us our most precious possession — hope. Hope is that moral activity which prompts us to challenge and to conquer evil. It gives us the courage "to take life strivingly." The philosophers who declare that the world is growing better *regardless* of our will are equally wrong with those who maintain that the world will remain bad *in spite* of our will. We alone can improve the world, and we can do it *because* of our will.

For this world is not a finished unit but "an aggregation of separate and contradictory elements." And here we come to the second point in James's philosophy — his *pluralism.* The world is not a *uni-verse* but a multi - -verse— a conflict of currents, some good, some evil. We must all of us try to conquer the evil and to establish the good. Is success certain? No. Is it possible? Decidedly yes. But if success is only possible at best, what is the good of striving? To this question James gives an answer which is not unlike that of the ancient Stoics. The mere chance of succeeding ennobles the struggle and makes it worthwhile. 'Suppose," writes James, "that the world's author put the case to you before creation, saying. 'I am going to make a world not certain to be saved, a world the perfection of which shall be conditioned merely, the condition being that each several agent does its own *level* best. I offer you the chance of taking part in such a world. Its safety, you see, is unwarranted. It is a real adventure, with real danger, yet it may win through... Will you join the procession? Will you trust yourself and trust the other agents enough to face the risk?'

"Should, you in all seriousness... feel bound to reject the offer as not safe enough?... If you are normally constituted, you would do nothing of the sort. There is a healthy-minded buoyancy in most of us which such a universe would exactly fit... It would be just like the world we practically live in, and loyalty to our old nurse Nature would forbid us to say no."

This is the old Stoic doctrine plus the modern American spirit. It is joy to fight the good fight even though the outcome may be in doubt. And after all, though the issue may be uncertain for the individual, it is pretty certain to be victorious for the race. For we have an efficient ally on our side — God. In the pluralistic philosophy of James, God is not supreme. He is merely one among many divine forces, "one helper... in the midst of all the shapers of the great world's fate." But he is *"primus inter pares,"* first among equals. He is our teacher, our leader, our friend in the glorious struggle for a better world.

Let us then, with God's help, struggle gallantly on. Let us shape the world to our needs. Let us, in other words, live a *practical life.* And this is the third and cardinal point in James's philosophy – his *pragmatism.* The world we live in is not a theory, but a fact. Indeed, it is a conglomeration of many facts. There is no such thing as *the* truth. What we call a truth is merely a working hypothesis, a temporary tool that enables us to transform a bit of chaos into a bit of order. What was true yesterday – that is, what was *helpful* yesterday– may not be true today. Old truths, like old weapons, tend to grow rusty and to become useless.

It is therefore impractical to try to reduce the universe to an "absolutely single fact." Truth is relative. Everything depends upon our individual point of view, and none of us has right to say that *his* point of view is the only correct one. "Neither the whole of truth nor the whole of good is revealed to any single observer, although each observer gains a partial superiority of insight from the peculiar position in which he stands." And that superiority insight which every individual has gained for himself is his own best tool in the struggle for the betterment of the world. Each man's faith, each man's church, each man's God is for him true if it enables him to cope with his legitimate daily problems.

That alone, therefore, is true which is expedient in practice. An idea is good only if it has a "cash value." Let us not, however, confuse the "cash value" pragmatism of William James with the crass materialism of our modern business life. The coinage of James's philosophical capital was not financial but moral. He looked down upon the mad scramble of his contemporaries for the accumulation of mere wealth. He scolded his fellow Americans for their worship of "that bitch goddess, success." His pragmatism was an ethical and therefore a practical urge to co-operation among the free members of a democratic society. The meaning of life, he believes, lies not in an isolated struggle as between man and man but in a united struggle of mankind against the forces of evil.

Pragmatism, said James, has no use for abstractions. It deals only with "concrete realities." It is not, strictly speaking, a system of philosophy. It is rather a "method for getting at the practical consequences" of all the philosophical systems. To quote the Italian philosopher Papini, James's pragmatism is "a collection of attitudes, and its chief characteristic is its armed neutrality in the midst of doctrines. It is like a corridor in a hotel, from which a hundred doors open into a hundred chambers. In one you may see a man on his knees praying to regain his faith; in another, a desk at which sits someone eager to destroy all metaphysics; in a third, a laboratory with an investigator looking for new footholds by which to advance towards wider horizons. But the corridor belongs to all."

IV

The corridor belongs to all. This is the very heart of James's philosophy. It was not his purpose to set himself up as the founder of a new school but as a guide for the practical interpretation of the old schools. He didn't want to be a master, and he asked for no disciples. Again and again he quoted to his students the passage from Ezekiel "Son of Man, stand upon thy feet and I will speak to thee." Let each man live upon his own spiritual capital. Let each one abide by his own truth. All that James was interested in doing was to stimulate man's mind, to release man's will and to encourage man's action. Above all, he wanted to widen man's interests. For he himself was a man of wide interests. His own stream of consciousness embraced a large part of the general stream of life. He raised his voice against the unjust oppression of Dreyfus; he advocated a more equitable distribution of wealth; he threw himself actively into every sort of movement for human welfare: and he was foremost in urging a moral equivalent for war — that is, a concerted effort to abolish disease, to drain marshes, to irrigate canals and to reclaim wastelands instead of an organized fight to kill men. In short, he wanted to open to others, as he had opened to himself, "the entire universe as an adventure." And he made the universe a familiar landscape, illuminating it to his students with the sudden flash of understanding, the happy phrase, the Socratic jest. "This universe," he said in one of his lectures, "will never be completely good as long as one being is unhappy; as long as one poor cockroach suffers the pangs of unrequited love."

He always tried to make his ideas picturesque, concrete, alive. He classified them in such a manner that his hearers might tuck them away in their minds like the neatly folded articles of clothing in a wardrobe, to be taken out for use at a moment's notice without any confusion or fumbling. For example, in describing the attitude of various types of people toward the world he divided them into the *tough-minded* and the *tender-minded.* The tough-minded, he said, are the hardheaded businessmen, the builders, the political leaders, the realists, the men who act. The tender-mined on the other hand, are the softhearted visionaries, the dreamers, the poets, the artists, the idealists, the men who think. James himself was an example of neither one of these extreme types. Instead he was an admirable synthesis of the two. He was *healthy-minded.*

He had a healthy mind but not in a healthy body. Throughout his adult life he suffered from a weak heart. During one of his summer vacations he lost his way in the Adirondacks. He overexerted himself in his effort to find the road, and when he finally arrived home he collapsed.

Although he recovered from his illness, he was never himself again. In 1907 he resigned from the Harvard faculty owing to his poor health. He lived just long enough to make a tour of Europe. He meant this to be a quiet and undisturbed health trip, but it turned out to be an exciting procession of triumph. Everywhere they followed the "great professor Weelyam Yams" with acclamation, and everywhere they insisted upon his public appearance.

The ordeal proved too much for his weakened heart. When he boarded the boat to return to America (in the summer of 1910) everybody knew that his days were numbered.

As he neared the end of his journey he sank back into his steamer chair and whispered, "It is so good to get home!"

****

Important Works By William James

The Principles of Psychology.

The Will to Believe and Other Essays in Popular Philosophy.

Human Immortality.

Talks to Teachers on Psychology and to Students on Some of Life's Ideals.

The Varieties of Religious Experience.

Pragmatism: A New Name for Old Ways of Thinking

A Pluralistic Universe.

The Meaning of Truth.

Essays in Radical Empiricism.

Some Problems in Philosophy.

Letters (edited by his son Henry James)

19

Henri Bergson

1859 – 1941

IN 1914 the armies of Europe were on the march. It seemed as if humanity had lost its soul. "Can anyone believe in progress and civilization in the face of what is going on?" people asked themselves.

At the College de France a soft-spoken professor with penetrating eyes gave answer. The very calmness with which he replied made one feel as if he were in the presence of a vision. "You are weary now," he said, "and bereft of hope. Never fear. Once I, too, was weary. But then in a flash I saw the meaning of destiny..."

II

HENRI BERGSON'S intellectual life was an evolution. He started out with a firm foundation in the physical sciences. He had a genius for mathematics. But he was an artist too. He possessed a fine feeling for language, a warm sympathy for the picturesque phrase. Indeed, he was a man with a dual tendency — a rigorous meticulousness and an exuberant imagination. He specialized in natural history and in Hellenic literature.

His was the soul of a poet in the mind of a scientist. And in the final struggle the scientist was compelled to yield to the poet.

Born in Paris in 1859, he entered the Ecole Normale Superieure at the age of seventeen. His inclinations were at this time "ruthlessly materialistic." He saw all life in terms of growth and decay. Like Spencer, he was convinced that societies and moralities disintegrate as inevitably as the human flesh. The noble thought, the mother's tear, the Christian deed — all are the products of chance, created in the wind and scattered in the dust. There is no purpose in life and no basis for hope. One glance into the microscope will dispel forever the vanity of the poet. So insistent was Bergson upon this theory that his fellow students at the Ecole Normale dubbed him "the atheist." Once, when he was librarian of his class, the teacher reprimanded him for keeping the shelves untidy. "How can your librarian's soul endure such disorder?" asked the teacher. Whereupon his classmates cried in chorus, "Bergson has no soul."

When he graduated he was offered a teaching position at the university town of Clermont-Ferrand, in the province of Auvergne. Here came the sceptic, and here his scepticism was conquered. He took long walks in the quiet of the countryside and the poet and rebel in him asserted themselves at last. The arguments of the laboratory, the formulas of the physicists, the smart phrases of the intellectual atheists were suddenly shamed into nothingness before the overwhelming majesty of nature. What, could it be true that a blind mechanism, a whirlpool of chance — guided atoms had formed the swelling breasts of these hills and levelled these plains? Only a clever little sophomore in the school of life could possibly believe that. How ridiculous were those men who tried to describe the infinite simplicity of creation in the complex language of formulas and specious theories! Good Lord, didn't the chemist have eyes to watch the sinking of the sun in these horizons? Yes, now he knew. Science was the refuge of the weary intellects of the world who had lost the courage to hope.

III

BERGSON'S transformation from a materialist to an idealist was not the result of a miracle. At first he had no positive idea as to the direction in which his impulses were leading him. But a growing sense of "poetical realization" had insinuated itself into his intelligence and was now striking out through "every fibre of his body and every cell of his mind." The impulse of intuition — that saving grace of women and poets- convinced him that there was more to life than he had formerly thought possible. Could an arbitrary embrace of atoms create the mind of Shakespeare? Could a scientific arrangement of the letters of the alphabet produce the Bible? And could the chemical and physical combination that was called Henri Bergson explain the spark of humour that sent a stream of anecdotes to his lips as he lectured and torrent of laughter from his audiences as they listened? Nor could the mere laws of physical energy have brought Bergson to Clermont a sceptic and returned him to Paris an idealist.

In his public addresses at the university town he gave

an indication of the new cast of his thoughts. Speaking of scientific research, he remarked: "You have all handled a microscope and may have noticed in its box those little slips of glass each of which encloses some anatomical preparation. Take one of these preparations, put it under the lens and look. You will see a tube divided into compartments. Slip the glass along and observe how one cell succeeds another cell, each clearly distinguishable. But what is the object, and what have you seen? If you want to get the answer to this question, you will be obliged to abandon the microscope and to consider as a whole, with your naked eye, that ugly spider's foot." Who put the ugliness into the spider's foot or the beauty into the spider's web, he might have added with a twinkle in his eye. And incidentally, in the name of the laws of science, who would have put the twinkle in Bergson's eye?

The difficulty with scientific analysis, reasoned Bergson, lies in the propensity of the human mind to map out its objects in space. Everything in human reason is conceived in terms of space. Geometry reduces the most abstract qualities of cosmic phenomena to points in space. Physics reduces the iridescence of the sunset to light rays travelling through space and the music of a symphony to wave lengths of sound vibrating in space. All quality is thus reduced to numerical quantity. The human reason is like a metronome. It *counts* the vibrations of reality. But it cannot *sound* reality. It divides the dynamic whole into static intervals. And thus, observes Bergson, there arises an absurdity. For the most essentially dynamic experience known to us is motion. Yet we represent motion, just as we represent everything else, in terms of a path or a series of static points extended in space. But in reality motion is no more a series of points in space than it is a series of snapshots on a roll of film flashed in succession upon the screen.

Science can merely *symbolize,* but it cannot *define,* the dynamic experience called motion. For the sake of simplicity we draw a line of chalk between two points on a blackboard and we compare the points in the chalk line to points in space. But there is no such thing as a point in space. For a point is a finite object, and space is infinitely divisible. Moreover, it is impossible to add points into a line. The true progress of our hand as it moves to make the line on the blackboard cannot be described as a series of immobile points. How can anyone create mobility out of immobility? Yet we persist in confusing the line of chalk with the motion of our hand.

In the same way we transfer the inward experience of time's *duration* to the path described by the hands of a clock passing through "points" in space. Science claims to count our *inner duration* because science can produce *clock time.* But time cannot be measured. The moments of time are not homogeneous points lying side by side in space. It is true that each second of our inner duration coincides with each sweep of the pendulum. The two occur simultaneously. And hence the confusion of time with space. Real time, however, has no limits, no extremes, no bounds. It is an inner duration that all of us can feel. But we cannot analyze it. Science has been unable to grasp it. Real time is growth and change and development and not an extension of points of seconds or hours or days.

IV

BERGSON had grasped the dynamic and immeasurable quality of the greatest of human experiences — the experience of *inner duration.* And in the face of this experience he was convinced that the rational part of the mind was helpless. For the rational function can only enumerate — that is, add, substract, multiply, divide. But it cannot *feel.* Feeling belongs to another province of the mind — intuition. Now intuition had been branded by all the rational philosophers as the black sheep of the mental family. It was considered the property of the ignorant masses, the chief instrument of superstition. But Bergson was determined to regenerate the dignity of intuition and to restore it to its rightful throne. "For intuition, wisely used, is a legitimate and noble province of the mind; indeed, it is the only means for perceiving the heart of things."

But intuition was a vague term. Just what did it mean? Was it a product of the nerve centres in the brain or was it an essential function of the mind quite apart from the orbit of the brain? The scientists had been assuming that there was nothing more to the mind than the brain and that the mind therefore was nothing more than matter. As one of them had put it — "No matter? Never mind."

Bergson now concentrated all his efforts on the study of the human mind. The most significant phenomenon of the mind, for the purposes of his study, was the memory. He became absorbed in this subject. He conducted numerous experiments in which he found that the victims of brain injury frequently managed to keep their memory intact. If the mind were merely a function of the brain, he concluded, then for every brain lesion there would be a corresponding impairment of the memory. On the other hand, he found that some patients were known to have lost their memory without any injury to the brain. Are recollections, then, stored up in the cells of the brain? In some cases yes. For example, after a certain number of attempts to drive an automobile we acquire the knack. We have absorbed the memory of each lesson automatically. Driving becomes a habit with us. It requires no conscious effort of recollection. And yet were we to recall the specific circumstances of any one lesson that we had taken, we would be obliged to make a conscious effort to remember those circumstances. For the circumstances of the lesson are unique by themselves. They have a quality all their own. They are the single units of an experience assimilated into a quantity of experience over a period of time, all these experiences constituting the process of habit formation. However, they are in themselves experiences of *quality* not of *quantity.* Now the faculty that can recall the quality of any one experience, maintains Bergson, is precisely the faculty that comprehends the quality of things in general. It is the faculty of the self underlying the brain. It is the fundamental "I" — the *ego* about which I cannot reason but which I can feel. This *ego* is known only to myself and cannot be communicated in words to any one else. Nor can the scientist take it apart and examine it just as the jeweller takes apart and examines the machinery of a watch. It is the personality area in which all our moods of hatred and of love and all the diversified shades of emotion that lie between these poles merge imperceptibly into one another. These moods are characterized by their dynamic intensity. They are not units of extensive measurement that obediently pass through the brain in review. They permeate the mind and "fill the soul." Nerve sensations may be measured according to the magnitude of their stimuli. But can anyone measure the magnitude of a thought? Does an emotion consist of so many calories of heat? Is the courage which impels men to lay down their lives for freedom to be regarded as nothing more than a bundle of sensory stimuli?

No, we shall find none of the inner nobility of man in the brain. The brain is a mechanism. It is not a soul. The brain adds units of quantity with an endless precision. But it cannot create. No mere machine can create Leonardo da Vinci's *Last Supper* by daubing one group of colours into another group of colours or Milton's *Paradise Lost* by piecing together the letters of the English alphabet. In the presence of any work that has been created by the grace of God the brain stands a helpless and uncomprehending alien. The great masterpieces in art and in nature, and greatest masterpiece of all, Man, can be grasped not by the brain but by the soul, the self — the *intuitive* self.

V

BERGSON calls our intuitive self, The *creative intellect*. It is the inner consciousness of our duration and growth — the "enduring withinness" of our life, our own profound sense of our unlimited depths. Indeed, our day-to-day thoughts and wishes and actions are but a small surface demonstration of the potential resources in the vast warehouse of our subconscious. It is only in times of great duress that we recognize our true souls and rise to feats of superhuman energy. In the ordinary course of events the brain keeps the lid down on the magic vessel of our personality. It functions like a military draft officer who calls up the relatively small number of ideas needed for present active service. It is a selective instrument that adapts us to our immediate needs. It grasps the temporary interrelationship of things and enables us to choose between them. It acts as a counsellor of the will. Yet the brain, as we have seen, is but a small part of the mind. In and by itself it can never transcend our daily experience. It is wholly material. It resides in the lower animals as well as in men. It functions only in space and develops its strength through the gradual and painful process of trial and error.

But true reality, observes Bergson, transcends our sensory experience. It is more fundamental than the fleeting present relationships of things. For the essence of true reality is growth — past, present and future. It is development not only is space but also and especially in time. John Smith, for example, is a portly individual of forty-five. As we observe him at this moment walking down the street, *whom* are we really looking at? John Smith? But it is obvious that at this particular moment he is no more John Smith than he was forty years ago when he romped about in short pants as a skinny boy of five. The real John Smith is not the person we see on any one day or at any split moment of his life. John Smith's *total reality* lies in his continuous development from the day of his birth to the day of his death. But obviously John Smith is the only person alive who can grasp and *feel* his true reality. For he is the only person who is experiencing every moment of his life. His reality as a living and growing soul is revealed only to his intuitive self — his *creative intellect.*

VI

IN 1900 Bergson was appointed to the chair of philosophy at the College de France. His books on *Time and Free will, Matter and Memory, Mind-Energy* and *Laughter and Metaphysics* raised a tempest of speculation in the intellectual horizons of the Old and the New World. Here was a fragile, unassuming and shy little David wielding a sling at the intellectual giants of materialism. Here was a professor who spoke softly and sedately of the spirit at a time when it was the fashion to speak spiritedly of the flesh. Here was a mathematician who dared to look beyond mathematics to the Bible. This was rank heresy.

Yet his lectures became extremely popular. "Silence would descend upon the hall and the audience would feel a secret tremble within when they saw him quietly approach from the back of the amphitheatre, seat himself beneath the shaded lamp, his hands free of manuscript notes and the finger tips usually joined." He spoke without hurry, with dignity, in a measured tone. His language was precise and musical. He formed his sentences with so little effort that few could detect his art. He shocked the graybeard professors when he asserted that philosophy must *cure,* not *obscure,* the ills of men. He refused to clothe his thoughts with factory-made phrases. He invented new words to supplant the old cut-and-dried formulas. He implored his audiences not to follow him but to examine his thoughts and to "think them out" in their own minds. He asked them to make an effort if they wished to sink a plummet into reality. "The sole purpose of my studies," he remarked, "has been to express precisely what each one of us is trying to find within himself."

It was true that "precise" conception was something precisely less than a revelation and precisely more than a headache to the common man. It is the uncommon man who feels at home in the black shadows of metaphysics. And yet it was not difficult for anyone to accept, Bergson's philosophy on faith; he had such a convincing smile! As in the case of Aristotle, his own definition of a gentleman could well be applied to himself. "The accomplished man of the world knows how to talk to any man on the subject that interests him; he enters into the other's views, yet he does not therefore adopt them; he understands everything though he does not necessarily excuse everything. So we come to like him when we have hardly begun to know him; we are speaking to a stranger and we are surprised and delighted to find in him a friend." Bergson was not only a philosopher but a master in social relationships. Imagine Nietzsche or Schopenhauer uttering such words!

Like the German thinkers across the Rhine, Bergson believed firmly in the power of man's instincts. We have seen what remarkably unholy conclusions the German philosophers had deduced from this belief. Schopenhauer had preached the religion of race annihilation. Nietzsche had promulgated the doctrine of ruthless aggression. But Bergson developed the philosophy of creative evolution. He had demolished the hypothesis that the mind is identical with the brain. The mind is far more than the brain, he had declared. Indeed, the fundamental quality of the mind eludes the brain. This fundamental quality is the *creative* mind as opposed to the brain which is the *analytical* mind. The creative mind alone can realize the fundamental truths of experience. For experience is a creative totality — a whole which is *not* the sum of its parts. We cannot add up a poem or a tree. We cannot produce points into a line and call this a line of progress. We cannot in reality combine seconds into minutes or minutes into hours. We do this with "dead" time that we ourselves have manufactured to symbolize "living" time. But each moment of living time represents not a *part* of time but the *whole* of time. For time, like a tree, is a creative whole.

And only the creative intellect, which is the ordinary man's intuition and the poet's inspiration, can apprehend the whole of reality at any given moment, from any vantage spot, under any circumstance. For though the analytical mind can act only in the present, the creative mind contains within it the evolution — that is, the growth — of the entire past, present and future.

This evolutionary growth of the inner consciousness of the creative intellect is life. It is the electric current that animates and moves us all. And Bergson gives it a picturesque name. He calls it the *Elan Vital,* the Vital Spark. Let the brain perish with the rest of the body. The Vital Spark, the inner consciousness, is immortal, just as time is immortal though all objects confined to space may perish. We have liberated time from the prison of space. We have given it its rightful throne in the inner consciousness. We have corrected the errors of the scientists. We have demonstrated a vital truth, asserts Bergson; *Man does not live in time, but time lives in man.* For time is not only *eternal* but *internal.* It lives within man's own creative intellect. He is not a slave to any exterior dimension erroneously called the passage of time. He is the master, the creator, the very soul of time. For time is the life of the mind just as growth is the life of the body.

Let us, therefore, stop lamenting that life is too brief. Life is eternal. Every living moment is an eternity, if only we break the mental bonds that bind us to our material environment. The vital spark within us is not material. Our life is not "harnessed like a yoked ox to a heavy task." The evolutionists have read a message of fatality into the cycle of struggle and survival and conquest. They have looked at the species of animals and men through a microscope and judged only from the external signs. They have scoffed at the idea that man's will is free. They have turned us into a factory of machines. They have transformed nature into a monster of levers and bolts and screws. They have counselled us to bend the knee to the Great God Resignation. For in resignation, they have told us, we shall find our security. This false doctrine appears to be true only because we accept the idea of time as the dead mechanical movement of temporal moments in space, like the dead mechanical movement of the hands on the face of a clock. If this were the true interpretation of the world, there would be as much life and freedom in the actions of man as there are in the puppet gestures of the celluloid characters imprinted on a movie film. In the case of the film the laws of mechanics rule supreme. Motion and time are controlled by the projection machine. The speed of the screen shadows can be slowed down or stepped up. The film can be run backward, and all the laws of chronology can be reversed. But the very essential of our real time — maintains Bergson — is its *irreversibility.* For time is growth, and growth belongs not to mechanics but to dynamics. The dynamic does not reverse itself. Nor does it repeat itself. Growth is progress, not repetition. Every experience in the past is an entirely unique experience. What has been done is done. Can the man become a child again? Can John Smith reverse himself? Can a moment reverse itself? The essential characteristic of the dynamic quality of time, as opposed to the static, quality of reason, is the vitality of time, its "livingness," its growth.

The future is not the mechanical product of the past. For if each *present* moment is unique each *future* moment is unique. Growth follows no inflexible laws. In the life of the mind there is no inevitable sequence of cause and effect. The preacher pronouncing a sermon over the dead body of John Smith may draw an "inevitable" moral from his life. He is in a position to view it as an external pattern of trial and error. He tries to reason that such and such a thing in Smith's life was influenced by his environment, such and such a characteristic was inherited from his mother, such and such a thought came from his schooling. But while John Smith lived there was nothing inevitable about each moment he experienced. Smith was his *own inevitability.* At every instant of his life he was his creative self. He was the mechanic of his own machine, the master of his own free will.

Once we have established the fact that man is free the whole theory of Darwinian evolution appears in a new light, maintains Bergson. Man is not the mechanical plaything of a sordid, inexorable struggle for the survival of the fittest. Life is not the product of mechanical laws, like a river carried by the force of gravitation from the cradle to the grave. The current of life drives man onward and upward on the path of evolution, and the driving power lies not outside him but within him. Life is a spontaneous artist. It promises at every moment to blossom into something new and unforeseeable. It wells up from the source of a glorious infathomable reality. The heart of divinity lies in its potential development. Indeed, the sum total of the creative life of man is God.

God is Life. And the urge of life is upward, ever upward. "The animal takes its stand on the plant, man bestrides animality, and the whole of humanity, in space and time, is one immense army galloping beside and before and behind each of us in an overwhelming charge able to beat every resistance and to clear every obstacle."

Even death. The current of life survives the death of the individual. It survives the chance of failure and the tendency of matter to destroy itself. When it strikes a blind path its manifold springs carve out a new.

channel and pour their irresistible torrents into new and greater achievements. Life cannot be stifled by a temporary defeat. It can never be stopped.

And this invincible urge of life, this *Elan Vital*, the Vital Spark, lies within us all. This energy that by an automatic insinuation into the lowest forms of matter becomes passively adjusted to it and slowly comes to dominate it finally frees itself in man and receives its mightiest expression in his creative self.

This creative self is the *universal* self, the impulse that sets every artist to produce the masterpiece that transcends his individual personality and becomes the collective heritage of man. And this creative urge resides not only in the artist but in every one of us. It is the power back of our every noble thought, the rapture experienced in the lover's kiss, the mother's joy in the act of giving birth to her child, the blessing that accompanies the doing of every good deed, the hope of all men who believe in their immortal destiny.

VII

BRAVE words, these! The words of a beautiful poem. Today the armies of the world are on the march again. And those who lived through the last World War and who listened to Bergson's philosophy of hope are now living through a second tragic war. Some of us may be inclined to smile sadly at the Frenchman who talks with such optimistic fervour about our human destiny. Perhaps we are a little puzzled by his joyous tale of creation, a little bewildered at this unfathomable energy of man — an energy directed toward starving and enslaving his fellow men. "What is this life," we are tempted to ask, "that can suddenly be extinguished by a bullet?"

But no doubt a "secret tremble" of light will come over the audiences in the lecture hall of time when the little professor quietly seats himself beneath the shaded lamp, his hands free of manuscript notes, and remarks with unhurried dignity: "Try to understand part of this with the mind and to divine the rest--with the heart."

It was both with the mind and with the heart that this Jewish-born philosopher of eighty-one reacted toward the anti–Semitic regulations of the Hitler-inspired French Government in 1940. In accordance with these regulations, all Jewish professors in France were ordered to resign from their positions in the state universities. Bergson was offered an exemption from this order. But he refused to accept the favour. He wanted no exemption from a cruelty dictated by Barbarians. He preferred to suffer the fate of his co-religionists. He resigned from the faculty of the *College de France*.

When this man had talked about the *Elan Vital*, the Vital Spark of nobility, he knew where he spoke.

****

Important Works By Bergson

Creative Evolution.
Time and Free Will.
Matter and Memory.
Mind-Energy.
Laughter and Metaphysics.
The Perception of Change.
The Meaning of the War (of 1914).

20

GEORGE SANTAYANA

1863 – 1952

SANTAYANA'S life, like his philosophy, is an echo of the past. Though born in Spain and educated in the United States, he is neither a Spaniyard nor an American. He is mentally as well as temperamentally the last of the ancient Greeks.

As a child he was brought up on tales of romantic adventure, faraway pageantry and fairyland enchantment. Before Santayana was born his father had been an official in the Philippine Islands. He had sailed three times around the world, and he had stocked his mind with many a tale of "interminable ocean spaces, coconut islands, blamless Malays and immense continents swarming with Chinamen," and with other fanciful and exotic persons and things. These exotic persons and things were to be the mental fare of Santayana during the formative years of his life. "From childhood," he tells us, "I have lived in the imaginative presence of (these) — lessons and wonders — It was habitual with me to think of scenes and customs pleasanter than those about me."

These words give us the keynote to Santayana's mentality as a philosopher and to his personality as a man. The flavour of the otherwhere and the antique has clung to him throughout his life. Santayana is an ancient poet writing a commentary on the modern world.

II

WHEN George Santayana was nine years old his mother separated from his father, who was her second husband, and migrated with her children to America. George was the only child of his mother's second marriage. There were three children by the first marriage, but they were considerably older than Santayana and therefore no congenial playmates or him. Nor did Santayana care to associate with any of the other children in the neighbourhood. "I played no games," he writes, "but sat at home all the afternoon and evening reading or drawing."

He received his early education at the Boston Latin School. Here, amidst the democratic influence of the "nailhoofed boys" who came "thundering down the steps of the schoolhouse... in an avalanche of forty or eighty or two hundred together," he learned to emerge somewhat from the shell of his aristocratic aloofness. He became at last approachable if not downright sociable.

When he entered Harvard he allowed the frost of his reserve to melt still further. Though he took no part in the college sports himself, he went to see the other students at their practice. He was especially fond of football — as a spectator on the sidelines. It was the poet in him, rather than the man of action, that found pleasure in the competitive struggle on the gridiron. "A football game," he writes, "is always a fine spectacle, but here upon the broad-backed earth, away from the town, nothing but sky and distant hills about you, where the wind always blows, the struggle has an added beauty... Here the heroic virtues shine in miniature and the simple joy of the ancient world returns as in a dream."

The memory of an ancient dream seen across the tussle of a modern game – such was Santayana's picture of the world in which he lived.

His social habits like his athletic contacts at Harvard were unexcited, impersonal, aloof. He frequently joined his classmates on their "visiting excursions" when "standing packed in the tinkling horsecar, their coat collars above their ears and their feet deep in the winter straw, they jogged in a long half-hour to Boston, there to enjoy the delights of female society, the theatre or a good dinner." But at the dinner table, too, just as on the football field, he looked on with an amused and kindly imperturbability. "At these dinners you talked half an hour with the lady on one side, then half an hour with the lady on the other side.. about ten minutes with the men... and finally, in the drawing room, you were able to choose the lady you wished to talk to."

He always talked to the ladies. He never danced with them. He didn't know how to dance.

He preferred the conversation of women to that of men. "I liked the ladies of Boston and enjoyed talking with them. They had travelled, read and were cultivated much more so than the men."

His attitude toward men was tolerantly sarcastic. On one occasion he was introduced to Governor Wolcott of Massachusetts. "I had looked forward to meeting him, but, I was very much disappointed. He had enough mind to have opinions but not enough to have the right ones."

This, too, was his attitude toward his Harvard professors. He had little respect for their opinions. He considered his own mentality too mature for the "elementary" teaching of James and Royce and Palmer. "I heard James and Royce with more wonder than serious agreement." As for Palmer, "he is still vegetating there," he wrote of him many years later. He disliked these men's "idealistic conception of the cruel and nasty world... as the model and standard of what ought to be." He had come to Harvard a confirmed materialist or "naturalist." "My naturalism," he said, "is no academic opinion; it is an everyday conviction which came to me, as it came to my father, from experience and observation of the world....it seems to me that those who are not materialists are not good observers....."

He was a product of his father's as well as of his mother's "irreligious religion." His parents had regarded all religion "as a work of human imagination." They had believed that "sacrifices, prayers, churches and tales of immortality were invented by rascally priests in order to dominate the foolish." To this belief Santayana subscribed fully. Yet– and here we have the first full glimpse into the complex mentality that was Santayana- - though his mind was the mind of a sceptic, his heart was the heart of a believer. "My sympathies," he writes, "were entirely with those other members of my family who were devout believers." To be sure "religions are the fairy tales of the conscience." But what inspiring fairy tales!

For Santayana, in spite of his materialistic protestations. was an enchanted prince living in magic world. He was a poet who tried to talk like a scientist. Indeed, his first literary efforts were poetical — sad, nostalgic laments over perished worlds and forgotten dreams. His was not, like Houseman's, the complaint that he had been born "a stranger and afraid in a world he never made," but the more bitter complaint that he was born too late in a world he would have ardently loved, had he come into it at the right time. A companion of Plato condemned to live among the Puritans of Boston — *that*, as Santayana saw it, was his great tragedy.

He wanted to spend his life in quiet conversation with Plato, Aristotle, Democritus, Lucretius and the other ancient spirits so congenial to his own. But he was compelled, by the trick of destiny, to become a teacher and to waste his time talking to college undergraduates. "I always hated to be a professor," he wrote in later years. Yet no one would have ever suspected it from the serenity of his lectures. It was the privilege of one of the authors of the present book to study under Santayana at Harvard. The experience was unforgettable. The poet-philosopher sat on the platform at Emerson Hall–pale hands folded on his desk under a pale face, black pointed beard giving his features an ethereal El Greco unreality, a spirit from afar flashing out of two fiery Spanish eyes and a voice filled with a cadenced wisdom that descended upon his students like a benediction. He spoke fluently but in a patient and unhurried tempo, as if he had before him all eternity in which to deliver his message. Sometimes he would stop for several seconds, searching in his mind for the right word. But his students waited expectantly, for they knew that when the word came it would be *the* inevitable word for that particular context – the perfect gem in the perfect setting.

Occasionally he directed the shafts of his gentle satire against the "false idols" of the human mind. But he never assailed them with the hammer of iconoclasm. He was amused rather than indignant at the foolishness of the human race.

He never married. He lived with a few intimates at Harvard, notably Hugo Munsterberg, a foreigner, aristocrat and poet like himself – and with his books. He still retained, however, his interest in football – his one concession to "the mummeries of contemporary life." One of his students, familiar only with his classroom aloofness and unaware of his interest in college athletics, was amazed when he saw him, "in his foreign cape and with his foreign cane," walking into the stadium on a Saturday afternoon. "Imagine Plato," exclaimed the student, "giving a regular cheer for Harvard!"

Aside from his little excursions into the present, however, he still spent the greater part of his leisure time in cultivating the friendship of the past. He had given up his poetry for philosophy – or, to be more exact he had given up his philosophical poetry for poetical philosophy. For though he now began to write in the medium of prose and in the language of metaphysics, he remained a poet to the end.

III

SANTAYANA'S philosophical work is a strange mixture of Platonism, atheism and Catholicism. First of all he believes, like Plato, in a world of ideas. Santayana calls them *essences.* The *essence* of Santayana, like the *idea* of Plato, is the form of everything that is, that ever was, that ever will be — and, Santayana would add -– that *never* will be. For not only the great ideas that have been written in novels and poems and dreams are essences; but the ideas that *have not* and *will not* be written are also essences. They are like the flowers that are "born to blush unseen and waste their sweetness on the desert air." Yet they "waste" their sweetness only insofar as our poor mortal senses are concerned but not insofar as eternal contemplation is concerned. And each of us can, to some extent at least, share in this contemplation. We can experience as *ecstasy, a standing out* from ourselves. As we plod along the narrow road of our existence from life to death, with the blinkers of our ignorance to thwart our vision, our spirits can, and sometimes do, lift us above ourselves, so that in a flashing moment we behold eternity. We experience such an eternal moment, for example, when we hear a beautiful sonata or see a beautiful painting of perform a beautiful deed. At such experiences of self--forgetfulness we see "the essences laugh from their Platonic heaven at this inconstant world into which they peep for a moment.

When an essence "peeps into the world"— that is, when it acts upon matter — it becomes an *existence,* in somewhat the same sense that the plan for a house becomes a house when it is formed into bricks and stones and glass and mortar. Santayana confesses that he doesn't know just exactly what matter is. "I wait for the men of science to tell me.... But whatever matter may be, I call it matter boldly, as I call my acquaintances *Smith* and *Jones* without knowing their secrets." Santayana doesn't understand the secret of matter, but he is sure of its existence. Whatever we may call it – "a confluence of atoms" or "an electric charge" or "a tension in either"-matter is that ever-present, all – pervading substance which goes to make the heavens and the earth and the leaves of the trees and the petals of the flowers and the bodies of men. Yes, and the *minds* of men. For the human mind, like the human body, is material. The mind, like the body, is subject to birth, growth, decay and death.

From a Platonist Santayana has now become an atheist. He has faith neither in immortality nor in God. "I believe there is nothing immortal," he writes. No doubt the spirit and energy of the world is what is acting in us, as the sea is what rises in every little wave; but it passes through us; and cry out as we may, it will move on. Our privilege is to have perceived it as it moved."

Life, the body, the mind, the earth, the heavens; the stars – all are reduced, in the philosophy of Santayana, to a machine. Man's actions are not free but mechanical. The mind, he declares, does not control the body. It is merely a "sideline spectator," observing the "automatic inward machinery" of the body sometimes with approval and sometimes with "impotent rebellion." There is no such thing as an immortal soul. "Belief in such a soul is simply belief in magic." What we call the "soul is merely a prodigious (and material) network of nerves and tissues, growing in each generation out of a seed."

In his denial of the power of the mind and of the freedom of the will Santayana is a Spinozist. Indeed, Spinoza is to him the only *complete* philosopher of the Christian era. "No modern writer is altogether a philosopher in my eyes except Spinoza." Yet Santayana rejects Spinoza's pantheism. "The word *nature,*" he maintains, "is poetical enough. It suggests sufficiently the generative and controlling function, the endless vitality and changeful order of the world in which I live." Pantheism implies the existence of God, and Santayana doesn't believe in God. Like Lalande, he searches the heavens with a telescope and cannot find him. Religion is a myth, and God is the fictitious hero of that myth.

But Santayana is not only an unbeliever but a poet, not only an atheist but a catholic. He asserts, as one of his biographers has put it, "that there is no God and that the Virgin Mary is His mother." But having rejected God from his intellect, Santayana then proceeded to enshrine him in his emotion. The story of Catholicism, especially the legend of the Virgin Mary, is the "fairest flower of poesy.' The myth of Christianity, though scientifically false, is poetically true." Catholicism is nothing but a dream, to be sure, but it is a *good* dream. And this, observes Santayana, is true of every other religion. God may be only a fictitious hero, but he is a splendid hero for men to follow. Let us not, then, scorn the fables of religion. Let us, rather, "honour the piety and understand the poetry embodied in those fables." Accept the fables of Christianity in their poetical rather in their literal sense, and you can even hope for immortality – of a sort. "The better a man evokes and realizes the ideal (of the Christian life)... the more pervasive becomes his presence in the society of the immortals. "Our immortality is not the extension of our personality in the *next* world but its repetition in *this* world – through our words, through our deeds and especially through our children. "We commit the blotted manuscript of our lives more willingly to the flames when we find the immortal text half engrossed in a fairer copy."

IV

SUCH is the inconsistent consistency of Santayana's philosophical system. It is the philosophy of a man who, in his own words, "was trying to dream with one eye open; to be detached from the world without being hostile to it; to welcome fugitive beauties and pity fugitive sufferings, without forgetting for a moment how fugitive they are."

It is with this detached though not unfriendly attitude that Santayana lived his entire life. He was the head of no family, the patriot of no country and — after 1912, when he resigned from Harvard — the professor of no school. Shortly before the World War of 1914 he left America and went to another hemisphere but a retirement to another age — the age to which he believed that he had always belonged. He settled down in Rome, "because there he felt closer to the past than anywhere else." Athens, he said, had been changed too much from its ancient Platonic days. Among the Roman ruins of a past glory he found himself most congenially at home. Here he adopted a quiet routine, walking in the "ignoble present" like the ghost of a nobler day. He took a modest suite in a hotel. When his friends suggested that he buys himself a home he replied that "possessions enslave a man." His habits were simple and inconspicuous. "I am the child of my father," he said. He had once asked his father why he always travelled third class, and his father had answered, "Because there's no fourth class." He enjoyed his few friends when they came to see him but he never sought them out if they stayed away. "I am like the Pope," he said; "I don't return visits."

He rarely attended religious services. "Sitting in church," he explained, "makes me tired in the small of my back." But he frequently went to the ruins of the Pantheon, to watch the statues of the ancient gods, and to San Pietro, to enjoy Michelangelo's *Moses*. He still preferred the poetry to the practice of religion.

His favourite haunt was a bench near the ruins of the temple of Esculapius, the ancient god of healing and one of the favourite divinities of Socrates. Here he sat for hours and dreamed himself back to the springtime of the world from which he had been so sadly divorced by the vicissitudes of fate.

Yet always there was a touch of humour to this sadness. He could look upon his own disappointments, as he looked upon the disappointments of other people, with an impersonal chuckle. Speaking of the unsuccessful sale of his books – prior to the publication of his novel, *The Last Puritan* – he laughingly remarked: "*The Sense of Beauty* is my first book and still my best seller.... It sells regularly a hundred copies a year."

Yet even disappointment, he observed, has its bright side — its impermanance. Nature amuses us for a moment with that silly bauble called life and then lulls us to a forgetful sleep. Let us make the best of that moment of wakefulness. Let us forget our fugitive misfortunes and be thankful for our fugitive joys. After all, "there is no cure for birth and death save to enjoy the interval."

And so Santayana gazed with a sad but amused and philosophical calm upon that "irrational spectacle" called life. In country after country, he saw civilization submerged and tyranny triumphant: yet like a visitor from another century he could look on undisturbed. He could even say, in detached and philosophic complacency, that he was "a great admirer of Mussolini." Before we condemn him too strongly for this attitude let us remember that Santayana always weighed his words with the carefulness of a Latin scholar. To admire, as he well knew and as he expected his readers to know, means not to *regard with approval* but *to observe with wonder.* He admired a Mussolini or a Caesar in the same sense that he admired a tornado or an avalanche. He wondered at their power, but he did not approve of their destructiveness. Indeed, Santayana shrank all his life from destructiveness, cruelty, injustice, oppression, war. "It is war," he writes, "that wastes a nation's wealth, kills its flower, narrows its sympathies, condemns it to be governed by adventures and leaves the puny, deformed and unmanly to breed the next generation... Instead of being descended from heroes, modern nations are descended from slaves."

"Heaven it is," he writes in one of his sonnets, "to be at peace with things."

In his attitude toward war, as in his attitude toward everything else, Santayana went back to the ancient Greeks. "The longer we think about the world," he concludes, "the more surely we return to Plato. We need no new philosophy; we need only the courage to live up to the oldest and the best."

****

Important Works By Santayana

Poems.

Lucifer, a Theological Tragedy.

The Sense of Beauty.

Interpretations of Poetry and Religion.

The Life of Reason, in five volumes.

Reason in Common Sense.

Reason in Society,

Reason in Religion.

Reason in Art.

Reason in Science.

Three Philosophical Poets (Lucretius, Dante and Goethe).

Winds of Doctrine.

Egotism in German Philosophy.

Character and Opinion in the United States.

Scepticism and Animal Faith.

Platonism and the Spiritual Life.

The Realm of Being.

The Last Puritan.

The Realm of Truth.

The Realm of Spirit.

Persons and Places.

The Middle Span.